Computer Communications and Networks

For further volumes:
www.springer.com/series/4198

The **Computer Communications and Networks** series is a range of textbooks, monographs and handbooks. It sets out to provide students, researchers and non-specialists alike with a sure grounding in current knowledge, together with comprehensible access to the latest developments in computer communications and networking.

Emphasis is placed on clear and explanatory styles that support a tutorial approach, so that even the most complex of topics is presented in a lucid and intelligible manner.

Shengming Jiang

Future Wireless and Optical Networks

Networking Modes and Cross-Layer Design

 Springer

Shengming Jiang
College of Information Engineering
Shanghai Maritime University
Shanghai
China

School of Electronic & Information
Engineering
South China University of Technology
Guangzhou
China

Series Editor
Professor A.J. Sammes, BSc, MPhil, PhD,
FBCS, CEng
Centre for Forensic Computing
Cranfield University
DCMT, Shrivenham
Swindon
UK

ISSN 1617-7975   Computer Communications and Networks
ISBN 978-1-4471-2821-2   e-ISBN 978-1-4471-2822-9
DOI 10.1007/978-1-4471-2822-9
Springer London Dordrecht Heidelberg New York

British Library Cataloguing in Publication Data
A catalogue record for this book is available from the British Library

Library of Congress Control Number: 2012932959

Printed on acid-free paper

Springer is part of Springer Science+Business Media (www.springer.com)

To my family, and the memory of my parents

Preface

This monograph collectively reports my research results on communication networking technologies since 2004, when next generation networking technologies for the future Internet and cross-layer design and optimization for high-performance wireless networks were among hot research topics in the community. Numerous research works have been conducted on these two topics, resulting in many new approaches and proposals published in the literature. This monograph is only a small leaf of this ever-growing tree, which focuses on some major networking issues of the future Internet.

Organization

This monograph begins with an introduction to major networking modes and their effect on the Internet development in Chaps. 1–2. Here "networking mode" is a general term used to collectively refer to the principle and methodology of networking.

Then in Chaps. 3 and 4, a new structure favorable for all-optical packet switching (AOPS) is discussed. This structure tries to simplify the current network structure such that an all-optical network can be realized simply by using optical processing technologies available today or in the near future, since the all-optical network node cannot all-optically process complex networking operations such as routing and congestion control.

Chapter 5 discusses a new quality of service (QoS) provisioning approach, which tries to overcome the weaknesses of the currently popular schemes, i.e., the scalability problem of IntServ and the coarse QoS granularity of DiffServ. A cost model corresponding to granular services is discussed in Chap. 6.

Chapters 7–9 formulate partially the famous end-to-end arguments, which are among the most influential principles for Internet design. The arguments suggest a design principle of putting the application-level functions at the network edge rather than inside a network as much as possible in order to simplify network design and implementation. However, in the development of some new types of networks, some function displacement into the network has become an option to improve network performance. These chapters discuss how to estimate both the performance gain and the implementation complexity that is potentially offered by a function displacement from the network edge into the network.

Inspired by the theoretical results reported in Chaps. 7–9, an approach decoupling the congestion control from the popular Transmission Control Protocol (TCP) is discussed for multi-hop wireless networks and all-optical networks in Chap. 10. This is studied because the original TCP fails to perform well in these kinds of networks, and incremental modification cannot solve this problem completely.

Chapters 11–12 discuss how to exploit the multiple-input-multiple-output (MIMO) technology to enable simultaneous transmissions at the medium access control (MAC) level at the same frequency from different nodes to improve network performance in centralized wireless networks. This approach is easier to implement in mobile terminals than other MIMO approaches.

Due to the ever-growing concern about global warming, green networking has become a hot research topic recently. This means that energy efficiency is also an important issue that should be addressed simultaneously in network design. Therefore, Chap. 13 conducts a brief survey of green networking strategies from a quantitative perspective.

Finally, this monograph is summarized in Chap. 14 with a brief discussion about possible developments of networking technologies for the future Internet.

Acknowledgements

I would like to take this opportunity to sincerely thank my students who contributed to this monograph through their studies of some relevant issues with me: Tianxiang Liang, Yibin Ye (master students graduated in 2007), Qin Zuo, Xuefang Teng, Tiejun Zhang, Linna You, Wenming Song, Guoxin Zhang, Xiaomeng Li, Min Zhang (master students graduated in 2008), Haiyan Hu, Weihui Zhong, Rongmei Chen, Zhe Wu (master students graduated in 2009), Yuanqing Lin, Mei Liu, Yegui Cai, Luyang Xu (master students graduated in 2010), Li Wang, Yan Lin, Aiqiao He (master students graduated in 2011), Quansheng Guan (Ph.D. student graduated in 2011), Quanmin Wu, Jianping Zhou, Hongxiao Hu, Shuhua Zhang, Xiang Gu, Wenwei Liang, Huachao Mao, Wanjuan Xie, Huarong Yang, Min Zeng (master students), Mian Guo, Xin Ao, Lin Tang, Hong Qiu, Binyi Guo, and Rongfeng Zhang (Ph.D. students).

I also want to thank the Editor, Prof. A.J. Sammes, for his support to this monograph.

Guangzhou, China   Shengming Jiang
January 2012

Contents

Acronyms

ACK	acknowledgement
ACPI	advanced configuration and power interface
ABR	available bit rate
AOA	angle of arrival
AOPS	all-optical packet switching
AQM	active queue management
AP	access point
ARQ	automatic repeat request
AS	assured service
ATCP	ad hoc TCP
ATM	asynchronous transfer mode
ATP	ad hoc transport protocol
BAC	buffer admission control
BER	bit error rate
BGP	border gateway protocol
BS	base station
CAC	call admission control
CBR	constant bit rate
CSMA	carrier sensing multiple access
CDMA	code division multiple access
CL	connectionless
CO	connection-oriented
COPAS	contention-based path selection
CRC	cyclic redundancy check
CSI	channel state information
CTS	clear-to-send
cwnd	congestion window
DBD	domain-by-domain
DBDR	domain-by-domain routing
DBF	distributed Bellman-Ford
DCF	distributed coordination function

DLSR	domain-level source routing
DQS	differentiated queueing service
DoS	denial of service
DTN	delay/disruption-tolerant network
EBB	exponentially bounded burstiness
ECN	explicit congestion notification
EDF	earliest deadline first
EEE	energy efficient Ethernet
ELFN	explicit link failure notification
EO	electrical-optical
EOR	end of optical route
ETE	end-to-end
ETES	end-to-end service
FDL	fiber delay line
FIFO	first-in-first-out
FEC	forward error correction
FTIF	forwarding table index field
FTM	field type mark
Gbps	gigabits/second
GNT	green network technology
GSM	global system for mobile
HBH	hop-by-hop
HOL	head-of-line
HSPA	high speed packet access
ICMP	Internet control message protocol
ICT	information and communication technology
IDR	intra-domain route
IDRN	intra-domain route number
IMS	IP multimedia subsystem
IoT	Internet of things
IP	Internet protocol
IPC	inter-process communication
IPSec	IP security
ISDN	integrated services digital network
ISO	International Standards Organization
JTCP	jitter-based TCP
kbps	kilobits/second
LAN	local area network
LP	loss preference
LPI	low power idle
LTE	long term evolution
LVF	long variable format
MAC	medium access control
Mbps	megabits/second
MEA	multi-element antenna

MEMS	micro-electro-mechanical system
MIMO	multiple-input-multiple-output
MPLS	multi-protocol label switching
NACK	negative acknowledgement
NAL	network adaptation layer
NDI	next domain identity
OBS	optical burst switching
OE	optical-electrical
OEO	optical-electrical-optical
OFDM	orthogonal frequency division multiplexing
OL	connection-oriented plus connectionless
OOO	optical-to-optical
OPI	output port index
OSI	open systems interconnection
PDB	per-domain behavior
PDS	per-domain segment
PHB	per-hop behavior
PHS	per-hop service
PLS	payload specification
PLSR	port-level source routing
PNS	per-node segment
PS	premium service
QoS	quality of service
RoF	radio over fiber
RAM	random access memory
RED	random early dropping
RSVP	resource reservation protocol
RTS	request-to-send
RTT	round trip time
SAP	service access point
SDMA	space division multiple access
SFF	short fixed format
SISO	single-input-single-output
SRS	source routing setting
SRT	source routing type
SSRL	station short retry limit
STC	space-time coding
Tbps	terabits/second
TCP	transmission control protocol
TCP-ADA	TCP with adaptive delayed acknowledgement
TCP-AP	TCP with adaptive pace
TCP-DCR	delayed congestion response TCP
TCP-DOOR	TCP detection of out-of-order and response
TDMA	time division multiple access
TLSR	two-level source routing

UN	United Nations
UWB	ultra-wide bandwidth
VBR	variable bit rate
VC	virtual channel
VCI	virtual channel identifier
VoIP	voice over IP
VPI	virtual path identifier
WAN	wide area network
WDM	wavelength division multiplexing
WLAN	wireless LAN
WMN	wireless mesh network
WWW	World Wide Web

Chapter 1
Introduction and Overview

Abstract A communication network is a complex system, and the International Standards Organization (ISO) has defined a seven-layer reference model for its construction. Although researchers have been studying network technologies for several decades and have successfully resolved many difficult issues, there are still many new challenging issues arising constantly, which have to be addressed adequately in order to support the ever-growing numbers of both new applications and users. This chapter summarizes some of the new issues that will be addressed by this monograph for wireless and optical networks in the future, with a brief overview of the relevant networking issues that have been studied extensively in the literature so far.

1.1 Introduction

A communication network is used to transfer application traffic (e.g., data, voice, and video) between source and destination. Source nodes generate application traffic, which leaves the network from destination nodes. These two types of nodes are henceforth called endpoints. As illustrated in Fig. 1.1, a network can be simply abstracted into a graph consisting of sets of nodes and links. A node can be either an endpoint or a relaying unit, which receives traffic from one node and forwards it to other nodes. A link, either a metallic cable or an optical fiber or even invisible wireless radio, is used to connect a pair of adjacent nodes for communication.

The key networking research issue is to design a network such that it can cost-effectively support all the applications it claims to support. Here the term networking mode is used to collectively refer to the principle and methodology for networking.

This chapter gives a brief overview of the fundamental network approaches and networking issues to be addressed in this monograph. The motivation and organization of the monograph are described at the end of this chapter.

1.2 Basic Network Approaches

The major network approaches described here include shared-media and switched-networks, connectionless and connection-oriented networks as well as circuit-switched and packet-switched networks.

S.M. Jiang, *Future Wireless and Optical Networks*,
Computer Communications and Networks,
DOI 10.1007/978-1-4471-2822-9_1, © Springer-Verlag London Limited 2012

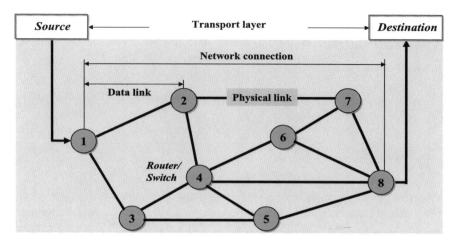

Fig. 1.1 Schematic illustration of the communication network

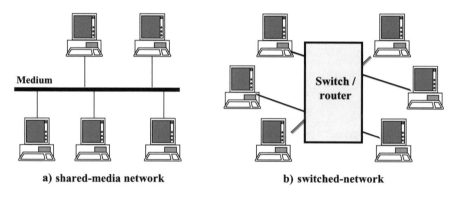

Fig. 1.2 Shared-media networks versus switched networks

1.2.1 Shared-Media and Switched Networks

A network is called a shared-media network if all nodes attached to this network share a common medium, such as a bus, a ring, or a portion of the electromagnetic spectrum band, as illustrated in Fig. 1.2(a). Typical shared-media networks include the classical Ethernet using a bus and wireless networks using electromagnetic waves as communication media. In this kind of network, a mechanism, namely medium access control (MAC), must be used to arbitrate media sharing among competing nodes.

In a switched network such as Internet Protocol (IP) networks and asynchronous transfer mode (ATM) networks, as illustrated in Fig. 1.2(b), each node is linked to a central relaying unit, which can be either a switch or a router using switching technology. In this case, each link has a full wired speed simultaneously, and no MAC is needed for the capacity sharing. Actually, there is still a contention issue to

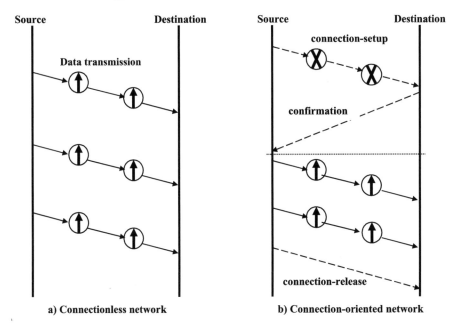

Fig. 1.3 Connectionless versus connection-oriented networks

be addressed for traffic to cross the switching fabric, but this issue is transparent to the nodes linked to the switching fabric, and will not be discussed further here.

1.2.2 Connectionless and Connection-Oriented Networks

According to whether a connection is needed for data transmission, networks are divided into connectionless (CL) and connection-oriented (CO) networks. In a connectionless network such as IP, data can be sent anytime they are available without a connection set up with the receiver, as illustrated in Fig. 1.3(a). In this case, routing is used by routers for data forwarding. This kind of network is suitable for non-delay-sensitive applications and short message transmission. However, it is difficult for this kind of network to guarantee quality of service (QoS), since it is impossible for a router to make a resource reservation for an instantly arriving packet.

In a CO network such as ATM, as illustrated in Fig. 1.3(b), a connection must be set up between source and destination before any data transmission occurs between them. In this kind of network, switching is used to accelerate data forwarding after a route has been set up by routing. Furthermore, during the connection setup, a resource reservation can be made simultaneously for QoS support, and the present location of a roaming mobile terminal can also be updated for mobility support in a mobile network. However, the connection setup is an overhead which consumes extra network resources and causes more delay, especially for short message transmission.

Table 1.1 Networking units involved in CL/CO services provided by the network and transport layers

CL/CO service in	Network units involved in service provisioning		
	Source	Router/Switch	Destination
Transport layer	yes	no	yes
Network layer	yes	yes	yes

Note that CL and CO services are also used to define end-to-end services in the transport layer (see Fig. 2.1 for the layer definition). The key difference between the CL/CO services provided by the network and transport layers is the networking units that are involved in the service provisioning, as listed in Table 1.1.

1.2.3 Circuit Switching and Packet Switching

According to the way in which a network resource such as bandwidth is shared, a network can be classified as a circuit-switched or a packet-switched network. In circuit-switched networks such as telephone networks and Global System for Mobile (GSM) cellular networks, the reserved network resource will be held by the reservation owner until the reserved resource is released. During this period, the unused network resource reserved by one user cannot be used by any other users. This kind of network is usually associated with CO networks, where a resource reservation can be made for a path set between source and destination. This network is suitable to transport constant bit-rate traffic such as voice applications but is not suitable for bursty traffic like data applications.

In contrast, in a packet-switched network such as IP and ATM, the network resource is allocated on demand at the packet level. This means that the network resource, albeit being reserved by a user, can be shared by other users if the reserved resource is not actually used by its owner. This kind of network is better than the circuit-switched network for transporting bursty and non-delay-sensitive traffic, but it is less efficient for transporting delay-sensitive traffic such as voice. As pointed out in [1], the packet-switched network is more efficient than the circuit-switched network in terms of network resource utilization due to the benefit from traffic multiplexing offered by packet switching.

1.3 Major Networking Issues

This section briefly describes the major networking issues to be addressed for network design, which include error control, MAC, routing and switching, flow and congestion control, transmission reliability control, mobility support, QoS, and network security.

1.3.1 Error Control

Part of the data may be corrupted during its transmission over a low quality channel, which leads to reception errors. Thus, error control has to be used to detect and correct errors. To correct errors, powerful error detection methods should be conducted by the receiver, which can use, e.g., the cyclic redundancy check (CRC) algorithm. Error correction can be carried out by the forward error correction (FEC) and automatic repeat request (ARQ) schemes. With FEC, error correction is carried out by the receiver based on redundant information sent by the sender along with the original data. With ARQ, error correction is conducted by the sender through re-transmission of the unacknowledged data using, e.g., the stop-and-wait, Go-back-N, and selective ARQ schemes. A hybrid of FEC and ARQ can provide more powerful error control.

1.3.2 Medium Access Control (MAC)

As mentioned earlier, in a shared-media network, several nodes are linked to a common medium. If more than one node tries to use the medium simultaneously, their signals may collide at the same receiver, resulting in a failed reception of all transmitted signals. This phenomenon is analogous to a situation in which two speakers are talking simultaneously, so that neither of them can be heard clearly. To solve this problem, a medium access control (MAC) protocol is necessarily in place to coordinate nodes to share a common and finite bandwidth efficiently in a fair manner. The design of a MAC protocol primarily depends on network topologies and application requirements. For example, in a start topology, a centralized MAC protocol such as polling can be used, in which a central coordinator can arbitrate medium sharing. In wireless sensor networks, since energy consumption is critical to prolong the network lifetime, energy efficiency is a major issue to be addressed by the MAC protocol.

1.3.3 Addressing, Routing, and Switching

Addressing deals with a numbering scheme that can uniquely identify every node attached to the network. The address will be used by the network to forward traffic between endpoints in the network. Popular addressing schemes include the telephone number and the IP address.

In order to deliver a packet from a source to destination nodes, at least one route between them must be found; this route searching process is called routing. Once a route is found, its information can be either stored in routers or carried by the packets themselves. In the former case, the basic operation performed by a router for packet forwarding is to look up the pre-established routing table according to the network address carried by the packets. In this table, the destination address is usually used as the key index to look for the next hop that corresponds to the destination of packets. This processing delay primarily depends on the routing table size and searching algorithms, both of which are affected by the size of the routing address space.

Alternatively, in the latter case, instead of storing routing information at routers, the source routing approach allows every packet to carry routing information on the route along which the packet is going to travel. This method can avoid looking up large routing tables, but at the expense of a large packet overhead.

Consider a large number of packets that are going to travel along the same route between a source and destination pair. Once a route has been found, the subsequent packets can be assigned with a short label, which is stored at relaying units along this route and used as the routing information instead of the full network address. Meanwhile, the label will also be carried by packets to find the next hop from switching tables. This technique is called switching. Usually the number of simultaneously active endpoints is much smaller than the number of total network addresses. Consequently, the label is much shorter than the address, so the switching table is much smaller than the routing table. Thus, switching is much faster than routing for packet forwarding.

1.3.4 Traffic Control Mechanisms

A traffic control mechanism is often used to control the amount of traffic to be injected into a network. Typical mechanisms are window-based and rate-based controls.

With a window-based control, the amount of traffic that a node can inject into the network depends on the window size; i.e., the node can send as much traffic as allowed by the window size at any time. See, for example, the sliding window illustrated in Fig. 1.4, which slides from the left to the right. Since this mechanism has been used by Transmission Control Protocol (TCP), the protocol unit here is the segment as used by TCP. The maximum size of the window here is set to 9 segments, which is jointly determined by the window size at the receiver (rwin). There are in total 15 segments numbered from 0 to 14. Among them, segments 0 to 3 have been sent and acknowledged positively, so they can be discarded. Only segments 4 to 12 are under the control of the window. Of these, segments 4 to 8 have been sent but are still waiting for the acknowledgements to be sent by their destinations. Here the term flight size is used to indicate the number of segments that have been sent but not yet acknowledged. These segments must be under the window control, since if any of them is lost, retransmission must be carried out. Segments 9 to 12 are waiting for the transmission service. The remaining segments 13 to 14 are still out of the window and cannot be transmitted until some of segments 4 to 8 have been acknowledged positively.

With a rate-based control, the amount of traffic to be injected into the network within a specific time interval is under control, for example, 5 packets per second.

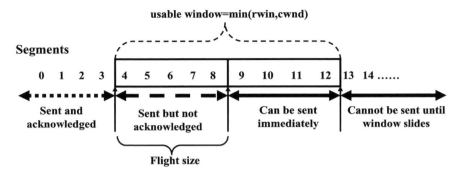

Fig. 1.4 An illustration of sliding window operation

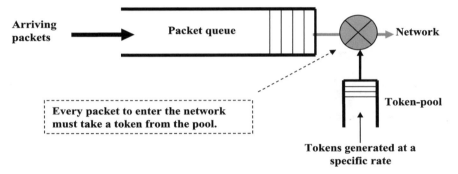

Fig. 1.5 Structure of the leaky bucket mechanism

A typical scheme is the leaky bucket as illustrated in Fig. 1.5, which consists of a token generator and a token pool. An arriving packet must take one token from the token pool in order to enter the network. If no token is available, the packet is stored in the buffer. The token is generated at a specific rate and is queued in the token pool if no packet is passing through. This mechanism can be used for traffic policing and traffic shaping. Traffic policing regulates incoming traffic according to a prior agreement set between the user and the network, while traffic shaping is used to shape traffic according to some traffic pattern, e.g., smoothing traffic burstiness.

1.3.5 Flow Control

Flow control is used to control the amount of traffic to be injected by a sending node into the network for a CO service. The objective of this control is to make traffic loads compliant with the pre-defined or pre-negotiated thresholds. Particularly in the transport layer, this control tries to limit the amount of traffic sent by a source

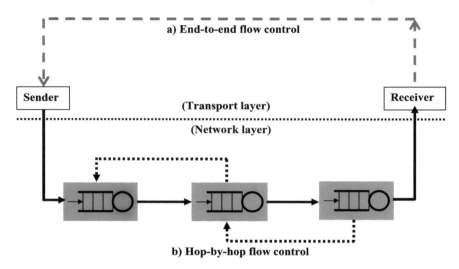

Fig. 1.6 Hop-by-hop flow control versus end-to-end flow control

node to prevent the buffer at its destination node from overflowing. For example, as illustrated in Fig. 1.6(a), TCP adopts the sliding window mechanism described above for an end-to-end flow control. In the network layer, this control tries to control the amount of traffic sent to other nodes along the route to the destination node according to the pre-negotiated agreement. To this end, a hop-by-hop flow control is needed, as illustrated in Fig. 1.6(b).

Obviously, a hop-by-hop flow control is more efficient than an end-to-end control since the former can be enforced more quickly than the latter. However, it is complex and costly to implement a hop-by-hop flow control since each node along a route should be involved in this kind of control. With an end-to-end flow control, only the source and destination nodes are involved in the control, so it is much simpler than the hop-by-hop flow control.

1.3.6 Congestion Control

Congestion control tries to relieve a congestion state as quickly as possible. A congestion state can be either physical or logical, as illustrated in Fig. 1.7. A physical congestion means that the maximum buffer capacity is reached. As a consequence, any newly arriving packets will be dropped immediately. A logical congestion state is defined artificially as a precaution to avoid physical congestion. Logical congestion states can be divided into multiple levels by setting different thresholds, as illustrated in Fig. 1.7.

In the network layer, once congestion occurs at a node, dropping packets is the fastest way to release the congestion state. In this case, which packet should be dropped is a major concern since packet dropping will affect the related applications.

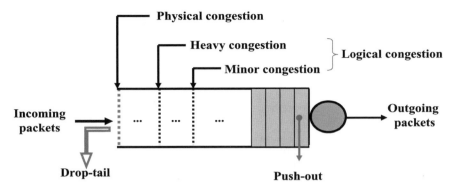

Fig. 1.7 Congestion states and control policies

Typically, there are three dropping policies. One is called drop-tail, in which all newly arriving packets are dropped in the case of congestion. This policy privileges those packets queued in the buffer over new arrivals. However, for delay-sensitive applications, if some packets have been queued too long to be meaningful even if they can reach their destinations, then dropping those packets makes more sense. Thus a push-out dropping policy is proposed to drop these packets on the head-of-line (HOL), as illustrated in Fig. 1.7. To support priority while maintaining fairness among arriving packets, a selective packet dropping policy is better such as the random early dropping (RED) policy [2].

An end-to-end connection, such as a TCP connection, may span over different types of networks. There is no guarantee that each network along an end-to-end connection will provide a proper congestion control. Therefore, from the transport layer's point of view, an end-to-end congestion control should be in place to maintain end-to-end transmission performance. This function is usually implemented in the transport layer to control the amount of traffic injected by source nodes so that the congestions at other nodes along the route to the destination can be released and even avoided. A typical example is TCP congestion control.

1.3.7 Transmission Reliability Control

Since channel error and congestion may affect a packet during its journey to its destination, packet loss or dropping may occur. In this case, the destination will not be able to receive what has been sent to it. A robust way to resolve this problem is to retransmit every lost or dropped packet, as illustrated in Fig. 1.8. To this end, a packet failure detection must first be performed. This can be realized by senders and receivers through the use of an acknowledgement scheme. An acknowledgement can be either positive (ACK) or negative (NACK). With the ACK, if a receiver has successfully received a packet, it returns a positive acknowledgement to the sender to confirm the reception. If the sender receives the ACK of the packets that have

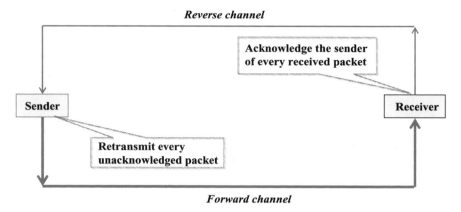

Fig. 1.8 Diagram of transmission reliability control

been sent in a pre-defined time period, it just retransmits them. In contrast, with the NACK, a receiver informs the sender of what has not been received successfully so far. Since a loss may also affect an acknowledgement packet, the positive acknowledgement is more robust than the negative one.

1.3.8 Quality of Service (QoS)

Quality of service (QoS) is used to measure the quality of the network service provided for the applications running over the network. Traditionally, one network is dedicated to one type of application with a fixed QoS. For example, the classical telephone network was designed for voice applications only by using the virtual circuit switching technology to provide a 64 kbit/s constant service rate for every voice session. The early IP networks adopted packet switching technology to provide only best-effort service for data applications. Later, with the development of the Integrated Services Digital Network (ISDN), QoS has received much more attention, because this network tries to support various applications with different QoS requirements. This issue has been studied for more than two decades, especially for ATM and IP networks.

In general, QoS mechanisms are divided into two levels: packet level and call level [3]. The most important mechanism at the call level is call admission control (CAC), which decides the call-level QoS by controlling the number of calls to be admitted by the network. The major packet-level QoS mechanisms include scheduling and buffering, which are fundamental to QoS provisioning. To guarantee QoS, these two mechanisms must be used jointly with traffic policing mechanisms, which enforce application traffic to be compliant with the contract negotiated between the user and the network.

1.3.9 Mobility Support

Since small and powerful mobile devices such as mobile phones, notebook computers, and iPads are becoming more and more popular, the support of communication for anything, anyhow, anywhere, and anytime has become an essential part of the modern communication network. To reach this goal, mobility support is the key element, and it actually can only be provided by wireless networks, especially as access networks. The fundamental mobility is usually jointly supported by two mechanisms at the call level and packet level. The call-level mechanism is called roaming, which is associated with location management that handles changes in user location. With roaming support, the user is allowed to change locations without suffering communication disconnection. The packet-level mechanism is called handoff, which deals with a user's motion during a communication in progress. With handoff support, the user can move during a communication in progress without suffering communication interruption.

1.3.10 Network Security

Numerous Internet attacks, such as the leaking of sensitive information and the denial of service (DoS) provided by important servers, have been reported, leading to immense economic and social damages. Since the Internet plays a critical role, not only in commercial applications but also in social activities, cyberspace security has been promoted to be part of national security in many countries. Therefore, network security as the basis of Internet security has become a networking issue of utmost importance which must be addressed thoroughly. Wireless networks in particular, due to their exposure and broadcast nature, are more vulnerable to security attacks than wired networks. Actually, this feature is a major hurdle in further deploying wireless networks in some important sectors such as governmental departments and financial-industrials. Furthermore, since the deployment of wireless networks is becoming more and more popular, the security of wireless networks will inevitably affect our daily life.

1.4 Motivation and Scope of the Monograph

As the number of applications and users, especially mobile users, continuously increases, the development of network technologies is moving toward a full integration of optical and wireless networks to meet the demand for both immense network capacity and pervasive computing. The current Internet has been developed primarily following the layered models and the end-to-end arguments. Typical layered models include the seven-layer Open Systems Interconnection (OSI) model defined by the International Standard Organization (ISO) and the 5-layer TCP/IP model to be discussed in Chap. 2. These models basically divide the system into multiple independent layers, each of which has explicitly defined functions and can interact only with its adjacent layers through service access points (SAPs) consisting of standardized primitives. Meanwhile, the end-to-end arguments basically suggest putting the application-level functions at the network edge rather than inside the network as much as possible in order to simplify network design and implementation.

Actually, both the layered models and the end-to-end arguments assume essentially the following conditions for networking. Nodes in the network, e.g., routers and switches, have powerful computing and buffering capabilities to support complex network operations and processing such as routing and congestion control. The reason for this is that the Internet was initially developed mainly for wired networks with almost stationary electronic computers. Now the development of optical and mobile wireless networks has radically changed the landscape of network technologies. First, the all-optical node in optical networks has only very weak computing and buffering capabilities, since no mature optical processing and buffering technologies are available today. Second, the channel quality of wireless networks is very different from that for wired channels in terms of capacity, reliability, and security, which are further impacted by terminal mobility.

To address these issues, many proposals with cross-layer design and optimization have been reported in the literature, somewhat suggesting a trend of reforming the layered models and the necessity of revising the end-to-end arguments for optical and mobile wireless networks in the future Internet. This monograph collectively reports the author's research results for these issues, which include an evaluation of networking modes for the Internet, all-optical packet switching (AOPS) networks, end-to-end QoS provisioning, the quantitative end-to-end arguments, an application of the multiple-input-multiple-output (MIMO) technology in wireless networks, as well as green networking strategies. Some preliminary results of the work have been published in international conferences and journals.

The remainder of this monograph is divided into eight parts and organized as follows.

1.4.1 The Internet Development versus Networking Modes

This part, i.e., Chap. 2, discusses the rationality of the layered models and the end-to-end arguments as well as their effects on the early development of the Internet. Challenges from the ever-growing number of new applications and users in the future Internet are also discussed, along with the major problems that the layered models and the end-to-end arguments may face in this case.

1.4.2 Structure for All-Optical Packet Switching

It is perceived that the all-optical network can provide immense network capacity that the other types of networks cannot offer with high energy efficiency. However, following the layered models mentioned earlier, the design of network protocols does not consider the characteristics of the physical layer except for physical transmission speeds. This type of design can avoid redesign and redevelopment of network protocols over different physical layers; however, the design principle is challenged by the big differences between conventional and all-optical communication systems. These differences strongly suggest that, in order to greatly improve network performance, an efficient interaction is required between the physical layer and the layers above to handle problems that cannot be resolved by the conventional layered model.

In all-optical networks, the all-optical node cannot process complex routing operations all-optically; however, this is essential and critical for networking. In this case, the current network structure needs to be reshaped such that all-optical networks can be developed with simple optical processing technologies available today or in the near future. To this end, a joint design of the network and physical layers is needed so that the routing function can be realized in the optical domain to avoid optical-electrical-optical (OEO) conversion. This topic is discussed in Chaps. 3 and 4, and some preliminary results were published in [4, 5].

1.4.3 Granular End-to-End QoS Provisioning

The future Internet should effectively satisfy different end-to-end QoS requirements of various applications in a heterogeneous network environment, which may integrate different types of wireless and wired networks. A possible solution available today is a combination of the per-flow IntServ and the per-class DiffServ, using DiffServ in backbone networks and IntServ in access networks to trade off between QoS granularity and implementation scalability [6]. But this combination is not a seamless end-to-end QoS solution, and QoS parameter conversion is needed between DiffServ and IntServ networks for every packet, which causes extra delay and consumes more energy.

Here a new QoS provisioning approach called Differentiated Queueing Service (DQS) is discussed. Unlike the per-flow IntServ and the per-class DiffServ, DQS is a per-packet QoS structure, by which the QoS requirement is clearly defined for each packet. By slightly increasing the packet overhead, DQS can provide granular end-to-end QoS without using sophisticated output schedulers. The principle of DQS is described in Chap. 5, and a cost model for DQS is discussed in Chap. 6. Some preliminary results of this part were published in [7–9].

1.4.4 Quantitative End-to-End Arguments

Reliable end-to-end transmission is one of the most important network services for many Internet applications. Conventionally, its design follows the famous end-to-end arguments [10], which as a whole strongly suggest a design principle of putting the application-level functions at the network edge rather than inside the network as much as possible in order to simplify network design and implementation. However, in certain new types of networks, such as multi-hop wireless ad hoc networks and all-optical networks, moving some functions from the network edge into the network is often considered to improve network performance but at the expense of an increased implementation complexity. Therefore, an important issue is to estimate both the performance gain and the implementation complexity potentially to be caused by a function displacement.

This part analytically studies some typical reliable transmission approaches by formulating some quantities for this issue. These formulas can be used to make a quantitative comparison between these different end-to-end reliable transmission approaches. This part consists of performance analysis in Chap. 7 and complexity estimation in Chap. 8, as well as a numerical discussion in Chap. 9. Some preliminary results of this part were published in [11].

1.4.5 Decoupling Congestion Control from TCP

Transmission Control Protocol (TCP) is the most popular and important transport layer protocol for end-to-end reliable transmission. However, it is well known that TCP cannot perform well in multi-hop wireless networks. Much research work has been carried out on this subject, but the problem has not been solved effectively. As inspired by the results of the quantitative end-to-end arguments discussed in Chaps. 7–9, shifting the congestion control function from the transport layer down to the lower layer can greatly improve the performance.

In this part, i.e., Chap. 10, we first discuss how to decouple the congestion control function from TCP and shift it down to the data link layer to overcome its problems in multi-hop wireless networks. In this case, the end-to-end congestion control of TCP is replaced by a hop-by-hop congestion control, which can be realized through a slight modification to the Request-to-Send (RTS)/Clear-to-Send (CTS) protocol used by the IEEE 802.11 MAC.

For all-optical networks, such decoupling also seems necessary, since the all-optical node with a limited buffering or even bufferless capacity will suffer high packet loss rates, not only due to congestion but also to collision if the capacity over provisioning is not in place. Therefore, we further discuss how to decouple the congestion control function from TCP and shift it down to the network layer to improve TCP performance. That is, a domain-by-domain congestion control is used to replace the end-to-end TCP congestion control. Some preliminary results of this part were published in [12].

1.4.6 Enabling Simultaneous MAC Transmission with MIMO

For the same reason as for all-optical networks, as mentioned in Sect. 1.4.2, cross-layer design and optimization is also very important for wireless networks. Therefore, Chaps. 11 and 12 will discuss how to exploit multiple-input-multiple-output (MIMO) technology [13] to enable MAC simultaneous transmissions at the same frequency from different nodes to improve network throughput. This approach, called logic MIMO (logMIMO), can improve the performance of wireless access networks, especially centralized mobile cellular networks. The major advantage of this approach is that it requires neither multiple antennas installed per terminal nor inter-node cooperative communication for an easier implementation. Some preliminary results of this part were published in [14].

1.4.7 Green Networking Strategies

Due to the ever-growing concern about global warming, green networking has becomes a hot research topic. It strongly suggests that energy efficiency should be addressed as an important issue in designing network protocols, algorithms, and infrastructure. Chap. 13 gives a brief survey of green networking strategies by formulating some fundamental elements of most green networking approaches. The implementation issue of each strategy is also investigated in terms of possible changes to be carried out in the existing network protocols and algorithms as well as the infrastructure. The discussion is intensified by evaluating how green networking efficiency is affected by some networking modes.

1.4.8 Summary and Vision

Last but not least, Chap. 14 first summarizes the major cross-layer efforts to improve network performance for all-optical and wireless networks discussed in the preceding chapters; these may be used by next generation networks in the future Internet. Then a strategic vision of network technology development is discussed with a super-layer model that allows cross-layer design and optimization for network research.

References

1. Kermani, P., Kleinrock, L.: A tradeoff study of switching systems in computer communication networks. IEEE Trans. Commun. **29**(12), 1052–1060 (1980)
2. Bonald, T., May, M., Bolot, J.C.: Analytic evaluation of RED performance. In: Proc. IEEE INFOCOM, Tel-Aviv, Israel, vol. 3, pp. 1415–1424 (2000)
3. Guérin, R., Peris, V.: Quality-of-service in packet networks: basic mechanisms and directions. Comput. Netw. **31**(3), 169–189 (1999)
4. Jiang, S.M.: A networking structure favorable for all-optical packet switching. In: Proc. IASTED Int. Conf. on Parallel & Distributed Computing & Systems (PDCS), Dallas, Texas, USA (2006)

5. Jiang, S.M.: An addressing independent networking structure favorable for all-optical packet switching. Comput. Commun. Rev. **37**(1), 19–28 (2007)
6. Rege, K., Dravida, S., Nanda, S., Narayan, S., Strombosky, J., Tandon, M., Gupta, D.: QoS management in trunk-and-branch switched Ethernet networks. IEEE Commun. Mag. **40**(12), 30–36 (2002)
7. Jiang, S.M.: Granular differentiated queueing services and cost model for end-to-end QoS: Principle. In: Proc. IEEE Int. Conf. Networks (ICON), Singapore, vol. 1, pp. 369–374 (2004)
8. Jiang, S.M.: Granular differentiated queueing services for QoS: structure and cost model. Comput. Commun. Rev. **35**(2), 13–22 (2005)
9. Jiang, S.M.: Differentiated queueing service (DQS) for end-to-end Qos provisioning: an evaluation from per-flow, per-class to per-packet. In: Wang, N. (ed.) Recent Advances in Providing QoS and Reliability in the Future Internet Backbone. Nova Science, New York (2011). ISBN 978-1-61761-858-1. Chapter 2
10. Saltzer, J.H., Reed, D.P., Clark, D.D.: End-to-end arguments in system design. ACM Trans. Comput. Syst. **2**(4), 277–288 (1984)
11. Jiang, S.M.: Quantitative end-to-end arguments: fundamental. In: Int. Conf. on Information, Communications and Signal Processing (ICICS), Macau, China (2009)
12. Jiang, S.M., Zuo, Q., Wei, G.: Decoupling congestion control from TCP for multi-hop wireless networks: semi-TCP. In: Proc. ACM MobiCom Workshop on Challenged Networks (CHANTS), Beijing, China (2009)
13. Alamouti, S.M.: A simple transmit diversity technique for wireless communications. IEEE J. Sel. Areas Commun. **16**(8), 1451–1458 (1998)
14. Jiang, S.M.: A logical MIMO MAC approach for uplink access control in centralized wireless. Guangzhou, China (2008)

Chapter 2
Internet Development Versus Networking Modes

Abstract In the 1970s, the ever-increasing application of computers pushed forward the development of computer networks. One famous project is the ARPANET, which was founded by the U.S. Department of Defense and laid the foundation for the Internet. Initially, the objective of developing a computer network was to enable data applications through interconnecting computers located in different sites for data sharing and message exchange. Typical applications available at that time included e-mail, news, File Transfer Protocol (FTP), and Telnet. Later, this technology spread quickly and widely and has now become a worldwide Internet, an essential part of our daily life. The applications supported by the Internet today include not only data applications but also real-time applications such as voice over IP (VoIP), IPTV, networked entertainment, and social networks, with new applications continuously being created. Although there have been many changes in both the number and types of applications and users on the Internet, the networking modes, which collectively refer to the principle and methodology for networking, have remained almost intact. This chapter briefly reviews the major networking modes and discusses the challenges that they may face for the future Internet.

2.1 Networking Modes

As discussed in Chap. 1, visibly a network can be abstracted into a collection of nodes and links. Invisibly, a network is composed of a set of functions which are used to provide network services. These functions must address the networking issues described in Chap. 1 by implementing relevant network protocols and algorithms. The network design must decide what functions to implement and how to distribute them as well as how to make them cooperate as a whole to provide network services. Generally, there are two design principles: the layered model, which governs a vertical distribution of network functions within one network node, and the end-to-end arguments, which mainly guide a horizontal distribution of network functions among different network nodes.

S.M. Jiang, *Future Wireless and Optical Networks*,
Computer Communications and Networks,
DOI 10.1007/978-1-4471-2822-9_2, © Springer-Verlag London Limited 2012

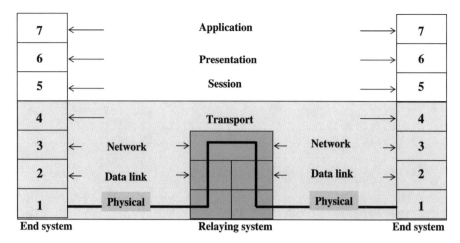

Fig. 2.1 ISO's OSI seven-layer reference model

2.1.1 *Layered Models*

The major issue to be addressed for interconnecting heterogeneous computers is the methodology to build a network. Obviously, building such a system is a huge and complex engineering task, and it is difficult for just a few companies or institutions to complete the whole system. Therefore, dividing this task into small pieces so that each piece can be solved relatively easily and independently is the basic idea of the layered model. Furthermore, different layers are made independent of each other in terms of layer internal design but with a standardized interface, through which the adjacent layers can interact and communicate with each other. There are three typical layered models: the OSI seven-layer reference model, the five-layer TCP/IP model, and the ATM reference model. However, since ATM is "going downhill," only the former two models are discussed below.

2.1.1.1 OSI Reference Model

In 1978, the ISO started to develop a standard for Open Systems Interconnection (OSI), which was enforced in 1983. This standard allows a system to communicate with any systems anywhere that are designed following the same standard. According to this reference model, an open system is divided into seven layers as illustrated in Fig. 2.1. The primary functions of each layer [1, 2] are briefly described below; some have been newly added following the recent development of networking technologies.

- Physical layer—handles the bit-level communication over media. It provides basic functions for digital communication such as modulation/demodulation, coding/decoding, synchronization, and error control.

- Data link layer—provides the frame-level communication over links. A frame is a formatted bit block. Since the physical layer cannot guarantee error-free communication, the primary function of this layer is error control that provides an error-free communication service for the network layer. For a shared-medium network in which multiple users share a common medium, a MAC protocol is especially needed to coordinate the medium sharing.
- Network layer—provides the packet-level communication across the whole network. A packet is also a formatted bit block. Addressing, routing, congestion control, QoS support, and network security are the primary functions of this layer.
- Transport layer—provides communications between endpoints, relying on the underlying network layer but providing network-independent services to higher layers. Its major functions include flow and congestion control as well as end-to-end transmission reliability control and security.
- Session layer—provides control functions for communications between cooperating applications at endpoints, including exchanging the identifications of endpoints, and establishing, managing, and terminating sessions between them.
- Presentation layer—provides independence for application processes from cooperating applications with different data representation, and services to the application layer by transforming data structures into a format agreed upon by the partners.
- Application layer—provides an interface with an application process requiring communication support, with standard services for transmission between user processes, database access, and running of processes on different computers.

From the above definitions, we find that only layer 1 through layer 4 are related to the networking issues discussed earlier.

Actually, each layer is composed of a set of functions. A function of one layer that can be seen by the layer above is called the service offered to its next higher layer. According to the model, each layer except the highest layer has a set of services that are provided for its next higher layer through the standardized service access points (SAPs). Thus, devices from different manufacturers can work together. Furthermore, only the adjacent layers can communicate with each other through SAPs. A network connection between source and destination must be set up first to provide the network service, particularly for the network layer. Therefore, the network defined by this model is a connection-oriented network.

2.1.1.2 TCP/IP Model

Although the ISO seven-layer reference model was theoretically considered as the ultimate model for worldwide interoperable networking, the TCP/IP model is the most popular and successful implementation in today's Internet. The mapping between the TCP/IP model and the OSI seven-layer model is illustrated in Fig. 2.2, where the function distribution of the TCP/IP model is also depicted. This model loosely follows the OSI reference model with only four layers, and its physical and data link layers are integrated into one link layer.

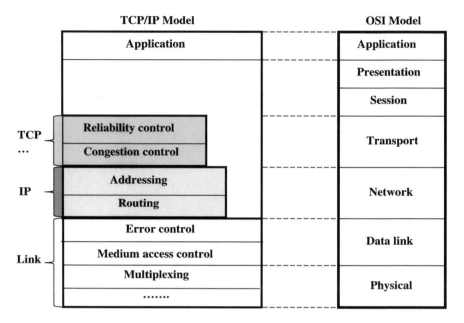

Fig. 2.2 ISO seven-layer model versus TCP/IP model

The key difference between these two models in terms of networking modes is that, with the ISO model, the connection-oriented service is provided in the network layer. Thus, packet switching can be used to accelerate packet forwarding. With the TCP/IP model, only the connectionless service using IP is provided, with which data packets can be transmitted anytime without a prior connection setup. In this case, routing has to be used. Due to its simplicity, this model has been widely implemented in the Internet. A brief comparison between these two models can be found in [2].

2.1.2 End-to-End Arguments

The end-to-end arguments [3] were among the most influential design principles for the Internet even before they were first explicitly articulated in the early 1980s. The arguments state that "functions placed at low levels of a system may be redundant or of little value when compared with the cost of providing them at that low level." Basically, these arguments as a whole strongly suggest a design principle of putting the application-level functions at the network edge rather than inside the network as much as possible in order to simplify network design and implementation. Doing so can also make the so-designed network protocols versatile for different types of networks.

One typical example following the arguments is the TCP/IP protocol stack. TCP is the most well-known protocol for end-to-end reliable transmission, and was first

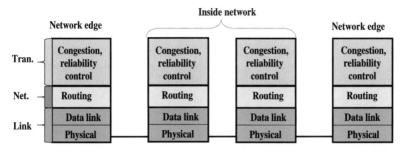

Fig. 2.3 A possible implementation without following the end-to-end arguments

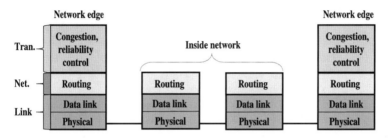

Fig. 2.4 An illustrative implementation following the end-to-end arguments

published in 1977 [4]. Although TCP was invented before the first explicit articulation of the arguments in 1980s, it follows them well [3]. As illustrated in Fig. 2.3, a possible networking mode is to allow every node to fully implement networking functions as depicted in Fig. 2.2. However, following the end-to-end arguments, only the source and destination of a TCP connection need to have the full functions as illustrated in Fig. 2.4. Similarly, the IP in the network layer is also as simple, using the connectionless networking technology and the first-in-first-out (FIFO) scheduling policy without the retransmission of lost packets. Actually, the end-to-end reliability control function is shifted to TCP in the transport layer. This design can simplify the implementation of relaying units such as routers so the protocols can run successfully over various types of networks [5].

2.2 Challenges of Wireless and Optical Networks

There is no doubt that both the layered models and the end-to-end arguments have played critical roles in the successful development of the Internet over the past three decades. These design principles allow a complex system to be decomposed into smaller subsystems for easy implementation and can guarantee the interoperability of devices produced from different manufacturers. They can also simplify the network structure and operation so that such a designed network can run over various communication systems for interconnection.

However, the user's expectations of the Internet today and in the future have been going far beyond the objectives of its original designers in terms of network coverage, capacity, and number and type of both users and applications. These new requirements greatly stimulate the development of new networking technologies for the future Internet, as discussed below.

2.2.1 New Requirements of Users and Applications

When the Internet was designed for the U.S. Department of Defense in the 1970s, the main objective was to share files in computers or storage media located in government offices and institutional organizations. These computers and storage media were mainly wired with metallic cables and were almost stationary. By default, the design of networking protocols and algorithms such as routing protocols and congestion control schemes assumes the availability of powerful computing and buffering technologies for the network service provisioning.

Today, the Internet is available almost everywhere. The ever-increasing number of users has already caused the address space of the original IP (i.e., IP version 4 or simply IPv4) to be exhausted. According to the statistics given by [6], the number of Internet users in the world was 360,985,492 on December 31, 2000, and reached 1,966,514,816 by June 30, 2010, which is equivalent to 28.7% of the world population, increasing at a rate of 444.8%.

On the other hand, mobile users, who may use mobile phones, laptop computers, or personal digital assistants, etc., constitute the largest population of electronic device users in the world. According to the report published by the United Nations (UN) on February 23, 2010 [7], two-thirds of the world's population (i.e., around 4.7 billion) were mobile subscribers, while this number was only about one billion in 2002. Meanwhile, the number of powerful and smart mobile devices such as Apple iPhone and iPad is growing rapidly. The number of smart phone users is expected to exceed one billion by 2013 [8]. Thus, more and more applications originally designed for stationary devices are expected to run on mobile devices too. This change requires the Internet be able to efficiently support mobile applications.

Regarding the Internet applications, besides the original data applications such as e-mail, FTP, and remote login, newly developed killer data applications include the World Wide Web (WWW) and e-commerce. Real-time applications have also been developed, for example, voice over IP (VoIP) and networked games as well as streaming applications like IP television (IPTV). Some other developing applications include cloud computing [9] and the Internet of Things (IoT) [10]. One can expect that more and more new applications will appear in the future as the number of Internet users is continuously increasing.

These radical changes in both the number and type of users and applications that the Internet should support pose a big challenge to networking modes. Although much incremental effort has been made to enhance the Internet, the networking modes mentioned earlier have been kept almost intact so far. The question is whether these networking modes can still guide us to foster the Internet to satisfy new requirements in terms of network capacity, pervasive networking, quality of service (QoS) provisioning, and network security support as well as green networking. These issues are discussed below.

2.2.2 Network Capacity

The ever-increasing number of users and applications requires immense network capacity to support them. For the time being, this level of capacity can only be provided by using optical communication technologies, particularly using optical fibers as communication media. For example, so far Gigabit Ethernet using metallic wires such as twisted copper pairs can only provide Gbps-level capacity over a maximum distance of less than 100 km, while a single optical fiber can provide Tbps-level (1 Tbps = 10^3 Gbps) transmission rates over much longer distances. Furthermore, optical fibers are much cheaper than metallic wires.

However, the ultra-high transmission rate of optical fibers cannot transfer into the same level of network speed if there is not the same level of high-speed packet forwarding technology. The successful development of the Internet is largely due to the mature electronic computer technology, which can provide high-speed computing and buffering support for realizing high-speed and quality networking. Many networking functions such as routing, QoS provisioning, and congestion control need complex computing and buffering, the key elements indispensable for networking. Unfortunately, cost-effective photonic computer and optical random access memory are not yet available, and it may still be a long time before they are available to provide ultra-high speed optical networking.

The following sections give a brief survey of optical networking technologies that aim at handling this issue.

2.2.2.1 Optical-Electrical-Optical Conversion

Today, many optical networks are implemented by jointly using electronic computers and optical fibers through optical-electrical-optical (OEO) conversion, as illustrated in Fig. 2.5. Optical fibers are used as transmission media while electronic computers are used for complex networking operations, particularly routing. To this end, optical signals are first converted into electrical signals, which are then routed electrically at the relaying units such as IP routers, and then recovered as optical signals for transmission over optical fibers. The major drawback of this approach is that the networking speed will be limited by the electronic computer speed, which will become a bottleneck of networking performance. The transmission speed of optical fibers is much faster than that of electronic computers, and the same applies to their speed increase rates, as discussed below.

According to Moore's Law [11], the speed of an electronic processor can be doubled almost every 18 months, while it can be doubled almost every nine months for

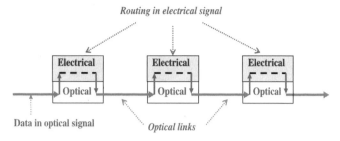

Fig. 2.5 Optical networks based on OEO conversion

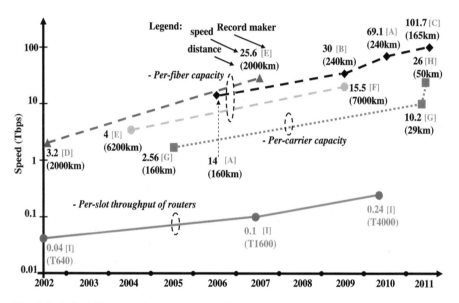

Fig. 2.6 Optical fiber capacity versus electronic router speed (Record makers: [A] = Nippon Telegraph and Telephone Corporation (NTT), [B] = KDDI R&D, [C] = NEC Laboratories in Princeton, [D] = Furukawa Electric (Japan), [E] = Alcatel-Lucent, [F] = Bell Labs, [G] = Fraunhofer Heinrich Hertz Institute (Germany), [H] = Karlsruhe Institute of Technology (Germany), [I] = Juniper Networks)

the optical transmission speed following Butters' Law [12]. Figure 2.6 depicts some optical carrier speed records and per-slot routing speeds of the electronic router T-Series from Juniper Networks [13]. We find that the routing speeds are much slower than those of the optical carrier, and the fiber speeds vary largely against the distances that the optical signal can travel without using a repeater. An inspiring fact is that the per-carrier capacity has increased rapidly recently, which will further improve the optical fiber capacity.

A carrier is associated with a wavelength or frequency. The capacity of an optical fiber is the sum of the capacities of all carriers multiplexed in this fiber by using wavelength division multiplexing (WDM) [14], which can allow multiple carriers

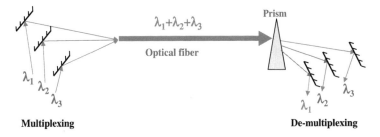

Multiplexing   **De-multiplexing**

Fig. 2.7 Principle of optical multiplexing and demultiplexing

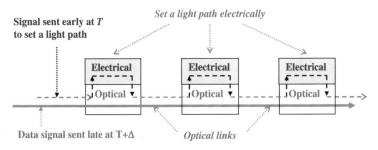

Fig. 2.8 Optical burst switching (OBS) network

to be multiplexed into one fiber and demultiplexed at the end of the fiber. As illustrated in Fig. 2.7, when it passes through a transparent medium such as a prism to another medium, light is refracted at an angle that varies with wavelength, and so a multiplexed signal can be demultiplexed in this way.

Another weakness of the OEO-based technology is its low energy efficiency due to the OEO conversion. As will be discussed in Chap. 13, energy consumption rather than transmission capacity will become one of the major hurdles that impact the Internet development, because the future Internet must be green.

2.2.2.2 Partial OEO Conversion

To avoid a full OEO conversion of every data signal for electronic processing, another approach suggests that the sender first transmit an optical signal along a dedicated light path to set a light path for data transmission. The data will then be sent subsequently in a Δ time after the path setup signal has been sent out. As illustrated in Fig. 2.8, upon arriving at a relaying unit, the path setup signal is converted into an electrical signal, which is processed electronically to set up a light path for the data transmission. In this case, no OEO conversion is carried out for the data signal, which travels in the optical domain all the way to the destination. This typical example is called optical burst switching (OBS) [15].

An OBS router can be composed of an array of mirrors, which can be tuned electrically through a micro-electro-mechanical system (MEMS) [16, 17] according

The same wavelength used along the whole path:

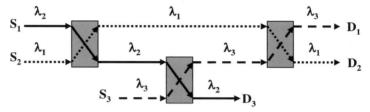

3 light paths: S$_1$D$_3$ with λ$_2$, S$_2$D$_2$ with λ$_1$ and S$_3$D$_1$ with λ$_3$

Fig. 2.9 Wavelength routing

to the routing information carried by the path setup signal. The major problem with OBS is the electronic processing with the OE conversion, which may become the bottleneck of the ultra-high-speed optical fibers. The major implementation issues include how to efficiently set up a light path for successful data transmission in the optical domain, which largely depends on the Δ setting. A large Δ will waste the fiber capacity, while a small one may cause data packets to be transmitted on an unavailable light path since no ACK on path setup is returned to the sender. Furthermore, since no global coordination is carried out for such a path setup, path collisions may occur if multiple paths are competing for the same carrier on the same link, causing packet losses.

2.2.2.3 All-Optical Networking

Two methods able to fully make use of ultra-high-speed optical fibers without any OEO conversion are wavelength routing and wavelength switching. These two methods exploit the same property of light as used for the demultiplexing mentioned above. The major difference between the routing and switching here is the number of wavelengths used in constructing a light path. With routing, the same wavelength is used all the way from source to destination; with switching, the wavelength can be changed hop by hop.

Figure 2.9 shows an example of wavelength routing, where three light paths are constructed, each of which is associated with one wavelength. That is, the same wavelength must be used along the entire light path. This requirement, called the wavelength continuity constraint [18], limits the number of light paths that can be set up by a given number of wavelengths. In contrast, wavelength switching exploits wavelength converters, which can covert the wavelength associated with the arriving signal on an input link into another wavelength and transmit it through an output link. As illustrated in Fig. 2.10, for the same set of three light paths as constructed in Fig. 2.9, two wavelengths are sufficient here.

However, for both wavelength routing and switching, a major problem is that the number of wavelengths with which the light signal can efficiently travel in optical fibers is very limited in comparison with the number of source-destination pairs. In

Input and output wavelengths can be different at one node:

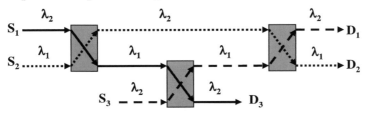

3 light paths: S_1D_3 with $\lambda_2\lambda_1\lambda_2$, S_2D_2 with $\lambda_1\lambda_2\lambda_1$ and S_3D_1 with $\lambda_2\lambda_1\lambda_2$

Fig. 2.10 Wavelength switching

Table 2.1 Summary of optical networking technologies

	Full OEO	Partial OEO	All-optical networking
Switching mode	Packet switching		Circuit switching
OEO level	Packet	Path setting	Control
Challenges	Slow electronic computing speed	Inefficiency of light path setting	Limited number of suitable wavelengths

this case, traffic aggregation and deaggregation need to be conducted at the network edges in order to use fewer wavelengths. To avoid OEO conversion at the time scale of a call level or packet level, a light path should be set up in advance for each node pair through a setting process with the OEO conversion at a larger time scale. However, once a light path has been set up, it cannot be adjusted dynamically on either call-level or packet-level time. Since the bandwidth of a light path is directly associated with the wavelengths, the bandwidth of a light path cannot be shared by other paths even if there is no traffic traveling along this path. This makes wavelength routing and switching essentially identical to electrical circuit switching in terms of bandwidth utilization, which cannot benefit from the traffic multiplexing that can be provided by packet switching.

2.2.2.4 Summary

Table 2.1 summarizes the major characteristics of the above-mentioned optical networking technologies. Without effective photonic computing and buffering technologies, a joint use of electronic computer and optical fibers for packet-level routing with OEO will be constrained by the electronic computing speed, which is much slower than the optical carrier speed and has a lower energy efficiency. The performance of OBS with partial OEO conversion relies on the efficiency of the light path setting. Wavelength routing and switching suffer from the limited number of wavelengths available for optical transmission.

Table 2.2 Comparison between wireless and wired networks

	Wired networks	Wireless networks
Channel reliability (BER)	About 10^{-9}	$10^{-2}-10^{-5}$
Channel capacity	Tbps-level or higher	Mbps-level
Channel security	Secure	Insecure
Mobility support	No	Yes
Node capability	Strong	Weak
Power supply	Unlimited	Battery-operated

2.2.3 Pervasive Networking

The ever-increasing number of mobile users greatly stimulates the development of mobile wireless networks toward supporting high mobility at high speeds as indicated in Fig. 2.11. This kind of network is usually used jointly with wired networks to provide the user with Internet access to anything anyhow, anywhere and anytime. However, as listed in Table 2.2, there are many radical differences between wired and wireless networks due to their distinct communication media. The major communication medium for wireless networks is radio, which by its nature is exposed and broadcast and thus vulnerable to interference and attack. Media for wired networks typically include metallic cables (e.g., twisted copper pairs) and optical fibers that are well protected. As listed in Table 2.2, wireless networks have the following distinguishing characteristics: low channel capacity, unreliable and insecure channels, and mobile terminals, which are less computationally powerful than stationary computers and often battery operated.

These differences are so significant that many networking issues that have been solved in wired networks must be readdressed in mobile wireless networks. A big challenge facing all wireless networks is how to efficiently use the scarce radio spectrum to support the ever-increasing number of both mobile users and mobile applications. As illustrated in Fig. 2.6, it is relatively easy for optical networks to have Tbps-level network capacity. However, for wireless networks, the fastest wireless technology available on the market is the ultra-wide bandwidth (UWB) network, which can provide up to 485 Mbps but within a distance of less than 2 meters. Furthermore, wireless network environments are usually highly dynamic due to interferences, multi-path propagation, and terminal mobility.

To achieve the above objectives in such a difficult and complex situation, much research has been conducted, and many proposals have been reported in the literature. Among them, the cross-layer design and optimization approach has recently attracted a lot of attention [19]. Unlike the layered models and the end-to-end arguments mentioned earlier, this approach tries to improve the performance of wireless networks and optimize wireless resource utilization by (i) sharing information available at different layers and (ii) redistributing networking functions or even adding new functions if necessary. In this case, changes in both the layered models and the end-to-end arguments are inevitable. Of course, some new challenging issues

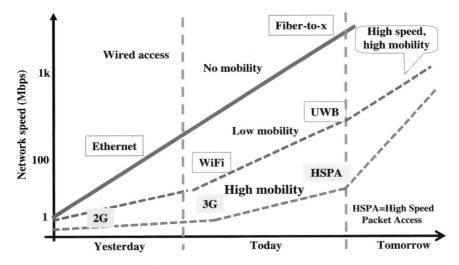

Fig. 2.11 Development of mobile wireless networks

may also arise from this approach. For example, we need to (i) study how to maintain interoperability for various cross-layer designed protocols and algorithms and (ii) determine whether the above changes are cost effective with respect to the performance gain and increased complexity caused by these changes.

2.2.4 Quality of Service

As the number of applications is continuously increasing, especially real-time and multimedia applications, an essential issue to be addressed for future networks is how to efficiently satisfy the quality of service (QoS) of various applications in a cost-effective way. QoS has been studied for more than two decades, especially for ATM and IP networks. ATM is regarded as a reference model for QoS support; many approaches originating from ATM are applied today for QoS support in other networks (e.g., IP) such as scheduling and call admission control. However, ATM is a connection-oriented network and is more complex than the connectionless IP network, leading to IP's dominance in today's Internet. This fact further stimulates the all-IP network approach, in which only IP is used as the network protocol in the network layer.

2.2.4.1 QoS Capability of IP

QoS support for the IP network has not been well resolved, since IP was originally designed to only provide a best-effort service at the packet level with the connectionless networking mode. Thus, IP has a property that is unfavorable for QoS support:

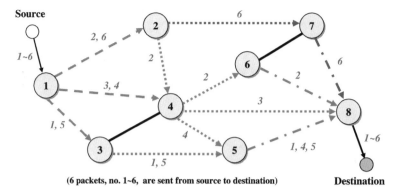

(6 packets, no. 1~6, are sent from source to destination)   **Destination**

Fig. 2.12 Example of dynamics of IP routes

at the packet level, it is impossible for a router to make any resource reservation for a packet that is going to visit it, since the router cannot know whether there is a packet visiting until the packet arrives. IP has been enhanced by introducing the flow approach on the top of packets. A flow is a series of packets traveling from source to destination. However, at the flow level, the route of a flow is not pinned [20] and is often adjusted during the flow lifetime to balance traffic loads and maximize fault tolerance capability. Therefore, there is not a dedicated route for a traffic flow between a source-destination pair since each packet is routed on-the-fly according to the route dynamically set by routing protocols. Figure 2.12 gives an example of this phenomenon, which shows that a series of packets may travel along different routes between node 1 (source) and node 6 (destination).

The best-effort service of the original IP using the FIFO scheduling policy has also been enhanced by using sophisticated output schedulers such as class-based scheduling. The flow-level resource negotiation and reservation method has also been standardized by the Resource Reservation Protocol (RSVP) [21, 22]. Call admission control (CAC) has also been proposed in order to further enhance IP's QoS capability. Actually, these efforts to improve the QoS capability of IP more or less follow ATM's philosophy for QoS provisioning. Note that ATM is a connection-oriented network, but the above enhancements to IP do not change its inherent properties, i.e., those of a connectionless network with unpinned routes. In this case, it is not cost effective to make a hard resource reservation for a flow to guarantee its QoS since the reserved resource is wasted if the route of the flow is changed. Therefore, RSVP only provides soft-state resource reservation, i.e., an amount of network resource reserved for a flow may be automatically released after a pre-defined time period even when the flow is still alive.

2.2.4.2 Per-Flow IntServ Versus Per-Class DiffServ

Two typical mechanisms proposed for IP to enhance its QoS capability include the per-flow IntServ [23] and the per-class DiffServ [24]. Similar to ATM, IntServ tries to provide granular QoS at the flow level by reserving resource for each flow, while DiffServ tries to provide QoS at the class level by aggregating flows with the same type of QoS requirements. However, the per-flow IntServ has a scalability problem in the case of a large number of flows present at a router, especially those in core networks. This occurs because the router needs to store per-flow QoS information for QoS provisioning. Although the per-class DiffServ can overcome this problem through flow aggregation, it cannot cost-effectively provide QoS support for each individual flow, since it must satisfy the individual flow with the most stringent QoS requirement in the aggregated flow.

To trade off between QoS granularity and implementation complexity, a combination of IntServ and DiffServ has also been reported [25]; i.e., DiffServ is used in core networks and IntServ in edge networks, such as access networks. In this combination, QoS parameter conversion must be carried out at the boundary between these two types of networks. Thus, this combination is not a seamless end-to-end QoS solution, and the conversion will cause extra delay and energy consumption. On the other hand, both IntServ and DiffServ as well as their hybrid largely depend on sophisticated output schedulers for QoS provisioning. Both parameter conversion and output scheduling will increase the implementation complexity as QoS granularity and the number of flows increase. The conversion point may become the performance bottleneck of end-to-end QoS provisioning, while a sophisticated output scheduler may become the bottleneck of high-speed links, since they have to make a decision on-the-fly for every incoming packet.

The adoption of CAC, resource reservation, and sophisticated schedulers for QoS provisioning very much increases the implementation complexity, which violates the simplicity principle of the original IP following the end-to-end arguments. Therefore, the capacity over-provisioning approach is proposed and implemented in practice to simplify QoS provisioning for IP by using a more-than-need network capacity [26]. Obviously, this approach wastes network bandwidth and is not green.

2.2.5 Network Security

Similar to QoS support, the Internet was initially designed without considering network security. This happened because the overwhelming majority of users at that time were people from governmental and institutional organizations, who are usually well educated and trustworthy. Thus, a lot of sensitive information such as user names and passwords for FTP and Telnet were sent in a plaintext over the Internet at that time. However, as the Internet has gone public, especially for commercial applications such as e-commerce and e-banking, attacks on the Internet are continuously increasing, causing immense economic and social damage. Thus, IP Security (IPSec) has been proposed to provide "access control, connectionless integrity, data origin authentication, rejection of replayed packets and confidentiality" [27]. Basically, IPSec builds a secure sublayer on top of the connectionless IP to provide secure network services for applications in higher layers.

Actually, it is almost impossible for a network to completely prevent a packet from being intercepted or modified during the journey to its destination, especially when traveling in a shared-media network such as wireless networks—everything transmitted over the air can be received by other parts due to its broadcast nature. Therefore, the actual confidentiality and integrity protection are realized through cryptographic mechanisms. That is, for confidentiality, if a packet is intercepted, it cannot be understood without a decryption using the proper key. Similarly, for integrity, if any modification is incurred to a packet, this incident can be detected by the receiver. However, these cryptograph-based protections in the network layer can also be equally provided by the transport layer on an end-to-end basis, and similarly for other secure services such as repudiation, which ensures that the sender of a message can be identified.

The confidentiality and integrity protections provided by the network layer are in an embarrassing situation. On one hand, many applications that do not want such protection avoid using these functions due to their computational expense. On the other hand, those applications requiring these security protections prefer to adopt the same protection provided by the transport layer since they are end-to-end based. This is because the application layer cannot be assured that the same protection can be provided by every network segment all the way from source to destination. If any of them fails in doing so, the end-to-end security may be compromised. Therefore, the network layer should focus on providing security protections that cannot be provided by higher layers.

Similar to the efforts made to enhance IP's QoS capability discussed above, IPSec does not change the connectionless nature of IP, which allows packets to be transmitted anytime to anywhere without requiring a connection setup. In this case, neither the sender nor the receiver has the chance to authenticate each other before any transmission incurs between them in the network layer. Furthermore, the destination has no way to control traffic loads approaching it and cannot judge whether the IP address of a sender is genuine. These features make it easy to launch many attacks, such as denial of service (DoS) attacks [28]. Since every packet is forwarded along a route that is dynamically set on-the-fly by routing protocols, attacks to routing information such as IP addresses or routing tables may lead to incorrect delivery of IP packets [29], probably leading packets to be sent to wrong receivers or to circulate in the network.

Today the Internet has become an indispensable part of our society, and Internet security has been delegated as a part of national security in many countries. Since both the number and type of users and applications are continuously increasing, it is still an open issue whether the enhanced IP security can satisfy the security requirements of a complex, important and even green cyberspace.

2.2.6 Green Networking

Due to the increasing number of disasters caused by global warming, carbon emission has become an important issue of almost every sector in the world today. As reported in [30], the energy consumed by the information and communication technology (ICT) sector is more than that consumed by the aviation sector. There is no doubt that the Internet has achieved great success over the past three decades. However, during this development, the privileged issues addressed by network researchers and designers have been mainly networking performance and reliability—energy efficiency has been more or less ignored.

High requirements on security and energy efficiency in the future Internet pose big challenges to network design. Therefore, it is necessary to conduct a timely revisit of the current networking modes with respect to the new requirements raised by the future Internet discussed above. We will discuss this issue in more detail in Chap. 13.

2.3 Conclusion

Table 2.3 summarizes the major characteristics of the Internet at different stages of its development. It is straightforward to understand the parts of the initial and current Internet, which have been discussed earlier. For the Internet in the future, we list some possible changes in both users and applications as well as networking modes that may be incurred to satisfy new requirements in the future.

First of all, "any media" is used here to indicate that unlimited types of applications may run over the future Internet, and the users will not be limited to humans only, but also objects. For example, the Internet of Things (IoT) tries to interconnect everything through the Internet. In terms of network design principles, cross-layered design and optimization should be applied in addition to the original layered models. Simplicity is always one of the major design objectives, but sometimes a tradeoff between simplicity and other important indicators is necessary. Although we do not know yet if it is necessary to invent new protocol units, there is no doubt that the packet and flow will still be basic protocol units in the future. Since both connectionless and connection-oriented networks have their own advantages and disadvantages, they should be used jointly to efficiently support various types of applications in the future Internet. For the QoS capability, more efforts should be made to improve QoS granularity for high cost-effectiveness and energy efficiency. Meanwhile, the structure of QoS support should be scalable in order to cost-effectively satisfy the QoS requirements of any media. Therefore, both soft- and hard-state resource reservations should be provided for different resource requirements. To this end, some new mechanisms need to be devised.

Network security and mobility support as well as green networking should become a cohesive part of the core network structure. Since optical fibers can provide much more immense capacity than traditional media cost-effectively, and also provide higher energy efficiency, optical networking is a promising technology for both wired and wireless networks. For wireless, the radio over fiber (RoF) technology can be applied to improve wireless coverage by using optical fibers. However, some new technologies need to be developed in order to narrow the gap between optical

Table 2.3 Evolution of network technologies for the Internet

	Initial Internet	Current Internet	Future Internet
Applications	Data (e.g., e-mail FTP, Telnet)	Multimedia (e.g., data voice, video, cybergames)	Any media (e.g., IoT cloud computing, new apps)
User characteristics			
Type	Limited types	Anyone	Anyone+anything
Number	Small number	Large number	Enormous number
Mobility	Stationary	Stationary+mobile	
Networking modes			
Vertical	Layered models		Cross-layered models
Horizontal	End-to-end arguments		Simplicity+tradeoff
Unit	Packet	Packet+flow	
CL/CO	Connectionless (CL)		CL+Connection-oriented
Stability	Unpinned routes		Unpinned+pinned routes
QoS structure			
QoS type	Best effort	Per-flow, per-class	Granularity+scalability
Scheduling	FIFO	Output scheduler	New mechanisms
Resource	No reservation	Soft-state reservation	Soft+hard reservation
Additional features			
Mobility	Not	Improved	Fully
Security	Supported	On top of IP	Integrated
Green	Not considered or optional		Compulsory
Enabling technologies			
Processing	Electronic computing+buffer		Optical processing+buffer
Media	Metallic cables	Cables+optical fiber	Optic fiber
Routing	Routing	OEO-based routing	All-optical switching
Switching	Switching	Wavelength routing	New methods

networking requirements and immature photonic computing and buffering technologies that are unable to effectively support optical networking. More discussions on these issues will be provided in the remainder of the monograph.

References

1. Stallings, W.: Data and Computer Communications, 5th edn. Prentice-Hall, New York (1997)
2. Tanenbaum, A.S.: Computer Networks, 4th edn. Pearson Education, Upper Saddle River (2003)

3. Saltzer, J.H., Reed, D.P., Clark, D.D.: End-to-end arguments in system design. ACM Trans. Comput. Syst. **2**(4), 277–288 (1984)
4. Postel, J.: Transmission control protocol. IETF RFC 793 (1977)
5. Clark, D.: The design philosophy of the DARPA Internet protocols. In: SIGCOMM '88: Symposium Proceedings on Communications Architectures and Protocols, pp. 106–114 (1988)
6. Internet World Stats – Usage and Population Statistics. http://www.internetworldstats.com
7. Available on line at http://www.mobilemarketingwatch.com
8. Available on line at http://www.telecoms.com
9. Hayes, B.: Cloud computing. Commun. ACM **53**(7), 9–11 (2008)
10. International Telecommunication Union (ITU): ITU Internet reports 2005: the Internet of things – executive summary (2005). http://www.itu.int/internetofthings
11. Schaller, R.R.: Moore's law: past, present and future. IEEE Spectr. **34**(6), 52–59 (1997)
12. Robinson, G.: Speeding net traffic with tiny mirrors. EE|Times News & Analysis **26** (2000)
13. Available on line at http://www.juniper.net
14. Mukherjee, B.: Optical WDM Networks. Springer, Berlin (2006)
15. Qiao, Q.M., Yeo, M.: Optical burst switching (OBS) – a new paradigm for an optical Internet. J. High Speed Netw. **8**(1), 69–84 (1999)
16. Wu, M.C., Li, F., Lee, S.S.: Optical MEMES: huge possibilities for lilliputian-sized devices. Opt. Photonics News, 25–29 (1998)
17. Rebeiz, G.M.: RF MEMS: Theory, Design, and Technology. Wiley, Hoboken (2003)
18. Borelia, M.S., Jue, J.P., Bankerjee, D., Ramamurthy, B., Mukherjee, B.: Optical components for WDM lightwave networks. Proc. IEEE **85**(8), 1274–1307 (1997)
19. Lin, X.J., Shroff, N.B., Srikant, R.: A tutorial on cross-layer optimization in wireless networks. IEEE J. Sel. Areas Commun. **24**(8), 1452–1463 (2006)
20. Handley, M.: Why the Internet only just works. BT Technol. J. **24**(3), 119–129 (2006)
21. Braden, R., Zhang, L., Berson, S.: Resource ReSerVation Protocol (RSVP) – Version 1 Functional Specification. RFC 2205, Internet Engineering Task Force (1997)
22. White, P.P.: RSVP and integrated services in the Internet: a tutorial. IEEE Commun. Mag. **35**(5), 100–106 (1997)
23. Braden, R., Clark, D., Shenker, S.: Integrated services in the Internet architecture: an overview. IETF RFC 1633 (1994)
24. Blake, S., Black, D., Carlson, M., Davies, E., Wang, Z., Weiss, W.: An architecture for differentiated services. IETF RFC 2475 (1998)
25. Chang, I.C., Chen, S.F.: An end-to-end QoS adaptation architecture for the integrated IntServ and DiffServ networks. In: IFIP Int. Federation for Information Processing, pp. 365–376 (2007)
26. Menth, M., Martin, R., Charzinski, J.: Capacity overprovisioning for networks with resilience requirements. In: Proc. ACM SIGCOMM, Pisa, Italy (2006)
27. Kent, S., Atkinson, R.: Security architecture for the Internet protocol. IETF RFC 2401 (1998)
28. Zhou, C.F., Leckiea, C., Karunasekera, S.: A survey of coordinated attacks and collaborative intrusion detection. Comput. Secur. **29**(1), 124–140 (2010)
29. Butler, K., Farley, T.R., McDaniel, P., Rexford, J.: A survey of BGP security issues and solutions. Proc. IEEE **98**(1), 100–122 (2010)
30. Tucker, R.S.: A green Internet. In: Proc. Annual Meeting of the IEEE Lasers and Electro-Optics Society, Acapulco, Mexico, pp. 4–5 (2008)

Chapter 3
Two-Level Source Routing (TLSR) for All-Optical Packet Switching

Abstract All-optical packet switching (AOPS) is one of the key technologies able to efficiently make use of the immense capacity offered by optical networks, by forwarding packets in the optical domain. However, due to the current lack of cost-effective optical processing technology, packet headers and table lookup must be processed electronically for packet forwarding. This not only increases the system complexity and energy consumption caused by optical-electrical-optical (OEO) conversion and related processing systems, but also limits packet forwarding speed because the electronic processing speed is much slower than the optical transmission speed. This chapter discusses a new AOPS network architecture called two-level source routing (TLSR) with domain-by-domain routing, which tries to facilitate AOPS realization with simple optical processing technologies. The basic idea of TLSR is to simplify a network structure so that less information needs to be processed and neither table lookup nor header rewriting is needed for all-optical packet forwarding.

3.1 Introduction

We have witnessed a rapid growth and evolution of the IP network over the past two decades. As IP becomes increasingly popular, more and more problems appear, such as its weak quality of service (QoS) capability, insecurity, and insufficient address space. More discussions on IP can be found in the literature; see, e.g., [1, 2]. The cause of the problems is simply that IP was not originally designed for what we expect it to do today and in the future. The network community is now studying new architectures for the Next Generation Internet such as the "100 × 100 Clean Slate" project [3] and the Future Internet Design (FIND) program in the United States [4]. Although there is not yet a clear picture of this new architecture, its design should take into account both the QoS requirements of various applications in high layers and the development, as well as the limitation of communication technologies in the physical layer. This is important because the communication capacity of the physical layer is the fundamental element for supporting high-layer applications. To improve networking efficiency and reduce networking overhead, inter-layer protocol conversions should be avoided as much as possible. For example, IP over optical

S.M. Jiang, *Future Wireless and Optical Networks*,
Computer Communications and Networks,
DOI 10.1007/978-1-4471-2822-9_3, © Springer-Verlag London Limited 2012

tries to enable IP to run directly over light paths. However, IP was not designed to process IP packet forwarding all-optically.

The physical network of the Internet has been evolving from electronic networks to all-optical networks [5] since the latter can provide much higher communication capacity than the former. Optical switching has an additional dimension for contention resolution by using different wavelengths to forward packets across switching fabrics. However, it is impossible to simultaneously assign different wavelengths for packet switching to many packets each going to different destinations, because only a limited number of wavelengths is available for efficient optical communication. Therefore, an all-optical packet switching (AOPS) technology has been studied to improve bandwidth utilization in optical networks. With AOPS, the signal is kept in the optical domain for processing to avoid the delay, additional energy consumption, and implementation cost caused by processing with optical-electrical-optical (OEO) conversion.

As discussed in Sect. 3.2, much research aiming to improve optical processing and buffering technologies for realizing AOPS is being reported in the literature. However, this chapter discusses a new direction for realizing AOPS networks, in which the network structure is simplified such that the limited optical processing and buffering technologies of today or the near future can be used to build fundamental all-optical network function blocks in order to realize AOPS networks. This is done because it may still take some time for optical technologies to become as mature as electrical ones to cost-effectively support complex networking processes. This new network structure, called two-level source routing (TLSR) with domain-by-domain routing, jointly uses the output port source routing originally proposed for electronic routers [6, 7] and hierarchical routing [8–10] to redistribute routing functions between AOPS nodes and domain edges. TLSR tries to (i) facilitate AOPS realization, (ii) be independent of addressing schemes used in higher layers, and (iii) support both connectionless and connection-oriented services as well as end-to-end QoS.

The remainder of this chapter is organized as follows. Some related works are briefly summarized in Sect. 3.2. The principle of TLSR is introduced in Sect. 3.3, and support of both connectionless and connection-oriented services with TLSR is discussed in Sect. 3.4. The major implementation issues of TLSR are discussed in Sect. 3.5, and a design is presented in Sect. 3.6. The chapter is summarized in Sect. 3.7.

3.2 Related Works

This section gives a brief survey of related works, including the topics of optical packet header processing, typical optical networks, and addressing issues.

3.2.1 Optical Packet Header Processing

Similar to electrical packet switching, optical packet switching also has to process packet headers to decide routes for every incoming packet. The key to all-optical packet forwarding is how to process packet headers all-optically. However, the limited optical processing and buffering technologies, especially the optical random access memory available today, only enable simple forms of all-optical header processing [11]. It is almost impossible to all-optically process long packet headers, table lookup, and packet header rewriting operations. As discussed below, it is possible, using the optical processing technologies available today or in the near future, to all-optically process short packet headers without requiring table lookup or packet header rewriting.

The fundamental function blocks for digital signal processing are logic gates such as AND and OR. Similarly, for all-optical processing, these gates include all-optical AND, all-optical OR, all-optical NOR, and all-optical NAND. Much research of all-optical logic gates has been reported in the literature, for example, 40 Gbit/s all-optical XOR [12], all-optical AND/NAND [13], all-optical AND/OR [14], and all-optical high speed NOR [15]. An all-optical header recognition method and a packet self-routing scheme for a 6-bit address at 100 Gbit/s were also reported in [16]. An all-optical header processing technique able to distinguish a large number of header patterns was demonstrated in [17]. Refer also to [18–22] for more results on these issues.

Other related works are also reported in the literature, such as all-optical buffers that can provide variable and adjustable queueing delays [23, 24], handling of packet contention of two simultaneously arriving optical packets [19], all-optically decreasing packet time-to-live [25], and separating a packet header from its payload [19, 26]. Furthermore, Lenslet Labs in Israel announced the world's first commercial re-configurable optics-based signal processing engine core, and a miniature photonic chip is also under development at the Macquarie University in Australia. Although those techniques are not yet comparable with electrical ones, and it may still take some time to develop them into mature technologies, one can expect that some practical techniques for simple all-optical computing and buffering in the optical domain will be available to realize simple AOPS networks.

3.2.2 Typical Optical Networks

One way to process long packet headers in optical networks is to extract the header from the packets and handle it separately. Such an example is the optical burst switching (OBS) network [27, 28]. With OBS, the OBS domain edge node first collects packets going to the same destination to form a burst. Then a control packet is sent first via a pre-established light path to set up a light path for the burst. To this end, the optical signal of the control packet is converted into the electrical signal for processing. It is usually suggested that the burst should be sent out within some time after the control packet has been transmitted, whether or not a light path has been successfully set up for the upcoming burst. Many issues may affect the performance of OBS networks. For example, the electronic processing speed may become the bottleneck of ultra-high speed optical networking, and the effective throughput will be affected by burst aggregation, the time interval between the sending time of a control packet and the departure of the associated burst, and burst loss caused by failure in light path setting and congestion [29], etc.

Although network technologies like ATM and Multi-Protocol Label Switching (MPLS) [30] have short packet headers, they are still too long to be processed all-optically since packet header rewriting has to be processed for switching labels. Moreover, table lookup is needed for switching operation in these networks, which cannot be easily processed all-optically [11]. Similarly for Pip [7], a source routing approach has been adopted to accelerate routing, and the routing information is a series of the indexes of the nodes to be visited by a packet, called forwarding table index field (FTIF) chains. However, this index is a long high-level logical identity and FTIF is used for forwarding table lookup for packet forwarding.

A self-routing address scheme was also proposed to realize AOPS such as the output port bitmap-based node address in [31]. With this scheme, each output port of a node is indicated by one bit in the port bitmap, which is set to 1 only if the associated route goes through this node via this port. A route is composed of these port bitmaps for each node along the route. One advantage of this scheme is that only simple bit processing is needed for AOPS, but at the expense of large packet overheads. This overhead increases rapidly with both the number of output ports at a node and the number of nodes along a route. Some proposals are also trying to provide a simple real-time calculation of the output port index upon a packet's arrival at an AOPS node, such as [32]. However, whether such a calculation can be carried out all-optically in a cost-effective way requires further studies.

Given a network architecture, the key implementation issue is the fabric switching block, which tries to automatically and rapidly pass a packet from the input port of its arrival at a node to the output port corresponding to its destination. Many methods have been proposed, such as the Manhattan network [33], wormhole routing [34], the Banyan network [35] and the proposal in [36], which jointly uses all-optical swapping techniques, electronic computing, and table lookup. These techniques had been used to design switches and routers for ATM and IP networks, and may also be enhanced for AOPS networks by extending them for all-optical routing in wide area networks (WANs).

3.2.3 Addressing Issues

Addressing is one of the most important networking issues. (Refer to [37] for a detailed discussion about addressing schemes.) IPv4 is facing an address starvation problem for its further growth. It is possible that all the IPv4 addresses may be exhausted by 2014 [38], because the IP address field was fixed, while the Internet size is growing fast beyond the expectation of its original designers. The IP address combines the identity of the endpoint and routing information to be processed by routers. Thus expanding the IP address space requires implemental changes in IP routers in order to support the new address formats.

IPv6 [39, 40] was proposed to provide a much larger address space than IPv4. However, fully deploying IPv6 is costly and may take time, since the network units in the current Internet, such as routers, all are based on IPv4. Moreover, it not clear whether the IPv6 address space will be sufficient in the future as more and more users and objects are linked to the Internet. The reasons for this are (i) it is almost impossible to accurately predict the Internet size in the future and (ii) whether every IP address can be effectively used largely depends on address allocation schemes. However, a fixed and hierarchical IP address, albeit favorable for routing, makes it difficult to allocate addresses according to user distributions.

An alternative solution, which tries to avoid the above problems, is to design a high-layer addressing independent network, which will not be affected by changes in addressing schemes used in high layers. To this end, one can separate routing information from a node's logical identity by using connection-oriented or source routing approaches [6, 41–43]. With the connection-oriented approach, a connection needs to be established between source and destination before any data transmission. However, this approach cannot efficiently support connectionless services for pervasive data applications, especially for short message transmission [44]. This approach also requires table lookup and packet header rewriting operations for switching. With source routing, a route is expressed in a concatenation of the identities of each router that a packet is going to visit from source to destination. As discussed in [41], source routing can simplify router implementation, since it does not require a large routing table to cover the global address space but a small one that only covers the neighbors of a router. Furthermore, its stateless characteristics avoid the need of per-flow information treatment, and routing does not require the packet header rewriting operation as required by switching. However, the packet overhead for carrying source routing information is much larger than for other routing approaches if they adopt the same address format.

3.3 Principle of TLSR

Routing is one of the most complex network operations since it requires extensive computation for route search and maintenance and packet forwarding, and the same is true for all-optical routing. The core of the proposed network structure is a new routing approach, called two-level source routing (TLSR) jointly using domain-by-domain routing. TLSR divides the routing operation into domain level and port level and displaces complex computations for routing and QoS to domain edge nodes so that it can be processed electronically. Inside a domain, only simple routing operations have to be carried out all-optically by processing a small amount of information without performing table lookup and packet header rewriting.

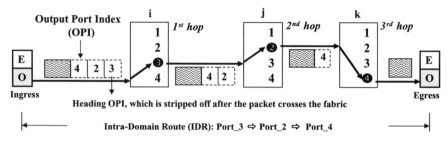

Fig. 3.1 Port-level source routing (PLSR), E/O = electrical/optical

Note that there are different definitions of addresses and routes in the literature [37, 45]. In this chapter, they are machine-friendly as defined below. The address indicates the identity of an endpoint in the network, while a route is a road
map at either the domain level or port level that indicates the travel sequence of a
packet between such addresses.

3.3.1 Port-Level Routing

Port-level routing is used by an AOPS node to all-optically forward an incoming
packet to an output port corresponding to its destination. The routing unit here is
the output port. This routing is based on an optical route, which is composed of a
series of output ports that a packet is going to visit in sequence and expressed in
a concatenation of output port indexes (OPIs). Within a domain, this optical route
is called an intra-domain route (IDR), which connects a pair of ingress and egress
nodes of the domain. To facilitate the AOPS implementation, port-level source routing (PLSR) is proposed, with which neither table lookup nor packet header rewriting
is needed. As illustrated in Fig. 3.1, the information on the output port via which an
incoming packet will leave is carried directly by the packet header. In this case, the
major operations to be performed by a node to forward a packet include (i) passing
the packet to the output port indicated by the heading OPI and (ii) stripping off the
heading OPI from the header once the packet crosses the switching fabric.

PLSR is the fundamental element for domain-level routing. With PLSR, an optical tunnel between source and destination can also be set up by letting a packet
header directly carry the information on the optical routes (i.e., IDR) used by each
domain that a packet is going to visit in the order of its visit sequence. In this case,
a packet always travels optically all the way to its destination without OEO conversion even at domain edge nodes. This tunnel can provide ultra-fast end-to-end
optical transmission, but at the expense of large packet overheads.

3.3.2 Domain-Level Routing

To reduce packet overheads caused by directly carrying the detail of optical routes used by PLSR, domain-level routing is further proposed to be jointly used with PLSR. At the domain level, the routing unit is the domain and routing is performed electronically at the domain edge nodes. When a packet arrives at a domain, the ingress node determines an IDR for the packet to cross the domain according to the domain-level routing information, and then passes the packet to PLSR for all-optical packet forwarding. Thus domain-level routing has to use PLSR to eventually route packets across a domain, while PLSR alone can route packets all-optically.

To efficiently support connectionless (CL) and connection-oriented (CO) services, domain-level routing is further divided into domain-by-domain routing (DBDR) and domain-level source routing (DLSR). DBDR is used to support CL services, while DLSR is used for CO services by using a domain-level route. This domain-level route is just a logical route between source and destination across the domain, and does not contain any detail of the optical route to be used by PLSR. The domain-level route is more stable than the optical route since changes in inter-domain links seldom occur. Actually, the Internet is divided into multiple autonomous systems (i.e., domains), each with its own administrative control and resource management [30].

3.4 Connectionless and Connection-Oriented Services

ATM is a CO network, while IP is a CL network. Thus ATM is inefficient at providing CL services, and similarly, IP is inefficient for CO services. As discussed in Chap. 2, to provide fundamental networking services for higher layers, it is necessary to efficiently support both CL and CO services. This section discusses how to exploit domain-level routing to achieve these objectives.

3.4.1 Domain-by-Domain Routing (DBDR)

To efficiently support connectionless IP which is based on hop-by-hop routing, domain-by-domain routing (DBDR) is proposed. With DBDR, the domain ingress node decides the next domain according to the destination address carried by a packet. DBDR is similar to hop-by-hop routing but different in terms of routing units, which is the domain for the former and the router for the latter. Once the next domain is determined, the ingress node decides on an optical route (i.e., IDR) to forward the packet across the domain. Since it is impossible to all-optically process hop-by-hop routing cost-effectively for long addresses, DBDR can be used as an option for IP by using the IP address to determine the next domain. Similar to the Border Gateway Protocol (BGP) used at the IP network border [30], a similar

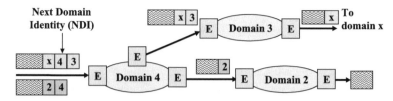

Fig. 3.2 Connectionless domain-level source routing (CL-DLSR, E = electrical)

protocol for DBDR can also be developed for domain edges to exchange domain-level routing information and traffic policies. DBDR can also make use of some routing information available for DLSR to find domains far beyond the neighboring domains toward the destination; this reduces the routing delay because fewer such operations are performed by each domain.

3.4.2 Domain-Level Source Routing (DLSR)

DLSR routes packets at the domain edge according to a domain-level route, which can be expressed in (i) a concatenation of the identities of the next domains that a packet is going to visit to reach its destination or (ii) a series of the indexes of every IDR used by each domain to forward a packet across it. Accordingly, DLSR is further divided into connectionless DLSR (CL-DLSR) using format (i) and connection-oriented DLSR (CO-DLSR) using format (ii).

3.4.2.1 Connectionless DLSR (CL-DLSR)

As illustrated in Fig. 3.2, in this case, a packet carries only next domain identities (NDIs). Upon the arrival of a packet, the domain ingress node has to determine an optical route across the domain (i.e., IDR) according to the heading NDI carried by the packet. Once an IDR is found, the ingress node replaces the heading NDI with the found IDR and passes the packet to PLSR for all-optical routing. This NDI-to-IDR mapping can be realized through table lookup to be processed electronically at the domain ingress node. Note that the NDI space should be much smaller than the IP address space, since the number of adjacent domains of a domain should be much less than that of network nodes. Therefore, this task can be performed much faster than the IP routing table lookup.

CL-DLSR can be used to support CO services at the domain level but CL service at the port level, because the domain-level route is available before data transmission but how to cross a particular domain is determined upon the arrival of a packet. This service is called connection-oriented plus connectionless (OL) service. Since the domain-level route can be shared by flows and packets and is relatively stable, OL can be more efficient in supporting CL services than DBDR in terms of end-to-end delay, especially for short message transmission, which usually does not require

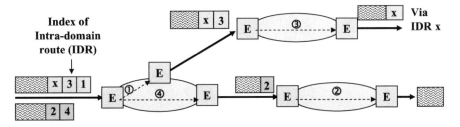

Fig. 3.3 Connection-oriented domain-level source routing (CO-DLSR, E = electrical)

resource reservation. CL-DLSR can also help balance the traffic load, since an IDR can be selected instantly according to the traffic load upon a packet's arrival.

3.4.2.2 Connection-Oriented DLSR (CO-DLSR)

As illustrated in Fig. 3.3, in this case, an optical route across a domain (i.e., IDR) is already available before the arrival of a packet. This route is indicated by the IDR number (IDRN) carried by the packet. The domain ingress node only replaces the heading IDRN with the detail of the indicated IDR. A dynamic IDR is set up only upon the arrival of such a request before data transmission. Alternatively, a static IDR, with which changes in connectivity seldom occur, can undergo pre-setup. Such a static IDR is similar to the ATM permanent connection and can be set up either through a signaling process or manually. For both dynamic and static IDRs, during the setting process, resource reservation can be made simultaneously to support QoS if necessary. The CL service can also be supported by CO-DLSR using static IDRs. Since IDRs are available upon a packet's arrival, there is almost no delay incurred in this case, in contrast to CL-DLSR. For the CO service, CO-DLSR with either dynamic or static IDRs can be used for support. For explicit resource reservation, using dynamic IDRs is a better choice.

3.4.3 Port-Level Routing Versus Domain-Level Routing

Table 3.1 compares the four routing schemes that make up TLSR in terms of the routing units, routing information, and physical support that they rely on. PLSR is the key physical support for DLSR and DBDR. Both PLSR and CO-DLSR need pre-setup routes so they are CO, while DBDR is CL. CL-DLSR is in between CL and CO networking modes since the domain-level route is already available before the arrival of a packet, but the setting of an optical route is launched only upon the arrival of a packet.

Note that an AOPS element that can pass an incoming packet at an input port to an output port according to the port number all-optically is the key to all-optical PLSR. An example of a PLSR realization based on a Banyan network will be discussed in Sect. 3.6.

Table 3.1 Comparison between PLSR, DLSR, and DBDR

Routing schemes	Routing unit	Routing information	Routing support	Networking unit	Signal domain	Networking modes
PLSR	port	IDR	AOPS	AOPS node	optical	CO
CO-DLSR	domain	IDRN	PLSR	edge	electrical	CO
CL-DLSR	domain	NDI	PLSR	edge	electrical	OL
DBDR	domain	DSN	PLSR	edge	electrical	CL

CL = connectionless, CO = connection-oriented, OL = CO plus CL, DSN = destination

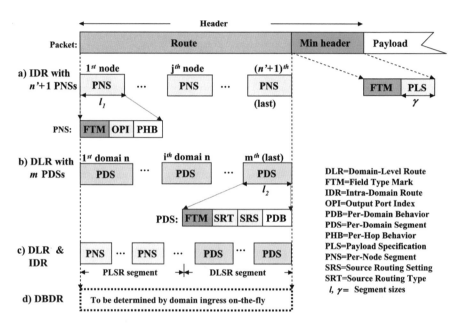

Fig. 3.4 Packet header format for PLSR, DLSR, and DBDR

3.5 Implementation Issues

With source routing, the complete routing information must be carried by every packet. An important issue is to design a packet header to carry as little routing information as possible for easy optical processing. This section briefly discusses a possible packet header format and its processing.

As illustrated in Fig. 3.4, the packet header consists of two parts: a minimum header and a route field that will be used by PLSR, DLSR, and DBDR for TLSR routing. There are two types of routes: the optical route (i.e., IDR) processed by PLSR all-optically, and the domain-level route processed electronically at the domain edge to find an optical route across the domain.

Table 3.2 Instance of settings for FTM, SRT and SRS

Field	Field type mark (FTM, 2 bits)				Source routing type (SRT, 1 bit)	
Setting	00	01	10	11	0	1
Meaning	PLSR	DLSR	DBDR	EOR	CL-DLSR	CO-DLSR
Note	CO	Ref SRT	CL	–	SRS = NDI	SRS = IDRN

3.5.1 Minimum Packet Header

The minimum header is located just before the payload of a packet. It consists of two parts: the field type mark (FTM) and the payload specification (PLS), as illustrated in Fig. 3.4. FTM indicates the type of information carried by the field just following it. For the minimum header, FTM indicates the end of an optical route (EOR). In other cases, FTM indicates whether a route is for PLSR, DLSR, or DBDR as illustrated in Table 3.2, where the source routing type (SRT) and source routing setting (SRS) fields are also set. Note that FTM always heads the packet and is processed all-optically at either domain edges or AOPS nodes within a domain.

PLS indicates whether the payload carries an IP packet or an ATM cell or other types of traffic so that it can be treated accordingly. This design attempts to increase TLSR's versatility while minimizing per-packet overhead. With this design, the information carried by the payload can be used by TLSR. For example, the "total length" of the IPv4 packet carried by the TLSR's payload can be used to delimit a packet at the domain level, and the IP address can be used by DBDR to decide next domains for domain-level routing as discussed in Sect. 3.4.1. The PLS-related operations are processed electronically at the domain edges.

3.5.2 Optical Routes

An optical route across a domain is called an intra-domain route (IDR). As illustrated in Fig. 3.4(a), an n'-hop long IDR is a concatenation of $n' + 1$ per-node segments (PNSs), each of which carries the information to be used by one node for routing and QoS support. The PNSs of an IDR are arranged in the order in which the nodes will be visited by the packet. Before the packet leaves the node under visit, the corresponding segment heading the packet is stripped off from the header. As illustrated in Fig. 3.4(a), a PNS is composed of an FTM, an output port index (OPI) and a per-hop behavior (PHB). The OPI indicates an output port via which an incoming packet should exit toward its destination. The PHB contains the information on the packet dropping preference for congestion control. The PNS is processed all-optically, and its delimitation can be realized through guard time intervals with a joint use of simple coding schemes, as discussed in [19, 26]. The use of PHB to support end-to-end QoS is discussed in Sect. 4.2.3.

The primary function of a domain ingress node is to set optical routes to domain egress nodes. To this end, it is necessary to maintain the information on domain topologies consisting of nodes and direct physical links between them, as we now discuss. Let n_p denote port p of node n and $(n_1\_p_1, n_2\_p_2)$ a link between two ports, where $n_1\_p_1$ is an output port (i.e., OPI) and $n_2\_p_2$ an input port. Given node i with output ports $1, 2, \ldots, o$, its direct physical links to the input ports of other nodes can be expressed as follows:

$$\text{Initial IDR format:} \quad (i\_1, 1\_1), (i\_2, 2\_h), \ldots, (i\_o, k\_j).$$

When the domain edge has this information for each node within the domain, an IDR between any pair of ingress and egress nodes can be constructed. Then, the IDR in Fig. 3.1 can be expressed as follows:

$$\text{Simplified IDR format:} \quad (i\_3, j\_x) \rightarrow (j\_2, k\_y) \rightarrow (k\_4, egress),$$

where x and y indicate an input port of nodes j and k, respectively. Since an input port does not affect the output port via which a packet will exit, while only the output port determines a route, the input port index can be removed, resulting in a simplified expression of the IDR as $i\_3 \rightarrow j\_2 \rightarrow k\_4$. Furthermore, the physical link between an input port of a node and an output port of another node is unique, so a packet will automatically visit them in sequence. Therefore, the node identity can also be removed from the expression, so that the final IDR can be simplified as

$$\text{Final IDR format:} \quad 3 \rightarrow 2 \rightarrow 4.$$

Once an optical route is set up, a packet will be routed all-optically along this route. Note that an optical route may span over just one domain (i.e., an IDR) or multiple domains, such as an optical tunnel between source and destination as discussed in Sect. 3.3.1. In the latter case, the optical route is the concatenation of the IDRs used by each domain along the route.

3.5.3 Domain-Level Routes

As illustrated in Fig. 3.4(b), an m-domain route is a concatenation of m per-domain segments (PDSs), each of which carries the information to be used by a domain for routing and QoS support. The PDSs of the same route are arranged in the order in which the domains will be visited by the packet. As illustrated in Fig. 3.4(b), a PDS is composed of an FTM, an SRT, an SRS, and a per-domain behavior (PDB). The SRT indicates whether DLSR is connectionless (CL) or connection-oriented (CO).

For CL-DLSR, SRS is set to the NDI that indicates the next domain for a packet to visit toward its destination. In this case, no optical route is available until the packet's arrival at the domain edge, which triggers the setting process. The optical route (i.e., IDR) is determined according to the heading NDI carried by the packet. For CO-DLSR, the IDR in each domain is already available before the arrival of a packet. To reduce the packet overhead for carrying source routing information, only the IDR number (IDRN) rather than the detail of the IDRs is carried by SRS. Upon the arrival of a packet, the domain ingress node simply selects the IDR following the IDRN carried by SRS in the heading PDS. The settings of SRT and SRS are listed in Table 3.2. For both CL-DLSR and CO-DLSR, the heading PDS is replaced by IDRs for all-optical processing with PLSR, as illustrated in Fig. 3.5.

3.5.4 Mixture of Optical and Domain-Level Routes

Figure 3.4(c) depicts a general packet header format that indicates both optical and domain-level routes. This format is used when a packet needs to travel across more than one domain. Only the heading domain-level route is replaced by an IDR to cross the indicated domain via PLSR; the remainder, along with the other parts of the packet, is kept intact when it is routed by PLSR.

3.5.5 Packet Header for DBDR

As illustrated in Fig. 3.4(d), neither an optical route nor a domain-level route is available for a new packet arriving at a domain, and the routing information at this moment is null; only the minimum header is available for CL services. When a do-main ingress node receives such a packet, it extracts the destination address from the payload according to the PLS carried by the minimum header. Then it further checks whether the packet needs to be forwarded to other domains. If it does, it determines the next domain according to the destination address as well as the corresponding IDR to be used by PLSR for all-optical routing. If the destination is located within the current domain, the ingress node just forwards the packet to the destination. In this case, if an optical route (i.e., IDR) is used to link the ingress node and the des-tination, this forwarding still goes through PLSR; otherwise, the packet is passed to the higher layer for electronic processing.

3.5.6 Flexible Packet Headers

Among the three elements of the per-node segment (PNS) as illustrated in Fig. 3.4(d), only FTM needs to be standardized. Since each OPI of an optical route is used only by the related node and will be stripped off once it is used, the remain-ing OPIs will pass through this node cleanly at the bit level. This feature allows a non-standardized OPI to be used without an impact on the connectivity between nodes. The OPI (and the same for PHB and PDB) signal is generated by the domain ingress node, and no node within the domain is involved in this operation provided that the domain ingress node knows the format of the OPI defined by each AOPS

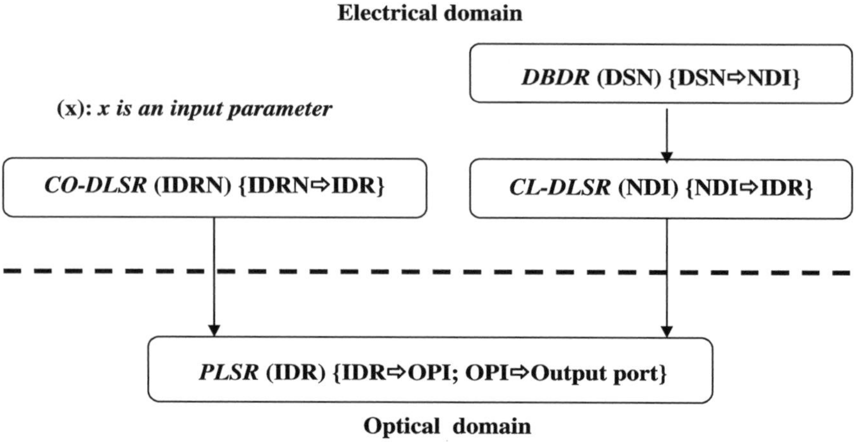

Electrical domain

DBDR (DSN) {DSN⇨NDI}

(x): *x is an input parameter*

CO-DLSR (IDRN) {IDRN⇨IDR}   **CL-DLSR (NDI) {NDI⇨IDR}**

PLSR (IDR) {IDR⇨OPI; OPI⇨Output port}

Optical domain

Fig. 3.5 Relationship between function blocks used by PLSR, DLSR, and DBDR

node therein. This information can be easily obtained during the configuration process, since the OPI format of one type of AOPS device can be kept unchanged once it is defined by its manufacturer.

This flexibility allows a manufacturer to define its proprietary OPI and optimize its design, since the OPI size affects the difficulty in realizing AOPS. For example, the port bitmap proposed in [31] may be adopted here for OPI, in which output port 1 is indicated by "1000..." and port 4 by "0001...". Furthermore, compared with standardized addresses and labels whose formats are open to the public, flexible OPIs can provide more secure networking, since it is not easy for other parts to learn the format of all the OPIs adopted by each AOPS node within a domain.

Similarly, a flexible format can also be adopted to identify neighboring domains, since a domain is only interested in interaction with its next domains with source routing. The NDI is only used by adjacent domains to find an optical route (i.e., IDR) and will then be replaced by the found IDR. Thus, a domain can identify its neighboring domains in its own way and broadcast its definition to its neighbors.

3.6 A Design for TLSR

Figure 3.5 shows the relationship between PLSR, DLSR, and DBDR. The fundamental function is expressed by *PLSR*(IDR), which takes the heading outport index (OPI) from the intra-domain route (IDR) and forwards the remainder of the packet to the corresponding output port. Both CL-DLSR and CO-DLSR functions use *PLSR*(IDR) for all optical packet forwarding. For *CO-DLSR*(IDRN), the function has to get the IDR first by searching its IDR table according to the IDR number (IDRN). For *CL-DLSR*(NDI), it requires a routing calculation to find an optical route (i.e., IDR) according to the next domain identity (NDI). Similarly for

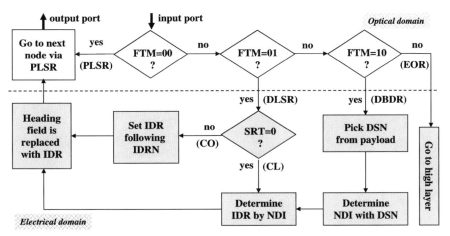

CO=connection-oriented, CL=connectionless, DSN=destination address, EOR=end of optical route
IDR=intra-domain route, NDI=next domain identity, IDRN=IDR number, SRT=source routing type

Fig. 3.6 Logical flow diagram for TLSR: FTM and PLSR are processed all-optically

DBDR(DSN), it also requires a routing operation, first to find the NDI of the next domain according to the destination (DSN), and then to call ***CL-DLSR***(NDI).

3.6.1 Module Structure

Figure 3.6 shows a logical flow diagram for TLSR, where FTM and PLSR are processed all-optically at every AOPS node, while the other fields are processed electronically at the domain edge. As illustrated in this figure, once an optical signal arrives at a node, its FTM, which always heads the signal, is checked first. According to the setting of FTM, the signal is diverted to different function modules as discussed below.

If FTM = 00, the signal is continuously forwarded to the corresponding output port in the optical domain via PLSR. In the other cases, the signal is converted into an electrical signal for higher layer processing at the domain edge. For DLSR (i.e., FTM = 01), if SRT = 0 (i.e., CO-DLSR), an IDR is picked up from the IDR table stored at the domain ingress node, according to the IDRN carried by the packet; otherwise (i.e., CL-DLSR), the domain ingress needs to find an IDR that can connect the domain indicated by the NDI carried by the packet. For DBDR (i.e., FM = 10), the ingress node has to determine (i) the destination address from the payload, (ii) the NDI of the next domain according to the address, and (iii) an IDR across the domain. For both DLSR and DBDR, since the signal still has to travel further in the optical domain, it is reconverted into an optical signal to be processed by PLSR. When FM = 11, which indicates the end of an optical route (EOR), the optical signal is converted into an electrical one for processing. Since the electrical signal can be processed by powerful computers, a detailed discussion is ignored here.

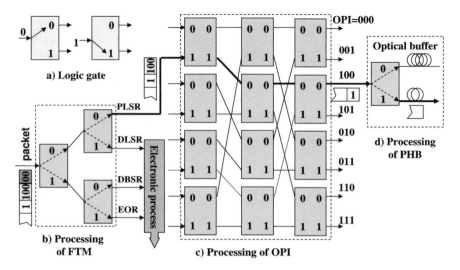

Fig. 3.7 A possible PLSR realization based on a Banyan network

3.6.2 PLSR Based on Banyan Network

An example is given here to show how to all-optically process FTM and PLSR by using the self-routing Banyan network [35]. This network was originally proposed for electronic switches and has been studied extensively over the past two decades for packet-switched networks such as ATM. Its principle is to use a logic gate array with two output ports, say 0 and 1. The self-routing capability is provided by the following feature of this type of gate: an incoming signal 0 will exit via output port 0, and 1 via port 1, as illustrated in Fig. 3.7(a). A sophisticated self-routing fabric can be constructed by using a multi-stage gate array. As mentioned earlier, there are many studies for all-optical logic gates, and it is possible to use this structure to implement PLSR, as discussed here.

As illustrated in Fig. 3.6, the all-optical processing for TLSR can be divided into two parts: FTM and PLSR. FTM processing is responsible for guiding an incoming packet to a proper function module according to FTM. The major task of PLSR is to forward the packet across the switching fabric according to the OPI. As illustrated in Fig. 3.7(b), a two-stage gate array can be used to process the 2-bit long FTM, and one gate is enough to process the 1-bit long per-hop behavior (PHB), as illustrated in Fig. 3.7(d). For OPI, as illustrated in Fig. 3.7(c), a three-stage Banyan network is used to construct a switching fabric with 8 output ports.

Now suppose an optical packet with FTM = 00 (i.e., a PLSR packet) and OPI = 100 (i.e., output port 4) arrives at the AOPS node. As illustrated in Fig. 3.7(b), the FTM processing forwards the packet to the PLSR module since FTM = 00 here. For the other FTM settings, the packet is forwarded to electronic processing modules. This packet is then forwarded to output port 4 following OPI = 100 by PLSR, as illustrated in Fig. 3.7(c). Note that a packet with OPI = 100 from any input port will be routed automatically to output port 4 with this Banyan network. Finally, the packet goes through another logic gate, which diverts the packet to different optical buffering structures according to PHB, as illustrated in Fig. 3.7(d). An intensive study of the detailed implementation is needed.

3.6.3 Buffering for PLSR

A weakness of TLSR is its large initial packet header, especially for long routes due to the routing information carried for source routing. It is very difficult to all-optically buffer and process long packet headers. As discussed below, a simple buffer is sufficient for PLSR when buffering is necessary.

As illustrated in Fig. 3.4(a), a node only needs to process an l_1-long per-node segment (PNS) for packet forwarding with PLSR. Since the PNS to be processed by a node is always located at the beginning of the packet, only this PNS must be buffered if necessary for processing. The remainder of the packet header is treated together with the payload and can be buffered in a fixed optical delay line buffer if necessary. Due to the fixed size (l_1), the processing time of the PNS is fixed too, so a fixed optical delay line buffer can buffer the remainder of a packet. No further processing is needed for the remainder of the packet, which will be passed through the node transparently once a route between the input and output ports is established. Usually l_1 is very small and largely depends on the number of output ports to be supported per node. As shown later in Table 4.3, for 512 ports per node with simple QoS, a 12-bit l_1 is sufficient, while only 7 bits are needed for 16 ports per node.

As illustrated in Fig. 3.8, the buffering requirement can be further simplified by dividing the PNS processing into three stages, each corresponding to FTM, OPI, and PHB, respectively. That is, once a packet arrives at a node, the heading FTM is first stripped off from the packet and processed by the FTM block. The remainder of the packet is buffered until the end of the FTM processing, as illustrated in Fig. 3.8(a), and then is passed to the OPI and PHB processing modules, respectively, as illustrated in Fig. 3.8(b)–(c).

3.7 Conclusion

This chapter discusses a new research direction to find an AOPS solution with a possible implementation of the proposed architecture TLSR. The basic idea of TLSR is to simplify a network structure such that neither table lookup nor header rewriting is needed for the AOPS operation, with less information to be processed. It is expected that the limited optical processing and buffering technologies available today or in the near future may be used to construct fundamental networking modules to realize AOPS networks. Addressing and major QoS issues are shifted from AOPS nodes to domain edges so that any changes in these issues do not change the AOPS network.

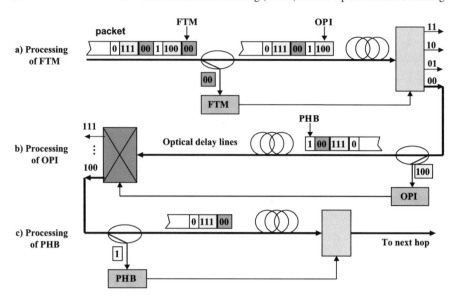

Fig. 3.8 PLSR processing using buffers

The work reported in this chapter is still far away from a solution to AOPS networks. Some issues of the practical implementation of TLSR are as follows:

(i) The Banyan network is adopted for the PLSR implementation, but it is a blocking network and more studies are needed.

(ii) A practical packet header considering preamble and guard time intervals between PLSR segments as well as between consecutive packets is necessary.

References

1. Molinero-Fernádenz, P., McKeown, N., Zhang, H.: Is IP going to take over the world (of communications)? In: Proc. ACM SIGCOMM WS. Hot Topics in Networks (HotNets), Princeton, New Jersey, USA (2002)
2. Handley, M.: Why the Internet only just works. BT Technol. J. **24**(3), 119–129 (2006)
3. 100 × 100 Clean Slate Project, http://www.100x100network.org/
4. USA NSF: Future Internet Design (FIND) – NSF 07-507, http://www.nsf.gov
5. Gladisch, A., Braun, R.P., Breuer, D., Ehrhardt, A., Foisel, H.M., Jaeger, M., Leppla, R., Schneiders, M., Vorbeck, S., Weiershausen, W., Westphal, F.J.: Evolution of terrestrial optical system and core network architecture. Proc. IEEE **94**(5), 869–891 (2006)
6. Cheriton, D.R.: Sirpent^{TM}: a high-performance internetworking approach. In: Proc. ACM SIGCOMM, Austin, Texas, USA, pp. 158–169 (1989)
7. Francis, P.: A near-term architecture for deploying Pip. IEEE Netw. **7**(3), 30–37 (1993)
8. McQuillan, J.: Adaptive routing algorithms for distributed computer networks. Tech. Rep. BBN Rep. 2831, Bolt Beranek and Newman Inc, Cambridge, MA, USA (1974)
9. Behrens, J., Garcia-Luna-Aceves, J.-J.: Hierarchical routing using link vectors. In: Proc. IEEE INFOCOM, San Francisco, USA, vol. 2, pp. 702–710 (1998)

10. Montgomery, M., De Veciana, G.: Hierarchical source routing through clouds. In: Proc. IEEE INFOCOM, San Francisco, USA, vol. 2, pp. 685–692 (1998)

11. Seppänen, K.: Optical time-division packet switch. In: Proc. 9th Summer School on Telecommunications, Workshop on Future Network Technologies, Lappeenranta, Finland, pp. 16–27 (2000). Research Report 73

12. Robinson, B.S., Hamilton, S.A., Savage, S.J., Ippen, E.P.: 40 Gbit/s all-optical XOR using a fiber-based folded ultrafast nonlinear interferometer. In: Proc. IEEE Optical Fiber Commun. Conf. (OFC), Anaheim, California, USA, pp. 561–563 (2002)

13. Ibrahim, T.A., Grover, R., Kuo, L.C., Kanakaraju, S., Calhoun, L.C., Ho, P.T.: All-optical AND/NAND logic gates using semiconductor microresonators. IEEE Photonics Technol. Lett. 15(10), 1422–1424 (2003)

14. Wu, Y.D.: All-optical logic gates by using multibranch waveguide structure with localized optical nonlinearity. IEEE J. Sel. Top. Quantum Electron. 11(2), 307–312 (2005)

15. Liang, T.K., Nunes, L.R., Tsuchiya, M., Abedin, K.S., Miyazaki, T., Van Thourhout, D., Dumon, P., Baets, R., Tsang, H.K.: All-optical high speed NOR gate based on two photon absorption in silicon wire waveguides. In: Proc. IEEE Optical Fiber Commun. Conf. (OFC), Anaheim, California, USA (2006)

16. Cotter, D., Lucek, J.K., Shabeer, M., Smith, K., Rogers, D.C., Nesset, D., Gunning, P.: Self-routing of 100 Gbit/s packets using 6 bit 'keyword' address recognition. IEE Electron. Lett. 31(25), 2201–2202 (1995)

17. Calabretta, N., Waardt, H.D., Khoe, G.D., Dorren, H.J.S.: Ultrafast asynchronous multioutput all-optical header processor. IEEE Photonics Technol. Lett. 16(4), 1182–1184 (2004)

18. Uenohara, H., Seki, T., Kobyayashi, K.: Four-bit optical header processing and wavelength routing performance of optical packet switch with optical digital-to-analogue conversion-type header processor. IEE Electronics Let. 40(9) (2004)

19. Dorren, H.J.S., Hill, M.T., Liu, Y., Calabretta, N., Srivatsa, A., Huijskens, F.M., de Waardt, H., Khoe, G.D.: Optical packet switching and buffering by using all-optical signal processing methods. J. Lightwave Technol. 21(1), 2–12 (2003)

20. Willner, A.E., Gurkan, D., Sahin, A.B., McGeehan, J.E., Hauer, M.C.: All-optical address recognition in next-generation optical networks. IEEE Opt. Commun., S38–S44 (2003)

21. Yu, B.Y., Runser, R., Toliver, P., Deng, K.-L., Zhou, D., Chang, T., Seo, S.W., Kang, K.I., Glesk, I., Prucnal, P.R.: Network demonstration of 100 Gbit/s optical packet switching with self-routing. IEE Electron. Lett. 33(16), 1401–1403 (1997)

22. Barry, R.A., Chan, V.W.S., Hall, K.L., Kintzer, E.S., Moores, J.D., Rauschenbach, K.A., Swanson, E.A., Adams, L.E., Doerr, C.R., Finn, S.G., Haus, H.A., Ippen, E.P., Wong, W.S., Haner, M.: All-Optical Network Consortium-ultrafast TDM networks. IEEE J. Sel. Areas Commun. 24(5), 999–1013 (1996)

23. Sakamoto, T., Noguchi, K., Sato, R., Okada, A., Sakai, Y., Matsuoda, M.: Variable optical delay circuit using wavelength converters. IEE Electron. Lett. 37(7), 454–455 (2001)

24. Yeo, Y.K., Yu, J.J., Chang, G.K.: A dynamically reconfigurable folded-path time delay buffer for optical packet switching. IEEE Photonics Technol. Lett. 16(11), 2559–2561 (2004)

25. McGeehan, J.E., Kumar, S., Gurkan, D., Nezam, S.M.R.M., Willner, A.E., Parameswaran, K.R., Fejer, M.M., Bannister, J., Touch, J.D.: All-optical decrementing of a packet's time-to-live (TTL) field and subsequent dropping of a zero-TTL packet. J. Lightwave Technol. 21(11), 2746–2752 (2003)

26. Nord, M., Bjornstad, S., Nielsen, M.: Demonstration of optical packet switching scheme for header-payload separation and class-based forwarding. In: Proc. IEEE Optical Fiber Commun. Conf. (OFC), Los Angeles, California, USA, vol. 1, pp. 2689–2693 (2004)

27. Turner, J.S.: Terabit burst switching. J. High Speed Netw. 8, 3–16 (1999)

28. Qiao, Q.M., Yeo, M.: Optical burst switching (OBS) – a new paradigm for an optical Internet. J. High Speed Netw. 8(1), 69–84 (1999)

29. Battestilli, T., Perros, H.: An introduction to optical burst switching for the next generation Internet. IEEE Optical Commun., S10–S15 (2003)

30. Tanenbaum, A.S.: Computer Networks, 4th edn. Pearson Education, Upper Saddle River (2003)

31. Yuan, X.C., Li, V.O.K., Li, C.Y., Wai, P.K.A.: A novel self-routing address scheme for all-optical packet-switched networks with arbitrary topologies. J. Lightwave Technol. **21**(2), 329–339 (2003)

32. Zhang, Y., Chen, L.K., Chan, C.K.: A multi-domain two-layer labelling scheme for optical packet switched networks with label-swapping-free forwarding. In: Proc. European Conf. Optical Commun. (ECOC), Rimini, Italy, pp. 3–5 (2003)

33. Madila, S.R., Zhou, D.: Routing in general junctions. IEEE Trans. Comput.-Aided Des. Integr. Circuits Syst. **8**(11), 1174–1184 (1989)

34. Ni, L.M., McKinley, P.K.: A survey of wormhole routing techniques in direct networks. Computer **26**(2), 62–76 (1993)

35. Sibal, S., Zhang, J.: On a class of Banyan networks and tandem Banyan switching fabrics. IEEE Trans. Commun. **43**(7), 2231–2240 (1995)

36. Blumenthal, D.J., Olsson, B.E., Rossi, G., Dimmick, T.E., Rau, L., Masanovic, M., Lavrova, O., Doshi, R., Jerphagnon, O., Bowers, J.E., Kaman, V., Coldren, L.A., Barton, J.: All-optical label swapping networks and technologies. J. Lightwave Technol. **18**(12), 2058–2074 (2000)

37. Francis, P.: Addressing in internetwork protocols. PhD thesis, University College London (1989)

38. Available online at http://www.potaroo.net/tools/ipv4

39. Deering, S., Hinden, R.: Internet protocol, version 6 (IPv6) specification. RFC 1883, Internet Engineering Task Force (1995)

40. 3COM: Understanding IP addressing: everything you ever wanted to know. White paper (2001)

41. Saltzer, J.H., Reed, D.P., Clark, D.D.: Source routing for campus-wide Internet transport. In: West, A., Janson, P. (eds.) Local Networks for Computer Communications, pp. 1–23. North-Holland, Amsterdam (1981)

42. Dixon, R.C., Pitt, D.A.: II. Source routing bridges addressing, bridging, and source routing. IEEE Netw. **12**(1), 25–32 (1988)

43. Cidon, I., Gopal, I.S.: Control mechanisms for high speed networks. In: Proc. IEEE Int. Conf. Commun. (ICC), Atlanta, GA, USA, vol. 2, pp. 0259–0263 (1990)

44. Jiang, S.M.: Logical ring with ATM block transfer to support connectionless services in ATM. In: IEEE ATM Workshop, Fairfax, VA, USA, pp. 154–158 (1998)

45. Shoch, J.: Inter-network naming, addressing, and routing. In: Proc. IEEE Comp. Soc. Int. Conf., pp. 72–79 (1978)

Chapter 4
Networking with TLSR

Abstract Chapter 3 discusses a new network structure called two-level source routing (TLSR). TLSR jointly uses domain-by-domain routing (DBDR) to realize all-optical packet switching (AOPS) with a lack of cost-effective photonic computing and buffering technologies available for networking. This chapter further discusses some networking issues of TLSR, which include addressing, congestion control, and end-to-end QoS, as well as interconnection with other types of networks such as ATM and IP. Since one major concern of TLSR is its packet overhead for carrying source routing information, an analysis of packet header sizes is also conducted in comparison with, e.g., the IP packet and the ATM cell.

4.1 Introduction

Chapter 3 discusses a new direction of AOPS solution by proposing a network structure called two-level source routing (TLSR), which jointly uses domain-by-domain routing (DBDR). With TLSR, it is expected that the limited optical processing and buffering technologies of today or the near future can be used to build fundamental all-optical networking functions to realize AOPS networks. This chapter will further address some networking issues of TLSR, which include addressing, congestion control, end-to-end QoS, and interconnection with other networks such as ATM and IP. This discussion is based on other approaches proposed in this monograph, i.e., differentiated queueing service (DQS), discussed in Chap. 5, for end-to-end QoS, and Semi-TCP, discussed in Chap. 10, for congestion control.

Since TLSR adopts source routing, which requires every packet to carry the information on the whole route for routing, its packet overhead is a major factor affecting protocol efficiency. Therefore, this chapter also conducts an analysis of packet header sizes. The numerical results show that, on average for the small Internet world [1], this overhead is comparable to those of the switching labels used by connection-oriented networks like ATM and the frame relay, and much smaller than those of addresses used by connectionless networks like IP, especially IPv6. This is because the information carried for TLSR includes shorter port indexes or domain identities rather than long network addresses like the IP address. Furthermore, stripping off the routing information on a visited node immediately once the packet leaves this node makes the overhead shorter and shorter as the packet approaches its destination.

S.M. Jiang, *Future Wireless and Optical Networks*,
Computer Communications and Networks,
DOI 10.1007/978-1-4471-2822-9_4, © Springer-Verlag London Limited 2012

The remainder of this chapter is organized as follows. Section 4.2 discusses some networking issues of TLSR, and interconnection with other networks is discussed in Sect. 4.3. An analytical evaluation of TLSR's packet overhead is given in Sect. 4.4. The chapter is summarized in Sect. 4.5.

4.2 Networking Issues

Here we discuss some important networking issues of TLSR such as addressing, congestion control, end-to-end QoS, and network interconnection.

4.2.1 Addressing with TLSR

Addressing is directly related to both high and low layers of a network. Major requirements and constraints imposed to addressing are summarized below.

- A sufficient address space means that the address space never exhausts against the increase in the demand for addresses. One solution is to remove the limit of the address space. However, this does not mean that an infinite address space is available at any time. Instead, an address space should be easily extended when necessary without invoking any modification to the implemented network infrastructure. With the current Internet, this is not possible, and a costly change in the implemented infrastructure is needed. For example, the transformation from IPv4 to IPv6 in order to resolve the exhaustion of the IPv4 address requires the IPv4 routers to be replaced by IPv6 routers.
- A flexible address size requires that the address size should not be fixed for all users. Flexible-size addresses can reduce packet overhead for addressing. For example, a short address is suitable for wireless networks since it is inefficient to transmit large packet headers over unreliable wireless channels. Therefore, header compression is often carried out for IP packets to be transmitted through wireless networks. Even in wired networks, the IP address, especially the IPv6 address, is too long compared to the payload for voice traffic.
- Simple routing means that an addressing scheme should simplify routing operations. To this end, a hierarchical addressing structure similar to the telephone numbering is an option, in which an address would consist of the identity of the user and high-level routing information. The former identifies the user, while the latter indicates where the user is located in the network.
- Network security requires that an addressing scheme should not jeopardize network security. Now most addressing schemes adopt fixed and open-standardized address structures such as the IP address, which actually combines the user identity and routing information into the address. This is necessary for public service provisioning. But it also allows the addresses of sensitive sites to be easily

guessed by malicious users to launch attacks. Therefore, it is necessary to separate the user identity from the address and provide multiple addressing schemes for different applications.

- Mobility support requires that the same address is able to be used in communications wherever the user is located. To this end, the user identity can be divided into two parts: fixed and temporary. The former cannot be changed once it is assigned, while the latter can be a private address or a temporary identity for mobility support. The private address can also facilitate private network deployment such as ad hoc networks that require a rapid setup. Most existing addressing schemes adopted fixed addresses (e.g., IP), with which triangle routing (e.g., mobile IPv4) or address binding (e.g., mobile IPv6) is needed to maintain the network connectivity of the roaming user [2].

However, it is very difficult to have one addressing scheme that satisfies all the above requirements; the coexistence of multiple addressing schemes is inevitable. Actually, different addressing schemes already exist, such as the IP address, the IEEE 802 MAC address, and the Integrated Services Digital Network (ISDN) address. New addressing schemes may also appear in the future. On the other hand, different types of networks are converging to one type of network, such as the all-IP network. To this end, the following issues must be addressed: (i) the low-layer network needs to be able to efficiently support different addressing schemes, and (ii) changes in the implemented addressing schemes or the addition of new ones should not require any change in the implemented low-layer network.

Therefore, addressing independent routing is necessary for low-layer networks, and TLSR is so designed, as discussed below. The routing units used by the TLSR core network are the basic elements of networks rather than logical identities like the IP address. These elements include output ports of network relaying units (e.g., routers or switches) and domains. A domain is a set of network relaying units located in the same area. These elements will not be changed by addressing schemes.

As illustrated in Fig. 3.5, port-level source routing (PLSR) provides routing functions in the optical domain, which is the base of TLSR. On top of PLSR, domain-level source routing (DLSR) and DBDR are further designed to meet different routing requirements of both connectionless and connection-oriented services. Only DBDR will be affected by high-level addressing schemes since it needs to use destination addresses for routing; but DBDR is not the core part of the TLSR network, as illustrated in Fig. 3.5. Both PLSR and DLSR are independent of addressing schemes, so any changes in addressing schemes or additions of new ones will not affect the core of the TLSR network. Every packet is routed all-optically in the same way by PLSR. Differences in addressing schemes are only present at the border of the TLSR network. Adding a new addressing scheme only requires implementing the corresponding component at the border of the TLSR network. A gateway is needed at the network border for the conversion between different addressing schemes and the TLSR routing structure, which will be discussed further in Sect. 4.3.

4.2.2 Congestion Control

Congestion will occur in a TLSR network, resulting in packet losses, particularly in AOPS nodes due to its poor optical buffering capability. The impact of congestion on network performance is very severe in the case of ultra-high optical transmission rates. This happens because a hop-by-hop retransmission of lost packets is infeasible for AOPS nodes because of the limited optical processing capability. Since powerful buffering and processing capabilities are available at domain edges, a domain-level congestion control is a reasonable option in this case through the use of a TCP-like flow control scheme over a domain. Actually, this is the idea of Semi-TCP, to be discussed in Chap. 10. The ingress and egress nodes of a domain have to (i) control the congestion within the domain and (ii) retransmit packets lost over the domain if necessary. Accordingly, the end-to-end congestion and transmission reliability control task is partitioned to domain-by-domain controls. As will be discussed in Chaps. 7, 8 and 9, a domain-by-domain control can tolerate more losses than an end-to-end control, which makes it more suitable than TCP for AOPS nodes with poor buffering capabilities.

Semi-TCP is also better in all-optical networks. In all-optical networks, packet losses can be caused either by congestion or by collision. The congestion in a domain may be caused by loose traffic control of its upstream domains. However, the collision in a domain is mainly due to traffic competition within the domain itself rather than the behavior of its upstream domains. With the conventional TCP, a domain may suffer from consuming more resources to retransmit lost packets actually caused by a collision in its downstream domains. The traffic load for such retransmission may also increase collision and congestion probabilities in upstream domains. Moreover, if a burst experiences congestion, all flows aggregated in this burst are affected. With Semi-TCP, every domain is responsible for the congestion control in its own domain, and a limited number of retransmissions across the domain is carried out for packets lost therein, thus improving the end-to-end transmission reliability.

4.2.3 End-to-End QoS

As illustrated in Fig. 4.1, TLSR decomposes an end-to-end QoS support into the domain level and the hop level. The domain-level QoS is supported by per-domain behavior (PDB), and the hop-level QoS by per-hop behavior (PHB). Given a route between a pair of source and destination nodes, the first domain of this route coordinates the determination of the PDB of each domain, while the domain ingress node decides the PHB of each node along a selected optical route (i.e., IDR) according to the PDB carried by a packet. To support PDB and PHB, QoS mechanisms such as call admission control (CAC) at the call level, and scheduling algorithms as well as buffer control schemes at the packet level [3] will be used jointly.

The QoS support of IP evolves from IntServ [4] to DiffServ [5]. DiffServ suggests shifting sophisticated QoS mechanisms from the core to the network border to keep the core network as simple as possible for implementation scalability. The same philosophy is adopted by TLSR to simplify the PHB of AOPS nodes in order to facilitate AOPS realization. That is, CAC only involves domain edges that provide scheduling and buffering functions. A simple or even zero buffer is used at AOPS nodes, and packet dropping is only a concern in case of congestion. Thus the domain-level QoS support is different from the hop-level one, as further discussed below.

At the domain level, each domain of a route is assigned a portion of the task for an end-to-end QoS provisioning in terms of the PDB defined earlier. Every packet needs to carry the PDB as shown in Fig. 3.4(c), and will be buffered and scheduled at the domain ingress node according to this PDB. Bounding delay and loss rates are the major responsibility of the domain ingress node rather than AOPS nodes within the domain, since the latter has no such capability. Therefore, the domain-level congestion control discussed in Sect. 4.2.2 is important to keep low packet loss rates inside the domain. To some extent, the PDB here is similar to that for DiffServ. Some related research on DiffServ can be found in [6, 7].

At the hop level, the domain ingress node needs to distribute its QoS support task to each hop along a selected IDR through defining PHBs. The PHB should be defined as simply as possible due to the limited optical processing capability of the AOPS node. For example, a 1-bit packet dropping preference can be adopted as the PHB to guide an AOPS node to drop packets in the case of congestion. A probabilistic dropping scheme for optical networks [8] may be adopted to perform smarter packet dropping.

As discussed in Chap. 5, the current QoS schemes can be of per-flow and per-class type. The former (e.g., ATM and IntServ) can provide granular end-to-end QoS but with a scalability problem. The latter (e.g., DiffServ) can overcome the scalability problem through flow aggregation but with problems of coarse end-to-end QoS and QoS over-provisioning [9]. To support granular end-to-end QoS in TLSR, the differentiated queuing service (DQS) discussed in Chap. 5 can be implemented at the domain ingress node to queue packets according to PDBs. With DQS, the end-to-end delay bound is projected into the delay bound provided by each domain that a packet will visit. Unlike per-class QoS schemes, with DQS, per-domain QoS (i.e., PDBs) can be different from one domain to another for the same application so that more granular end-to-end QoS can be provided.

4.3 Network Interconnection

A TLSR network may be composed of one or multiple TLSR domains, as illustrated in Fig. 4.1. There are two types of physical routes here: the intra-domain optical route (IDR) and the optical tunnel. This tunnel is a concatenation of the IDRs and interconnects a source and destination nodes. The domain-level route for DLSR or DBDR needs to be projected into physical routes to be used by PLSR for all-optical

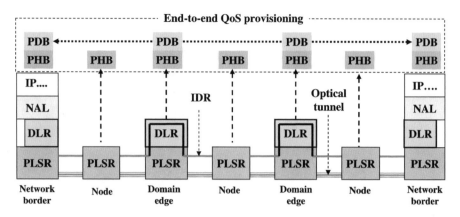

Fig. 4.1 TLSR network connections (DLR = domain-level routing, NAL = network adaptation layer)

packet routing. This projection is carried out with optical-electrical-optical (OEO) conversion at the ingress node of each domain along the route between source and destination. With an optical tunnel, the signal of a packet always travels in the optical domain via PLSR all the way to its destination.

When a TLSR network connects with other types of networks such as IP or ATM, a network adaptation layer (NAL) is needed above TLSR, as illustrated in Fig. 4.1. The major functions of this layer include the conversion of routing information and QoS parameters as well as packet encapsulation for the interconnection with other networks, as discussed below.

4.3.1 Routing Information Conversion

This function converts the routing information used by non-TLSR networks (e.g., IP address) into that used by TLSR. The routing information to be used by the TLSR network includes the destination address (DSN), the next domain identity (NDI), the IDR number (IDRN), and the output port index (OPI). The format of DSN needs further studies. Which of the above conversions should be carried out largely depends on which service is used, i.e., either connectionless (CL), connection-oriented (CO), or CO plus CL (OL) service, as listed in Table 4.1. This table also compares different conversions in terms of end-to-end delay, packet overhead sizes, and conversion complexity, which depends on the amount of information to be used for conversion.

Particularly for IP, a gateway can be implemented at the TLSR network border to transfer the IP address into the TLSR routing information. This gateway for DBDR is similar to an IP router. However, with IP, a packet has to go through IP routing at every router in order to reach its destination. With TLSR, after passing the gateway, a packet travels along an optical route (i.e., IDR) to cross the domain. The IP address can be used directly as the destination address used by TLSR. Then a database for

Table 4.1 TLSR routing information conversions

Information conversion	TLSR services	Suitable for	End-to-end delay	Packet overhead	Conversion complexity
Routing info→DSN	DBDR	CL	long	small	simple
Routing info→NDI	CL-DLSR	CL	↑	|	|
Routing info→IDRN	CO-DLSR	OL	|	↓	↓
Routing info→OPI	PLSR	CO	short	large	complex

CL = connectionless, CO = connection-oriented, OL = CO plus CL, DSN = destination

the projection of the IP address and NDI can be built up at the domain ingress node. Since the details of the destination are useless for routing at the domain level, only part of the IP address rather than the whole address is necessarily stored in this database.

In this case, DBDR can be used to transport IP packets over TLSR. When a packet arrives at a domain, its ingress node extracts the IP destination address from the payload, and looks for an NDI from the database following this address. Once an NDI is found, then CL-DLSR is invoked for the remaining operation. (Refer to Sect. 3.4.2 for more details on CL-DLSR.) CO-DLSR and PLSR can also be used to support the connectionless IP if the corresponding routing tables are available at the domain ingress node. However, constructing and maintaining these databases is more costly than those of DBDR since more details of the network topology are needed.

4.3.2 Packet Encapsulation

There are two schemes that can be used for packet encapsulation for interconnection between TLSR networks and non-TLSR networks: tunneling and shortcut. With tunneling, a non-TLSR packet is encapsulated into a TLSR payload without any change in this packet. Its major advantage is simplicity, but at the expense of long packet overheads. This scheme is more suitable for the CL service, since the original routing information carried by a packet will still be useful on the remaining journey of the packet. Tunneling can also be used for the CO service. With shortcut, the original routing information, such as IP addresses, ATM virtual channel identifier (VCI)/virtual path identifier (VPI) and Multi-Protocol Label Switching (MPLS) labels, is removed from every packet (or cell), and only the remaining information, especially the payload, is encapsulated into the TLSR payload. Shortcut is suitable for the CO service, since the removed information is useless when a packet is traveling along an established route directly linked to its destination [10, 11].

As shown in Fig. 3.4, the payload type is indicated by the payload specification (PLS) in the packet header. Table 4.2 gives an example of a 4-bit PLS (which has

Table 4.2 Example of the setting of the payload specification (PLS) for packet encapsulation

PLS	Payload type	Supported by	Service	Encapsulation
0000	TLSR	DBDR, DLSR	CL, CO	Tunneling, Shortcut
0001	IPv4 packet	DBDR, DLSR	CL, CO	Tunneling
0010	IPv4 w/n address	CO-DLSR	CO	Shortcut
0011	IPv4 payload	CO-DLSR	CO	Shortcut
0100	IPv6 packet	DBDR, DLSR	CL, CO	Tunneling
0101	IPv6 w/n address	CO-DLSR	CO	Shortcut
0111	IPv6 payload	CO-DLSR	CO	Shortcut
1000	ATM cell	CO-DLSR	CO	Tunneling
1001	ATM payload	CO-DLSR	CO	Shortcut
...	...	...	...	...
1111	Management info	DBDR, DLSR	CL, CO	NA

the same length as that of the "version" field of IPv4) setting for different types of payloads. PLS = 0000 means that the payload is just of the TLSR network itself, and is supported by both DBDR and DLSR and suitable for both connectionless (CL) and connection-oriented (CO) services. Here only the domain-level routing is listed. "IPvX w/n address" means that only destination and source addresses are removed from the IPvX packet since the addresses are too long especially with IPv6, while the other information is kept intact. The last row is for the management information on the TLSR network.

4.3.3 QoS Mapping

This function converts QoS parameters of a non-TLSR network into those of TLSR. As mentioned earlier, TLSR jointly uses the PDB and the PHB for QoS support. A PDB defines a per-domain effort to support end-to-end QoS and is determined according to end-to-end QoS requirements such as delay bound and packet dropping ratio. Accordingly, PHB defines a per-hop effort to support the PDB along a selected optical route (i.e., IDR) across a domain. For an optical tunnel, PHB is set according to end-to-end QoS requirements, especially packet dropping rate because of the poor buffering capability of AOPS nodes. In this case, the end-to-end delay is not an important issue due to the ultra-high speed of optical fibers. Therefore, QoS requirements from a non-TLSR network must be converted into a PDB corresponding to an intra-domain route (IDR) or directly into PHBs corresponding to an optical tunnel.

4.4 Analysis of Packet Headers

One concern about using source routing is large packet overheads, since every packet needs to carry the routing information on the entire route. This issue is discussed analytically here with a comparison between TLSR and other typical network architectures including ATM and IP.

4.4.1 Packet Header Sizes

For simplicity, we assume that an IDR in each domain consists of the same number of nodes, i.e., $(n' + 1)$, and that there are in total $m(n' + 1)$ nodes, where n' indicates the number of hops along a domain-level route. The size of the per-node segment (PNS) for PLSR (l_1) and the size of the per-domain segment (PDS) for DLSR (l_2) are also assumed identical for different nodes and domains. Refer to Fig. 3.4 for the packet format and the definitions of parameters l_1 and l_2 as well as γ, where γ indicates the size of the PLS field.

The packet header (refer to Fig. 3.4) size depends on the number of domains that a route goes through (m). The average per-node packet header, denoted by $A(m, n')$, is also calculated. $A(m, n')$ is defined as the ratio of the sum of header lengths of the packet to be present in each node to the total number of nodes that the packet has visited. For DLSR, the packet header size is $(m - 1)l_2$ in the first domain, since only the information on the next domains needs to be carried. Due to the header stripping operation (see Fig. 3.1), this header size becomes $(m - 2)l_2$ in the second domain and zero in the last one. Thus, the sum of lengths of the DLSR header for a route consisting of m domains is calculated as follows:

$$\text{DLSR header length} = \frac{m}{2}(m - 1)l_2. \tag{4.1}$$

For PLSR, the size of the IDR at the first node is $(n' + 1)l_1$, and l_1 at the last node within the same domain. Therefore, the sum of lengths of the PLSR header for an IDR per domain is calculated as follows:

$$\text{PLSR header length per domain} = \frac{(n' + 1)(n' + 2)l_1}{2}. \tag{4.2}$$

To be conservative, here an IDR is still assumed to be necessary in the last domain to route a packet to its destination. Then, the total PLSR header length for m domains is

$$\text{PLSR header length} = \frac{m(n' + 1)(n' + 2)l_1}{2}. \tag{4.3}$$

The minimum header with a length of $(2 + \gamma)$ is associated with every packet, where the field type mark (FTM) field can always be set to 2 bits, as indicated in Table 3.2.

Therefore, we have

$$A(m, n') = 2 + \gamma + \frac{1}{m(n'+1)}\left[m(m-1)\frac{l_2}{2} + m(n'+1)(n'+2)\frac{l_1}{2}\right]$$

$$= 2 + \gamma + \frac{l_1(n'+2)}{2} + \frac{l_2(m-1)}{2(n'+1)}. \tag{4.4}$$

The maximum packet header is the packet present at the ingress node of the first domain of a route, since this packet must carry both DLSR and PLSR segments of each domain along this route. The DLSR segment is $(m-1)l_2$ bits long, as mentioned above. For the maximum size of the packet header as a packet is passed to the first node of the route, denoted by $M(m, n')$, due to the $(n'+1)l_1$ bits for the PLSR segments of the nodes along the route and the $(2+\gamma)$-bit long minimum header of every packet, we have

$$M(m, n') = 2 + \gamma + (m-1)l_2 + (n'+1)l_1. \tag{4.5}$$

As shown in Eqs. (4.4)–(4.5), both $A(m, n')$ and $M(m, n')$ increase linearly with m at an increase rate of $\frac{l_2}{2(n'+1)}$ and l_2, respectively, given that the other parameters are unchanged. When $m = 1$, Eqs. (4.4)–(4.5) corresponds to an all-optical route consisting of $(n'+1)$ AOPS nodes. In this case, we have

$$A(1, n') = \frac{l_1}{2}(n'+2) + 2 + \gamma \tag{4.6}$$

and

$$M(1, n') = l_1(n'+1) + 2 + \gamma, \tag{4.7}$$

each of which is just a linear function of n' at an increase rate of $\frac{l_1}{2}$ and l_1, respectively.

Furthermore, from

$$\frac{\partial A(m, n')}{\partial n'} = \frac{l_1}{2} - \frac{(m-1)l_2}{2(n'+1)^2}, \tag{4.8}$$

it can be found that $A(m, n')$ also increases almost linearly with n' if m is small. There is an inflection point of having the smallest $A(m, n')$ against n' as follows:

$$A_{\min} = 2 + \gamma + \sqrt{(m-1)l_1 l_2}, \tag{4.9}$$

which can be used to optimize the IDR selection. Equation (4.9) is obtained by setting

$$n' = \sqrt{\frac{(m-1)l_2}{l_1}} - 1, \tag{4.10}$$

which is given by letting

$$\frac{\partial A(m, n')}{\partial n'} = 0. \tag{4.11}$$

4.4.2 Sizes of Per-Hop and Per-Domain Segments

Now we discuss how to determine l_1 and l_2 by assuming that every node has the same number of output ports (x) while every domain has the same number of adjacent domains (y). The length of the output port index (OPI) is bounded by $\lceil \log_2^x \rceil$. The per-hop behavior (PHB) is set to 1 bit for the packet dropping preference, similar to ATM. With a 2-bit FTM, we have

$$l_1 = 3 + \lceil \log_2^x \rceil. \tag{4.12}$$

Similarly for l_2, 1 bit is enough for the source routing type (SRT), as indicated in Table 3.2. For the per-domain behavior (PDB), it consists of two parts for each domain, one for the packet dropping preference and the other for the delay bound. Two bits are allocated to the packet dropping preference to have more granular packet dropping preferences at the domain level. The delay bound depends on its expression format. Here a packet should carry the index rather than the real value of a delay bound as proposed in [12] to reduce the overhead. That is, a domain assigns an index to each delay bound, which is carried by PDB. Given b sets of delay bounds available per domain, the size of PDB is $2 + \lceil \log_2^b \rceil$. For the source routing setting (SRS), it will be set to either the next domain identity (NDI) if SRT $= 0$ or the intra-domain route number (IDRN) if SRT $= 1$, as indicated in Table 3.2. The size of NDI is $\lceil \log_2^y \rceil$ for CL-DLSR. For CO-DLSR, the size of IDRN is $\lceil \log_2^z \rceil$, where z is the maximum number of IDRs available per domain. With a 2-bit FTM, we have

$$l_2 = 4 + \lceil \log_2^b \rceil + \lceil \log_2^X \rceil, \tag{4.13}$$

where $X = y$ for CL-DLSR and $X = z$ for CO-DLSR. Usually, z is larger than y since the number of neighbors of a domain is small.

4.4.3 Numerical Discussion

Here, we use Eqs. (4.5) and (4.4) to calculate the maximum packet header size $M(m, n')$ and the average packet header size $A(m, n')$ with a 2-bit FTM and a 1-bit PHB for DLSR and PLSR. The results are plotted in Figs. 4.2 and 4.3, respectively.

As illustrated in Fig. 4.2, $M(m, n')$ for $m = 15$ and $n' = 49$ (i.e., a route consisting of 15×50 nodes) as well as $x = 1024$ (i.e., the number of output ports per node) is still much shorter than the header of the IPv6 packet, and $M(m, n')$

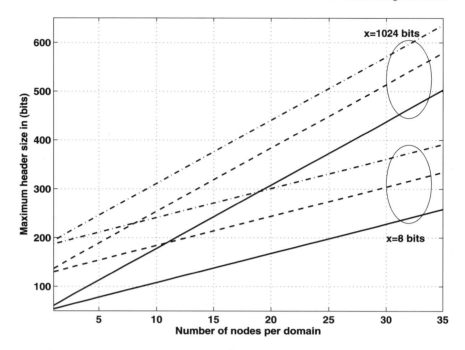

Fig. 4.2 Maximum packet header sizes $M(m, n')$ against the number of nodes per domain $(n'+1)$: $x = 1024$, $b = 32$, $\gamma = 8$ bits

for $x = 8$ is less than 600 bits. As illustrated in Fig. 4.3, $A(m, n')$ for $x = 1024$, $m = 15$, and $n' = 19$ is still less than the header of the IPv4 packet, and $A(m, n')$ for $x = 8$ is shorter than 80 bits. Moreover, $A(m, n')$ almost increases linearly with n' when $n' > 14$ roughly, and is almost insensitive to m in this case. We also see that for $n' = 34$, $A(m, n')$ for $x = 1024$ is less than 250 bits, while $A(m, n')$ for $x = 8$ is around 125 bits. However, with the port bitmap address structure-I proposed in [13], the initial overhead just for routing is given by $x \times n$, where n is the number of hops of the route. Particularly for the case discussed above, the initial overhead is $1024 \times (15 \times 35)$ bits. But the header size for DBDR is always equal to the length of the minimum header, i.e., $2 + \gamma = 10$ bits here.

Table 4.3 lists l_1 and l_2 as a function of x and X. It shows that l_1 increases very slowly with x and is much shorter than the headers of typical networks listed in the column "Typical headers." This is why PLSR can simplify optical processing. According to the small Internet world reported in [1], the average length of the Internet at the domain level is less than 4, while that at the router level is shorter than 10. From $M(m, n')$ and $A(m, n')$ with $X = 512$ for $m = 4$ and $n' = 2$ listed in this table, we can see that $A(m, n')$ is equivalent to the size of the ATM cell header while $M(m, n')$ is almost half of the IPv4 header size.

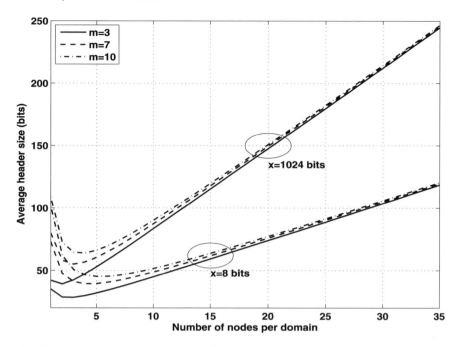

Fig. 4.3 Average packet header sizes $A(m, n')$ against the number of domains (m) and the number of nodes per domain $(n' + 1)$: $x = 1024$, $b = 32$, $\gamma = 8$ bits

Table 4.3 Packet header sizes (in bits): TLSR versus typical networks ($\gamma = 8$ bits and $b = 32$ sets)

X, x (bits)	PNS $l_1(x)$	PDS $l_2(X)$	$m = 1, n' = 39^{\dagger}$ $M(m, n')$	$A(m, n')$	$m = 4, n' = 2^{\ddagger}$ $M(m, n')$	$A(m, n')$	Typical headers (bits)
16	7	13	360	188.5	88	33.5	Frame relay = 24~56
32	8	14	410	214	91	35.5	MPLS = 32
64	9	15	460	239.5	94	37.5	ATM = 40
128	10	16	510	265	97	39.5	Ethernet = 112
256	11	17	560	290.5	100	41.5	IPv4 = 192
512	12	18	610	316	103	43.5	IPv6 = 1280

†For optical tunnel, ‡for the "small Internet world" [1]

4.4.4 Comparison of Network Structures

We now further compare the PLSR of TLSR with some typical network structures including ATM, MPLS, and IP in terms of operations and information required for routing and/or switching.

Table 4.4 Per-node operation for routing/switching

Network tech.	Per-con info storage	Routing info storage	Table lookup	Header rewriting	Header stripping	R-info size (bits)	Fixed R/S-info
ATM	yes	no	yes	yes	no	8/12/16[†]	yes
MPLS	yes	no	yes	yes	no	20	yes
IPv4	no	yes	yes	no	no	32[‡]	yes
IPv6	no	yes	yes	no	no	128[‡]	yes
TLSR	no	no	no	no	yes	$\lceil \log_2 x \rceil$	no

[†]VPI = 8 or 12 (bits), VCI = 16 bits, [‡]destination address, x =port number per node, R/S-info = information for routing and/or switching, Per-con info = per-connection information at each switch, Routing info = per-router routing information

As shown in Table 4.4, for both the connection-oriented ATM and MPLS, per-connection information has to be stored at each node of a connection for switching, and both table lookup and header rewriting are needed. For the connectionless IP, the routing information is stored at every router, and table lookup is needed for routing. The sizes of the information used for routing or switching carried by ATM cells, MPLS, and IP packets are fixed, while that for PLSR depends on the number of output ports to be supported by a node (x). For IP, its address can be further organized in a hierarchical structure to reduce the size of the routing information stored at routers. For example, for PLSR with x equal to 64, $\lceil \log_2 x \rceil = 6$. Processing such short routing information all-optically without table lookup and header rewriting operations can be much easier than processing with long routing or switching information, requiring table lookup and/or header rewriting operations. Therefore, this type of PLSR design is expected to facilitate AOPS realization.

4.5   Conclusion

This chapter discusses some major networking issues of TLSR, including addressing, congestion control, QoS support, and inter-networking. The analysis of the TLSR packet header shows that the size of the header on average is comparable with those of existing network structures for the typical Internet size. Therefore, the source routing approach adopted here can simplify routing operations at the AOPS nodes by avoiding routing table operation and packet header rewriting without a big increase in packet overheads for routing information carrying.

References

1. Albert, R., Barabási, A.L.: Statistical mechanics of complex networks. Rev. Mod. Phys. **74**(1), 47–98 (2002)
2. Perkins, C.: IP mobility support. IETF RFC 2002 (1996)

3. Guérin, R., Peris, V.: Quality-of-service in packet networks: basic mechanisms and directions. Comput. Netw. **31**(3), 169–189 (1999)
4. Braden, R., Clark, D., Shenker, S.: Integrated services in the Internet architecture: an overview. IETF RFC 1633 (1994)
5. Blake, S., Black, D., Carlson, M., Davies, E., Wang, Z., Weiss, W.: An architecture for differentiated services. IETF RFC 2475 (1998)
6. Jiang, Y.M.: Per-pomain packet scale rate guarantee for expedited forwarding. In: Proc. Int. WS Quality of Service (IWQoS), Berkeley, CA, USA, pp. 422–439 (2003)
7. Bless, R., Nichols, K., Wehrle, K.: A low effort per-domain behavior (PDB) for differenticated services. RFC 3662 (2003). Available on line http://www.faqs.org/rfcs/rfc3662.html
8. Yang, L.H., Jiang, Y.M., Jiang, S.M.: A probabilistic preemptive scheme for providing service differentiation in OBS networks. In: Proc. IEEE Global Tele. Conf. (GLOBOCOM), San Francisco, CA, USA, vol. 5, pp. 2689–2693 (2003)
9. Jiang, S.M.: Granular differentiated queueing services for QoS: structure and cost model. Comput. Commun. Rev. **35**(2), 13–22 (2005)
10. Firoiu, V., Kurose, J., Towsley, D.: Performance evaluation of ATM shortcut connections in overlaid IP/ATM. CMPSCI Technical Report TR 97-40, University of Massachusetts, Department of Computer Science, University of Massachusetts (1997)
11. Jiang, S.M., Ding, Q.L., Jin, M.: Flexible encapsulation for IP over ATM with ATM shortcuts. In: Proc. IEEE Int. Conf. Networks (ICON), Singapore, pp. 238–242 (2000)
12. Stoica, I., Zhang, H.: Providing guaranteed services without per flow management. In: Proc. ACM SIGCOMM, Cambridge, MA, USA (1999)
13. Yuan, X.C., Li, V.O.K., Li, C.Y., Wai, P.K.A.: A novel self-routing address scheme for all-optical packet-switched networks with arbitrary topologies. J. Lightwave Technol. **21**(2), 329–339 (2003)

Chapter 5
Differentiated Queueing Service (DQS) for Granular QoS

Abstract The future Internet will have to provide granular end-to-end quality of service (QoS) for different applications to cost-effectively satisfy their QoS requirements. Conventional packet-level QoS mechanisms largely rely on sophisticated schedulers. This, however, results in a scalability problem for increasing QoS granularity, since the more granular the QoS, the more complex the scheduler will be. This chapter proposes a per-packet QoS approach, called differentiated queueing service (DQS), which is evaluated in comparison with the per-flow IntServ and the per-class DiffServ. DQS aims to provide granular end-to-end QoS to satisfy various QoS requirements using buffer admission control (BAC) rather than sophisticated output schedulers. BAC, which is to be installed at networking units like routers and domain ingress nodes, queues packets according to their end-to-end delay requirements and drops or downgrades the service qualities of those packets whose end-to-end delay guarantees are perceived to fail as early as possible to reduce network resource waste.

5.1 Introduction

The subject of how to support QoS has been studied for a long time with many proposals reported in the literature. Most of them try to trade off between QoS granularity and the simplicity and scalability of implementation. Typically, there are two QoS provisioning approaches: per-flow such as IntServ and per-class such as DiffServ. To provide per-flow QoS, the scheduler must know the QoS requirement of every flow in order to treat it accordingly. This per-flow treatment has to store per-flow QoS information in relaying units, which causes a scalability problem for implementation. To avoid this problem, the per-class QoS method suggests aggregating flows with the same QoS requirement into a class so that relaying units only need to handle classes instead of every individual flow for QoS provisioning. The major disadvantages of per-class over per-flow QoS provisioning approaches include (i) a lack of QoS granularity for different applications and (ii) the possibility that flow aggregation may cause QoS over-provisioning to some individual flows.

With per-class QoS, a packet carries a class tag that will not be changed during its journey to the destination. Consequently, the same class service will be provided by each node along the route, since a class tag indicates one type of service

S.M. Jiang, *Future Wireless and Optical Networks*,
Computer Communications and Networks,
DOI 10.1007/978-1-4471-2822-9_5, © Springer-Verlag London Limited 2012

class that will be treated in the same way across the whole network. Therefore, the number of end-to-end QoS services provided by per-class QoS cannot exceed the number of QoS services provided by a node. For DiffServ in particular, only the premium service (PS) and assured service (AS) can be provided. PS and AS are designed, respectively, for delay-sensitive but loss-tolerable applications (e.g., voice and video) and delay-tolerable but loss-sensitive applications (e.g., data). The question is whether they are able to cost-effectively support new applications in the future. For example, there are other applications which cannot be simply classified as delay-sensitive or loss-sensitive such as inter-process communication (IPC) between remote systems and network remote control. They require not only QoS but also control quality [1, 2]. The traffic from those applications may be sensitive to both delay and loss or be even more delay constrained than voice and video. A diversity of QoS requirements and various QoS requirements mixed within one flow may also be required by new applications such as grid computing and cloud computing.

DiffServ suggests aggregating individual flows with identical QoS requirements into one big flow. This aggregation makes it difficult to support a flow containing two types of packets: one better served by PS, and the other better served by AS. In fact, an aggregated flow should be served such that the most stringent individual QoS requirement can be satisfied [3]. Consequently, each flow should be treated equally against the most stringent QoS and charged accordingly. However, from the end-to-end point of view, this treatment may be unnecessary and the subsequent charge is unfair to some flows even for the same type of application. Although the end-to-end QoS requirements of the same application are identical, the difficulty of per-hop QoS provisioning depends on and varies with route situation, particularly the number of hops along a route. In general, for the same end-to-end QoS requirement, the less hops in a route, the easier for a node to support it. However, with DiffServ, a flow going through a short route and another through a longer route will be tagged with the same class and aggregated accordingly if they belong to the same kind of application. Therefore, a flow may not be able to obtain an end-to-end QoS service that can cost-effectively satisfy its end-to-end QoS requirement according to its route situation.

There are also many proposals for improving the QoS granularity of DiffServ. For example, reference [4] suggests decoupling end-to-end QoS provisioning from service provisioning at core routers so that a flow can choose different service classes to have granular end-to-end QoS. Stateless per-flow QoS guarantee approaches can provide per-flow QoS guarantee with fewer scalability problems; see, e.g., [5–7]. However, they still rely on sophisticated output schedulers for QoS provisioning. The output scheduler becomes more complex with QoS granularity and is a performance bottleneck, especially for high-speed links since it must make a decision on-the-fly for every packet. Therefore, an approach not using output schedulers but still using per-flow virtual queue management was proposed in [8]. There are also some incremental upgrading proposals such as [9, 10], which did not successfully address the above-mentioned issues.

To provide granular end-to-end QoS with scalability, a per-packet DQS is discussed in this chapter. DQS suggests using BAC instead of sophisticated output schedulers to provide granular packet-level QoS.

The remainder of this chapter is organized as follows. A brief comparative discussion about the per-packet DQS versus the per-flow IntServ and the per-class DiffServ is given in Sect. 5.2, while the major implementation issues of DQS are discussed in Sect. 5.3. This chapter is concluded in Sect. 5.4.

5.2 Evaluation from IntServ, DiffServ to DQS

The following notation is used in the discussion:

- a: packet arrival time
- c: node link rate (bits/s)
- n: number of links along a route
- $\tilde{d}$: delay experienced by a packet at a node on its past journey, which is an interval between its arrival at and departure from this node
- $\dot{d}$: delay to be experienced by a packet at a node on its remaining journey
- $\hat{d}$: actual maximum delay allowed for a packet to stay at a node
- $\mathbf{e}$: latest departure time of a packet from a node
- $\mathbf{D}$: maximum end-to-end delay to be experienced by a packet, which is initially set to its lifetime.

Unless specified elsewhere, the subscript i is associated with node or hop i. To simplify the discussion, propagation delay is ignored here, since it is a constant given a route.

5.2.1 Overview of DQS

The principles of DQS are summarized below.

1. Buffer admission control (BAC): BAC is used to provide packet-level QoS for every packet by queueing it according to its end-to-end QoS requirement, particularly delay bound. The service order of a queued packet is determined by its queueing position in the buffer, so the role of the output scheduler in QoS provisioning becomes trivial.
2. Call admission control (CAC): BAC can drop packets whose end-to-end delays are perceived unable to be guaranteed in order to reduce network resource waste. For those perceived to probably fail in end-to-end delay guarantee, their service qualities are downgraded. In this sense, the issue of end-to-end delay guarantee becomes an issue of packet dropping ratio guarantee. Similar to packet losses caused by congestion, it is expected that packet dropping rate can also be bounded statistically by using a CAC algorithm.
3. End-to-end QoS service: This service along a route is just a combination of the per-hop services (PHSs) provided by each node along the route. The number of these combinations can be large, to satisfy different end-to-end QoS requirements. This results because a PHS is defined by a node itself rather than being

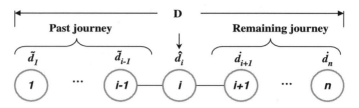

Fig. 5.1 Relationship between $\tilde{d}$, $\hat{d}$, and $\dot{d}$

classified by others, and the PHS set of a node can be different from one to another.

4. QoS information handling: To avoid the scalability problem of IntServ, DQS lets each packet carry its end-to-end QoS requirement, which will be used by BAC to queue the packet upon its arrival.

The key to enabling DQS to provide granular end-to-end QoS is the queueing operation carried out by BAC. Upon a packet's arrival at node i, in order to queue this packet at a proper position in the buffer, BAC first determines $\mathbf{e}_i$ as follows:

$$\mathbf{e}_i = a_i + \hat{d}_i, \tag{5.1}$$

where $\hat{d}_i$, as illustrated in Fig. 5.1, is calculated by

$$\hat{d}_i = \mathbf{D} - \sum_{j=1}^{i-1} \tilde{d}_j - \sum_{j=i+1}^{n+1} \dot{d}_j, \tag{5.2}$$

where $\dot{d}_j$ needs to be estimated and will be discussed further in Sect. 5.3.4.

The position of a packet to be queued in the buffer is determined according to its $\mathbf{e}$ and those of the packets already in the buffer. That is, it will be located between two consecutive packets, say packets j and $(j+1)$, satisfying the following conditions:

$$\mathbf{e}(j) \leq \mathbf{e}(j+1) \tag{5.3}$$

and

$$\mathbf{e}(j) \leq \mathbf{e} < \mathbf{e}(j+1), \tag{5.4}$$

where $\mathbf{e}(j)$ is the $\mathbf{e}$ of packet j. This means that packets with different $\mathbf{e}$ are ordered according to their $\mathbf{e}$ settings, while those with an identical $\mathbf{e}$ are queued according to their arrival sequences following the first-in-first-out (FIFO) policy. Packets with smaller j are closer to the head-of-line (HOL) and will always be served earlier.

Without using pre-emption to any packet, a successful packet queueing into the queue should satisfy the following buffer admission conditions:

1. $\mathbf{e} \geq a + \frac{\tilde{l}}{c}$, where $\tilde{l} = \sum_{i=0}^{j} l(i) + l$, $l(i)$ is the length of packet i ($i = 0$ indicates the packet that is currently under service), and l is the length of the newly arriving packet. This condition means that the delay requirement of this packet can be supported if it is admitted.

Table 5.1 Comparison between IntServ, DiffServ, and DQS

Compared items	IntServ	DiffServ	DQS
QoS treatment level	Per-flow	Per-class	Per-packet
QoS granularity	Fine	Coarse	Fine
QoS over-provisioning	Unlikely	Likely	Unlikely
Key to QoS provisioning	Scheduler	Scheduler	BAC
Different QoS support within a flow	No	No	Yes
Per-router's PHSs for one flow	Different	Identical	Different
QoS adaptive to route situation	No	No	Yes
Number of end-to-end QoS	Unlimited	Limited	Unlimited
Scalability for QoS granularity	Better	Worst	Best
Implementation complexity	Highest	Lowest	High

2. $e(j') \geq a + \frac{l'(j')}{c}, \forall j' \geq (j+1)$, where, $l'(j') = \sum_{i=0}^{j'} l(i) + l$, which means that for all packets to be affected by this packet insertion, their delay bounds provided by node i will still be assured if this packet is admitted.

With a finite buffer, these conditions are further limited by the buffer capacity. That is, there should be enough buffer space to insert a new packet without pushing out or dropping any queued packets.

5.2.2 DQS Versus IntServ and DiffServ

This section compares DQS with IntServ and DiffServ as summarized in Table 5.1. A comparison among these three QoS provisioning approaches based on computer simulation can be found in [11].

DQS is a per-packet QoS provisioning approach, with which the QoS for each packet is explicitly defined and carried by the packet itself. The key element of DQS is BAC, rather than the output scheduler that has been used by both IntServ and DiffServ. The major difference between using BAC and using output schedulers is the point at which the service time of a queued packet can be determined. With the output scheduler, this decision is made by the scheduler almost as soon as the server becomes available to serve new packets. Thus the service decision must be made as fast as possible to avoid having the server wait for a queueing decision. The amount of time required for making such a decision depends on how many competing packets and how much information are to be considered in this operation. Particularly for IntServ, the QoS information is stored for every flow, and the number of competing packets is almost proportional to the number of flows under consideration. This is the major reason why IntServ cannot be scalable to the number of flows.

With DiffServ, the scalability problem of IntServ does not exist, because the number of classes is much less than that of flows in a network. But, with a large number of classes, DiffServ will also face a similar problem since the number of queues will increase with the number of classes to be supported. With the BAC of DQS, the service time of a packet exactly corresponds to its position in the buffer, which is determined upon its arrival at the buffer through the queueing operation. The amount of time required for queueing a packet is proportional to the number of packets queued in the buffer and determined by searching algorithms used to locate the position of an arriving packet in the queue.

As mentioned earlier, DQS lets each data packet carry its end-to-end QoS requirement, which will be used by BAC to determine its position in the buffer during its admission. In this case, whether the end-to-end delay of a packet can be bounded can be perceived upon its arrival. Therefore, BAC can drop, as early as possible, those packets that are perceived to surely fail in their delay bound guarantee, or it can downgrade the service quality for those perceived to probably fail, in order to reduce network resource waste. Consequently, end-to-end delay guarantee becomes an issue of packet dropping ratio guarantee. Therefore, DQS somewhat converts packet-level delay guarantee into call-level packet dropping ratio guarantee. Generally, it is more difficult to implement packet-level schemes than call-level ones, since the former often requires on-the-fly operation for every packet while the latter does not.

With DQS, a node treats every packet according to its end-to-end QoS information carried by the packet. Therefore, if packets from the same flow have different QoS requirements, a node can also treat them differently. However, this is impossible with per-class DiffServ; every packet of the same class will be treated identically by a node, because the class tag is the only QoS information that a route can use to handle every incoming packet. Similarly, for per-flow IntServ, QoS information is only stored at the flow level, so each packet from the same flow will be treated equally by a node.

With IntServ, a per-flow resource reservation can be made through the Resource Reservation Protocol (RSVP). This process allows each router along a route to allocate a certain amount of network resource to one flow according to the QoS provided for this flow. This means that different routers may have different PHSs for the same flow, and can adapt to route situations. However, this adaptability is at the call level, since this PHS is determined during the resource reservation process and will not be changed at the packet level. With DQS, the PHS is also defined by each node and can be different from one to another. An end-to-end QoS is just one of the combinations of the PHSs of each node along a route, and the number of such combinations can be large, to satisfy different end-to-end QoS requirements. Therefore, for both IntServ and DQS, due to their flexible PHSs, the number of end-to-end QoS services is unlimited theoretically. However, for per-class DiffServ, with the currently defined per-hop behaviors (PHBs), it can provide only two types of end-to-end QoS: premium service (PS) and assured service (AS).

Since QoS information is carried by every packet, DQS can allow a node to adjust its PHS for an incoming packet at the packet level according to the current situation as indicated by Eq. (5.2), as we discuss below. Typical QoS information to be carried by a packet includes its lifetime on its remaining journey to the destination

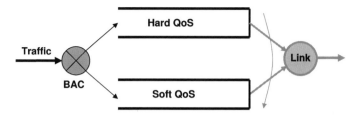

Fig. 5.2 A queue structure for DQS implementation

and a pre-defined PHS to be provided by every node along the route. Therefore, every node can adjust its PHS for an incoming packet instantly. For example, if a packet has been served better than the pre-defined PHSs by upstream nodes, the present node can relax its PHS for this packet by the service margin offered by the upstream nodes, resulting in a looser PHS than the pre-defined one. Furthermore, if the situation on its remaining journey can be estimated, the node can also adjust its PHS to accommodate more traffic. However, this feature cannot be provided by either IntServ or DiffServ, because no such information is available to them.

5.3 Implementation Issues

The major implementation issues of DQS include queue structure, BAC, CAC, an estimation of **e**, and the carrying of end-to-end QoS information. Besides the notation defined in Sect. 5.2, the following are also used in this discussion:

- **d**: per-hop maximum delay determined by CAC
- ω: size of QoS information field per packet.

5.3.1 Queue Structure

DQS can only use a single queue to support different applications with various QoS requirements. However, there may be differences in QoS guarantee degrees required by different applications and even by the same application from different users. For example, some users emphasize QoS without concern about cost, while others try to find a better tradeoff between QoS and cost. Therefore, QoS guarantee degrees can be classified into hard and soft QoS. With hard QoS, QoS enforcement cannot be compromised, but it can with soft QoS. Hard QoS is important to certain applications such as critical real-time control. Soft QoS not only can support some applications, but it can also provide a last chance for those packets initially associated with hard QoS but perceived to probably fail in their end-to-end QoS guarantee. Therefore, a two-queue structure is proposed as illustrated in Fig. 5.2, i.e., one queue for hard QoS traffic, and the other for soft QoS traffic. The link service will always be given to the hard-QoS queue first if there is any traffic therein.

Note that some traffic such as network control traffic often needs a privileged service over application traffic, since it is important to network operation and performance. But this kind of traffic usually does not have explicit QoS requirements. There are two methods to handle this issue: (i) quantifying its QoS requirement and (ii) adding another queue. The queue structure illustrated in Fig. 5.2 can be used to support method (i) without any change. With method (ii), a privileged FIFO queue should be added to the above structure. In this case, the link service will always be given to the privileged queue first if there is any traffic therein, and then to the hard QoS queue.

Although multi-queue structures are also used in ATM, IntServ, and DiffServ, they are significantly different from the queue structure proposed for DQS. In the former multi-queue structures, a sub-queue is needed per class or even per flow. For example, in ATM, even a virtual sub-queue has been proposed for each connection, while DiffServ uses a per-class queue structure for aggregated flows. A sub-queue can be a physical one, in which each sub-queue is allocated with a physical buffer. It can also be a logical one, in which a physical buffer is divided into sub-buffers, each of which is allocated to a sub-queue. The complexity of both types of queue structures increases with the number of traffic classes or the number of flows to be supported, as the number of sub-queues required to support them also has to increase accordingly. However, this will not happen to the queue structure for DQS since only maximally three sub-queues are sufficient for this case.

5.3.2 Buffer Admission Control

BAC decides whether a newly arriving packet is allowed to enter the queue, and if yes, queues it properly subject to its QoS requirements and resource availability. A BAC unit is usually located at the entrance of a queueing system, and multiple queues can share a BAC unit (see Fig. 5.2). For this structure in particular, BAC checks every incoming packet for buffer admission and queues it accordingly if it is admitted; otherwise, BAC can either drop the packet or downgrade its service quality. In the latter case, the packet is queued in the soft QoS queue. Since every admitted packet is queued according to its **e** that exactly defines the forwarding sequence, the output scheduler here is simple for packet forwarding.

BAC operates according to the conditions discussed in Sect. 5.2.1. The crucial part is how to queue arriving packets as quickly as possible, and the key operation is packet queueing according to **e**; these operations have to be carried out almost on-the-fly upon the arrival of every packet. How fast a packet can be inserted into the queue depends on algorithms used to locate the proper position for an arriving packet in the queue, for example, binary search tree. Due to the similarity between DQS and the earliest-deadline-first (EDF) scheduling algorithm, we can refer to some implementations of EDF or similar schedulers such as [12, 13] for implementing DQS.

For packet queueing operations carried out by BAC, the situation in which the link transmitter keeps waiting for a queueing decision on arriving packets can be avoided with a proper queueing algorithm, as we now discuss. All queued packets are ordered according to their latest departure time (**e**) in an ascending order starting from the HOL of the queue. If an arriving packet needs to be queued at the HOL, this insertion can be done easily and quickly. If no packet is in the queue upon a new packet's arrival, this packet can be queued at the HOL immediately or passed to the link transmitter directly if the transmitter is free. If there are some packets to be served earlier than this newly arriving packet, i.e., packets from 1 to j defined in the queueing operation discussed in Sect. 5.2.1, the time used to serve those j packets is just the maximum time that can be used by BAC to complete queueing this packet and is proportional to j. The bigger j, the more time that BAC has to insert a new packet into the queue. So a fast search algorithm can be used to prevent the link transmitter from waiting for a queueing decision made for the new packet.

5.3.3 Call Admission Control (CAC)

As discussed in Sect. 5.2.1, DQS tries to convert delay bound guarantee into packet dropping ratio guarantee since packets that may not be guaranteed will be dropped or their service qualities downgraded. A packet may also be lost due to congestion. So a CAC for DQS must be able to evaluate packet loss caused by congestion and packet dropping due to packet lifetime overdue to make call admission decisions. An end-to-end CAC operation will be eventually broken down to per-hop operations. Therefore, the following paragraphs will discuss some basic ideas of per-hop CAC rather than detailed algorithms, since the latter require more information on traffic model, traffic shaping, and policing algorithms.

Per-hop CAC is used to check whether QoS can be guaranteed for both the admitted flows and that under consideration. For packet dropping, as discussed in Sect. 5.2.1, only if the buffer admission conditions are satisfied can a newly arriving packet be admitted into the buffer. Therefore, this CAC has to calculate how often these conditions may be violated if a new flow is admitted. For packet loss, this CAC must calculate the probability for the buffer to be congested if a new flow is admitted for a given buffer capacity and link rate.

However, it is difficult to directly apply existing CAC schemes for DQS for the following reasons. (i) Many schemes only consider packet loss caused by congestion. (ii) Most priority queueing schemes such as that discussed in [14] are designed for HOL-like fixed priority systems. However, the priority in DQS is not a discrete quantity, and it is impossible to distinguish between high and low priorities in the same queue. Thus it is difficult to determine parameters used by these algorithms, such as mean arrival rates of low- and high-priority traffic. Experience from ATM, IntServ, and even DiffServ has shown that CAC is an important but complex element for QoS guarantee and must be studied in depth separately. Below we discuss some existing CAC schemes which we may refer to in designing the CAC for DQS.

DQS is similar to the EDF scheduling algorithm in terms of differentiating service order. In particular, EDF is equivalent to the condition of determining a packet's position in the queue discussed in Sect. 5.2.1. Therefore, we can refer to some CAC schemes based on EDF scheduling algorithms for DQS CAC schemes. For example, CAC in [15] applies the EDF-schedulable condition given in [16] for a work-conserving server to serve a set of flows, each characterized by a minimum envelope describing an upper bound on the flow's arrival pattern. This condition basically limits the total amount of traffic injected to the server from exceeding the maximum service capacity available during any time interval subject to an end-to-end delay bound. Then it derives the admission conditions for a set of flows policed in terms of their peak rates, average rates, and maximum burst sizes.

As mentioned, the CAC for DQS should be able to consider both call-level and packet-level issues. This is similar to the work reported in [17] in terms of this requirement. Reference [18] discusses a method exploiting the interaction of call blocking at the call level and ATM cell loss rates at the packet level, and demonstrates that the perceived cell loss can be significantly lower than that set by CAC with a properly dimensioned network. Similarly, reference [17] proposes a resource allocation strategy subject to joint packet-level and call-level QoS constraints in wireless networks, and shows that there is a significant improvement in terms of resource utilization.

To reduce the processing burden and signaling traffic load caused by CAC, especially in core networks, some CAC approaches proposed for DiffServ can be borrowed to simplify the CAC design for DQS. For example, the capacity over-provisioning [19] suggests "providing sufficient bandwidth to make overload in network unlikely" to support QoS. However, it shows that QoS guarantee with this approach is costly and not green. With the advantage of DQS for QoS provisioning listed in Table 5.1, the efficiency of QoS guarantee can be further increased. Furthermore, by jointly considering call-level and packet-level issues as discussed above, the amount of over-provisioned capacity can be reduced, which can be further endorsed by DQS's adaptability of packet-level QoS treatment discussed in Sect. 5.2.1. This adaptability may also be jointly used with measurement-based CAC [20] to reduce the impact caused by measurement errors on QoS guarantee. Basically, this type of CAC shifts the task of traffic characterization from the user to the network, and CAC decisions are made based on traffic measurement rather than on a pre-defined traffic specification provided by the user, as this specification is often unavailable.

5.3.4 Estimation of Latest Departure Time

As discussed in Sect. 5.2, $\mathbf{e}$ is the key parameter for a node, say node i, to perform BAC to a newly arriving packet and decide its position in the queue. But it is difficult to determine $\mathbf{e}_i$ according to Eqs. (5.1)–(5.2), since it is impossible for node i to know precisely, upon a packet's arrival, its travel time on the remaining journey, i.e., $\dot{d}_j$ for $j > i$. This is due to the stochastic nature of traffic loads in the network. Therefore, some approximation methods are discussed below.

In practice, $\hat{d}_i$ given by Eq. (5.2) can be approximated by $\mathbf{d}_i$, and accordingly Eq. (5.1) can be rewritten as follows:

$$\mathbf{e}_i \approx a_i + \mathbf{d}_i. \tag{5.5}$$

This approximation will not compromise the end-to-end delay bound as proofed below.

Proof Given an end-to-end delay bound $\mathbf{D}$, actually, $\mathbf{d}_j$ is determined by CAC to define how long a packet can be delayed maximally at node j, i.e.,

$$\sum_{j=1}^{n+1} \mathbf{d}_j \leq \mathbf{D}. \tag{5.6}$$

Therefore, if every upstream node of node i has bounded the delay as promised by CAC, then $\tilde{d}_j \leq \mathbf{d}_j$ for $j \leq i$, hence

$$\sum_{j=1}^{i-1} \tilde{d}_j \leq \sum_{j=1}^{i-1} \mathbf{d}_j. \tag{5.7}$$

Similarly, if every downstream node of node i can also bound the delay as promised by CAC, we have

$$\dot{d}_j \leq \mathbf{d}_j \quad \text{and} \quad \sum_{j=i+1}^{n+1} \dot{d}_j \leq \sum_{j=i+1}^{n+1} \mathbf{d}_j. \tag{5.8}$$

Therefore, with the proposed approximation, the end-to-end delay perceived by the packet at node i is bounded by

$$\sum_{j=1}^{i-1} \tilde{d}_j + \mathbf{d}_i + \sum_{j=i+1}^{n+1} \dot{d}_j \leq \sum_{j=1}^{n+1} \mathbf{d}_j \leq \mathbf{D}. \tag{5.9}$$

$\square$

Alternatively, node i can send probing packets to measure the travel time of the remaining journey, i.e., $\sum_{j=i+1}^{n+1} \dot{d}_j$. However, the accuracy of this measurement largely depends on the probing frequency. The more frequent the probes, the more extra traffic will be generated. To reduce this cost, we can exploit some information available for other network functions such as routing. For example, with the Distributed Bellman-Ford (DBF) routing protocol, node i has to maintain a delay vector $[\mathbb{D}_{i,1}, \mathbb{D}_{i,2}, \ldots, \mathbb{D}_{i,m}]$ through a periodical inter-neighbor updating process. Here $\mathbb{D}_{i,j}$ is the latest estimation of the minimum delay from nodes i to j, and can be used by DQS to estimate the delay over the remaining journey, i.e., $\sum_{j=i+1}^{n+1} \dot{d}_j$. Recently, such a cross-layer design using DBF to estimate $\mathbf{e}$ for wireless mesh networks (WMNs) has been reported in [21].

Note that for the first approximation, when CAC determines $\mathbf{d}_i$ for node i, it has to take into account the inherent delay imposed by node i to every packet. This inherent delay may consist of packet transmission time and switching delay, which is the delay experienced by packets for crossing the switching fabric. Actually, this inherent delay is the minimum delay that every packet will experience. Therefore, any flow requiring a $\mathbf{d}_i$ smaller than this inherent delay will be rejected immediately by CAC.

5.3.5 Carrying of QoS Information

With DQS, the QoS information to be carried by a packet includes packet delay and loss preference (LP). Similar to ATM, LP here is also used to decide which packet to be dropped first in the case of congestion, and a binary expression (i.e., 0 or 1) is sufficient for it. The issue here is the packet overhead due to carrying QoS information (ω), which depends on how the QoS information is to be carried, especially for delay. There are two formats for QoS information: either the real value or the index of QoS requirements. For example, for *delay* = 125 μs, with a real value, a packet has to carry 125 μs directly; with an index, only 01 is carried if 01 is pre-defined to refer to this delay. Usually, ω with the index is shorter than that with real values, while a real value can express continuous delays. Both formats can be implemented simultaneously if necessary. According to ω, here we discuss two methods: a short fixed format (SFF) and a long variable format (LVF).

5.3.5.1 Short Fixed Format (SFF)

With SFF, a packet uses a fixed field in its header to carry the QoS information, and the overhead is only one field long, i.e., ω. For the delay, there are two further formats, as discussed below.

With the first format (F1), the remaining lifetime of a packet can be carried. The lifetime of a packet is initially set to $\mathbf{D}$ and then deducted by the delay incurred at a node once it passes this node. So upon its arrival at node i, this node can have $\mathbf{D} - \sum_{j=1}^{i-1} \tilde{d}_j$ to determine $\mathbf{e}_i$ by estimating the delay on its remaining journey. Its major advantage is that a service margin offered by upstream nodes, i.e., $\sum_{j=1}^{i-1}(\mathbf{d}_j - \tilde{d}_j)$, can be exploited by node i to accommodate more traffic. The reason is that $\mathbf{e}_i$ given by Eq. (5.1) may be larger than the promised one (i.e., $a_i + \mathbf{d}_i$), because at least the maximum delay at node i satisfies

$$\hat{d}_i \geq \mathbf{d}_i + \sum_{j=1}^{i-1}(\mathbf{d}_j - \tilde{d}_j). \tag{5.10}$$

However, this method may disorder packets belonging to the same flow because $\hat{d}_i$ of an early arriving packet may be still larger than that of a later arrival, probably due to dynamic traffic loads at upstream nodes. Consequently, this later arriving packet is still queued before an early arriving packet according to their $\mathbf{e}$ settings.

To avoid packet disorder with F1, alternatively (format F2), a packet only carries a typical per-hop delay requirement $\mathbf{d}$ along with LP. The $\mathbf{d}$ here is determined by the selected service according to, for example, the most stringent per-hop delay bound, i.e., $\min[\mathbf{d}_1, \mathbf{d}_2, \ldots]$, or an averaged value determined according to an end-to-end delay. Given $\mathbf{d}$, the packet will be treated identically by each node on its journey, which is similar to DiffServ. The difference is that DiffServ only has a few options of service classes, but DQS can provide many different services. However, in this case, the margin in service time given by upstream nodes cannot be exploited by downstream nodes.

5.3.5.2 Long Variable Format (LVF)

A route often consists of multiple nodes, each of which may give different PHSs for the same flow. However, these different PHSs cannot be supported with SFF. To carry the service provided by each node, an LVF is needed, whose size increases with the number of nodes along the route. For example, the QoS information on end-to-end delay can be carried in a form of $\mathbf{d}_{n+1}\mathbf{d}_n \cdots \mathbf{d}_2\mathbf{d}_1$, which is arranged following a travel sequence from nodes 1 to $n + 1$. Once a packet has been served by a node, the related QoS information is stripped away to reduce packet overhead, and the above chain becomes $\mathbf{d}_{n+1}\mathbf{d}_n \cdots \mathbf{d}_2$ after the packet has been served by node 1. Therefore, the average overhead for a packet to travel over an $(n + 1)$-node route is equal to $\frac{1}{2}(n + 1)(n + 2)\omega$.

5.3.5.3 SFF Versus LVF

SFF is a simple and economical format and is not affected by route lengths, similar to those used in IP and ATM. This format can be implemented to support both connection-oriented (CO) and connectionless (CL) services to have more end-to-end QoS granularity. However, given a connection or a route, LVF is more accurate than SFF to reflect an end-to-end QoS requirement of each node along a route, but at the expense of longer overheads. Because it is less accurate, SFF may either lead to lower resource utilization due to the most stringent QoS requirement to be provided by every node or fail to provide hard end-to-end QoS by using the average QoS requirement. For LVF, a connection is needed, so it is inefficient for supporting CL services. Table 5.2 provides a comparison between these two formats. We find that only F1 with SFF can benefit from the service margin given by upstream nodes, as mentioned earlier.

5.4 Conclusion

This chapter discusses a per-packet QoS approach called differentiated queueing service (DQS) and compares it with IntServ and DiffServ. Many networking approaches today assume that application traffic can be well studied for network design; therefore, once a new application appears, the existing network may have to

Table 5.2 Short fixed format (SFF) versus long variable format (LVF)

Compared items	SFF-F1	SFF-F2	LVF
Packet disorder	yes	no	no
QoS information accuracy	better	worst	best
Gain from upstream service margin	yes	no	no
Remaining journey time estimation	yes	no	no
Per-packet average overhead for QoS	ω	ω	$\frac{1}{2}(n+1)(n+2)\omega$
Support of CL and CO services	CL, CO	CL, CO	CO
Cost efficiency for QoS support	worse	worse	better

be changed accordingly. DQS tries to make the packet-level service provisioning unaware of traffic characteristics as much as possible by converting packet delay into packet dropping ratio in QoS provisioning. Packet dropping can be considered jointly with packet loss at the call level by CAC.

An ideal CAC able to achieve the above objective should be able to satisfy various packet failure criteria with less packet-level intervention and less over-provisioned bandwidth to provide QoS at high bandwidth utilization. However, more studies are required on this topic. Another issue is how to implement BAC, especially jointly using buffer management to reduce overall complexity. Simulation studies are also needed to investigate the relationship between traffic characteristics, BAC, and queueing policies as well as end-to-end performance.

References

1. Lian, F.L., Moyne, J., Tilbury, D.: Network design consideration for distributed control systems. IEEE Trans. Control Syst. Technol. **10**(2), 297–307 (2002)
2. Cucinotta, T., Palopoli, L.: QoS control for pipelines of tasks using multiple resources. IEEE Trans. Comput. **59**(3), 416–430 (2010)
3. Benameur, N., Fredj, S.B., Oueslati-Boulahia, S., Roberts, J.W.: Quality of service and flow level admission control in the Internet. Comput. Netw. **40**, 57–71 (2002)
4. Yang, J., Ye, J., Papavassiliou, S., Ansari, N.: A flexible and distributed architecture for adaptive end-to-end QoS provisioning in next-generation networks. IEEE J. Sel. Areas Commun. **23**(2), 321–333 (2005)
5. Stoica, I., Zhang, H.: Providing guaranteed services without per flow management. In: Proc. ACM SIGCOMM, Cambridge, MA, USA (1999)
6. Zhang, Z.L., Duan, Z.H., Gao, L.X., Hou, Y.W.T.: Decoupling QoS control from core routers: a novel bandwidth broker architecture for scalable support of guaranteed services. In: Proc. ACM SIGCOMM, Stockholm, Sweden (2000)
7. Jiang, Y.M.: LBFA: a stateless approach to scalable support of end-to-end per-flow service guarantees. In: Proc. IFIP Networking Conf., Athens, Greece (2004)
8. Guérin, R., Kamat, S., Peris, V., Rajan, R.: Scalable QoS provision through buffer management. In: Proc. ACM SIGCOMM, Vancouver, Canada (1998)
9. Dovrolis, C., Stiliadis, D., Ramanathan, P.: Proportional differentiated services: delay differentiation and packet scheduling. In: Proc. ACM SIGCOMM, Cambridge, MA, USA (1999)

10. Mamatas, L., Tsaoussidis, V.: Differentiating services with non-congestive queuing (NCQ). IEEE Trans. Comput. **58**(5), 591–604 (2009)
11. Guo, M., Guan, Q.S., Mao, H.C., Jiang, S.M.: Comparison of IntServ, DiffServ and DQS for QoS support in IP converged IMSs. In: Proc. IEEE Int. Conf. Inf. Theory & Inf. Security (ICITIS), Hangzhou, China (2011)
12. Zhang, F.X., Burns, A.: Schedulability analysis for real-time systems with EDF scheduling. IEEE Trans. Comput. **58**(9), 1250–1258 (2009)
13. Lou, J.Y., Shen, X.J.: Frame-based packet-mode scheduling for input-queued switches. IEEE Trans. Comput. **58**(7), 956–969 (2009)
14. Berger, A.W., Whitt, W.: Extending the effective bandwidth concept to networks with priority classes. IEEE Commun. Mag. **36**(8), 78–83 (1998)
15. Firoiu, V., Kurose, J., Towsley, D.: Efficient admission control for EDF schedulers. In: Proc. IEEE INFOCOM, Kobe, Japan, vol. 1, pp. 310–317 (1997)
16. Liebeherr, J., Wrege, D., Ferrari, D.: Exact admission control for networks with bounded delay services. Tech. Rep. CS-94-29. University of Virginia (1994)
17. Cheung, M., Mark, J.W.: Resource allocation in wireless networks based on joint packet/call level QoS constraints. In: Proc. IEEE Global Tele. Conf. (GLOBOCOM), San Francisco, USA, vol. 1, pp. 271–275 (2000)
18. Beshai, M., Kositpaiboon, R., Yan, J.: Interaction of call blocking and cell loss in an ATM network. IEEE J. Sel. Areas Commun. **12**(6), 1051–1058 (1994)
19. Menth, M., Martin, R., Charzinski, J.: Capacity overprovisioning for networks with resilience requirements. In: Proc. ACM SIGCOMM, Pisa, Italy (2006)
20. Grossglauser, M., Tse, D.N.C.: A frame work for robust measurement-based admission control. IEEE/ACM Trans. Netw. **7**(3), 293–309 (1999)
21. Teng, X.F., Jiang, S.M., Wei, G., Liu, G.K.: A cross-layer implementation of differentiated queueing service (DQS) for wireless mesh networks. In: Proc. IEEE Veh. Tech. Conf. (VTC) – Spring, Singapore (2008)

Chapter 6
Cost Model for Granular End-to-End QoS with DQS

Abstract Chapter 5 discusses the principle of the per-packet QoS approach called differentiated queueing service (DQS). This chapter further discusses a cost model corresponding to the QoS service provided by DQS. Since the objective of DQS is to cost-effectively satisfy the QoS requirements of applications, it is necessary to have a cost model that can properly reflect the cost for a QoS service provided by the network for and actually received by an application. This model is useful both for establishing a reasonable charging scheme and for preventing users from abusing QoS services provided by the network.

6.1 Introduction

A proper cost model corresponding to granular services is equally important for both the network service provider and the user. Many references such as [1] discuss the leverage of pricing for quality of service (QoS) provisioning and congestion control as well as revenue optimization for network service providers [2]. A pricing structure based on effective bandwidth was also proposed in [3]. A cost-based pricing structure for adaptive applications is discussed for DiffServ in [4], and a survey can be found in [5]. However, differentiated queueing service (DQS) is different from both DiffServ and the effective bandwidth approach in terms of QoS provisioning.

Therefore, this chapter further discusses a cost model for the DQS service, which is more appropriate than the original one proposed in [6] to measure the amount of bandwidth needed by a DQS service for each flow with respect to its QoS requirement. Since this cost model is based on call admission control (CAC) algorithms, accordingly, a preliminary CAC for DQS with the exponentially bounded burstiness (EBB) traffic model is also discussed.

The remainder of this chapter is organized as follows. The services provided by DQS are discussed in Sect. 6.2, and the proposed cost model is described in Sect. 6.3. An example of using the proposed cost model is discussed in Sect. 6.4, and numerical results of the per-flow QoS requirement and the corresponding cost are discussed in Sect. 6.5. This chapter is concluded in Sect. 6.6.

S.M. Jiang, *Future Wireless and Optical Networks*,
Computer Communications and Networks,
DOI 10.1007/978-1-4471-2822-9_6, © Springer-Verlag London Limited 2012

Table 6.1 PHSs provided by each node: $\mathbb{S} = (\mathbf{f}, \mathbf{d})$

Node	PHSs			
	$\mathbb{S}^1$		$\mathbb{S}^2$	
	$\mathbf{f}\,(10^{-3})$	$\mathbf{d}$ (ms)	$\mathbf{f}\,(10^{-3})$	$\mathbf{d}$ (ms)
N_1	0.1	10	0.01	50
N_2	0.25	4	0.025	20
N_3	0.75	1.25	0.075	12.5
N_4	1.25	1	0.125	10

6.2 DQS Services

A DQS service is defined in terms of delay bound and packet failure ratio. It consists of two types of services: the per-hop service (PHS) provided by a node and the end-to-end service (ETES) provided by a route. The PHS is fundamental, and the ETES of a route is constructed by combining the PHSs provided by each node along this route.

Besides the notation defined in Chap. 5, the following notation is also used in this discussion:

- $\mathbf{f}$: CAC-level packet failure (i.e., packet loss plus packet dropping) ratio for a delay bound $\mathbf{d}$
- $\mathbb{S} = (\mathbf{f}, \mathbf{d})$: a per-hop service in terms of $\mathbf{f}$ and $\mathbf{d}$ provided by a node
- $\mathbf{F}$: maximum end-to-end packet failure ratio, which is the ratio of the sum of dropped and lost packets to the total number of transmitted packets
- $\mathbb{T}$: traffic descriptor of a flow
- $\mathbf{r}(\mathbb{T}, \mathbb{S})$: average amount of bandwidth to be allocated to a flow with the traffic described by $\mathbb{T}$ and using service $\mathbb{S}$
- θ: per-hop cost rate (bits/s) for a flow using a service at a node
- $\mathbb{C}$: end-to-end cost rate (bits/s) for a flow using an end-to-end service
- ψ: initial mean packet arrival rate of a flow.

6.2.1 Per-Hop Service (PHS)

A PHS ($\mathbb{S}$) is described as tuple $(\mathbf{f}, \mathbf{d})$, where a superscript is used to indicate different PHSs provided by the same node in a form of $\{\mathbb{S}^j, j = 1, 2, \ldots\}$, where $\mathbb{S}^j = (\mathbf{f}^j, \mathbf{d}^j)$. Unlike per-class service such as DiffServ, the PHS here can be fully determined by a node itself, so different nodes can have various PHSs to provide granular QoS services. For example, consider a route consisting of four nodes, namely, $N_1 \sim N_4$, where each node provides two PHSs as defined in Table 6.1.

Table 6.2 All possible combinations of PHSs for ETES over the four-node route

ETES index	PHS combinations				D (ms)	F (10^{-3})	Reordered by	
	N_1	N_2	N_3	N_4			D	F
1	$\mathbb{S}^1$	$\mathbb{S}^1$	$\mathbb{S}^1$	$\mathbb{S}^1$	16.25	2.3	1	15
2	$\mathbb{S}^1$	$\mathbb{S}^1$	$\mathbb{S}^1$	$\mathbb{S}^2$	25.25	1.2	2	8
3	$\mathbb{S}^1$	$\mathbb{S}^1$	$\mathbb{S}^2$	$\mathbb{S}^1$	27.5	1.7	3	12
4	$\mathbb{S}^1$	$\mathbb{S}^1$	$\mathbb{S}^2$	$\mathbb{S}^2$	36.5	0.5	5	3
5	$\mathbb{S}^1$	$\mathbb{S}^2$	$\mathbb{S}^1$	$\mathbb{S}^1$	32.25	2.1	4	14
6	$\mathbb{S}^1$	$\mathbb{S}^2$	$\mathbb{S}^1$	$\mathbb{S}^2$	41.25	1	6	6
7	$\mathbb{S}^1$	$\mathbb{S}^2$	$\mathbb{S}^2$	$\mathbb{S}^1$	43.5	1.4	7	9
8	$\mathbb{S}^1$	$\mathbb{S}^2$	$\mathbb{S}^2$	$\mathbb{S}^2$	52.5	0.3	8	2
9	$\mathbb{S}^2$	$\mathbb{S}^1$	$\mathbb{S}^1$	$\mathbb{S}^1$	56.25	2.3	9	16
10	$\mathbb{S}^2$	$\mathbb{S}^1$	$\mathbb{S}^1$	$\mathbb{S}^2$	65.25	1.1	10	7
11	$\mathbb{S}^2$	$\mathbb{S}^1$	$\mathbb{S}^2$	$\mathbb{S}^1$	67.5	1.6	11	11
12	$\mathbb{S}^2$	$\mathbb{S}^1$	$\mathbb{S}^2$	$\mathbb{S}^2$	76.5	0.5	13	4
13	$\mathbb{S}^2$	$\mathbb{S}^2$	$\mathbb{S}^1$	$\mathbb{S}^1$	72.25	2	12	13
14	$\mathbb{S}^2$	$\mathbb{S}^2$	$\mathbb{S}^1$	$\mathbb{S}^2$	81.25	0.9	14	5
15	$\mathbb{S}^2$	$\mathbb{S}^2$	$\mathbb{S}^2$	$\mathbb{S}^1$	83.5	1.4	15	10
16	$\mathbb{S}^2$	$\mathbb{S}^2$	$\mathbb{S}^2$	$\mathbb{S}^2$	92.5	0.2	16	1

6.2.2 End-to-End Service (ETES)

Given a route consisting of $n + 1$ nodes indexed from 1 to $n + 1$, an ETES is just one combination of PHSs provided by each node along the route. Let $\mathbb{S}_i^j = (\mathbf{f}_i^j, \mathbf{d}_i^j)$ denote the j-th service provided by node i. An ETES can be expressed as a series of PHSs as follows:

$$\text{ETES} = \left\{ \mathbb{S}_1^{j_1}, \mathbb{S}_2^{j_2}, \ldots, \mathbb{S}_{n+1}^{j_{n+1}} \right\}. \tag{6.1}$$

Then the QoS of this ETES in terms of end-to-end delay bounds ($\mathbf{D}$) and failure ratio ($\mathbf{F}$) of packets is given, respectively, by

$$\mathbf{D} = \sum_{i=1}^{n+1} \mathbf{d}_i^{j_i} \quad \text{and} \quad \mathbf{F} = 1 - \prod_{i=1}^{n+1} \left(1 - \mathbf{f}_i^{j_i}\right). \tag{6.2}$$

The maximum number of ETESs that can be provided by this route is $\prod_{i=1}^{n+1} |\mathbb{S}_i|$, where $|\mathbb{S}_i|$ indicates the number of PHSs provided by node i. Table 6.2 lists 16 ETESs over the four-node route listed in Table 6.1, which are sorted according to $\mathbf{D}$ and $\mathbf{F}$ in ascending order in the rightmost two columns. If two ETESs have an identical $\mathbf{F}$, they are further distinguished by $\mathbf{D}$, and vice versa.

6.3 Cost Model

In order to charge the user reasonably according to the QoS service offered by the network and to prevent network services from being abused, it is necessary to quantify the cost of the QoS service that has been provided by the network and actually received by the user. Below, such a cost model is discussed for PHS and ETES.

6.3.1 Cost for Per-Hop Service

Given a service selected by a node for a flow, the cost to provide this service should be measured from two sides: (i) the benefit that the flow actually obtains from this service (β) and (ii) the degree of difficulty for the network node to provide this service as promised (ξ). Then the final cost (θ) should be a product of these two quantities as follows:

$$\theta = \beta \xi. \tag{6.3}$$

The benefit can be measured in terms of the effective throughput expected by a flow with an initial mean rate ψ when using this service, i.e.,

$$\beta = (1 - \mathbf{f})\psi. \tag{6.4}$$

However, this quantity alone is insufficient to measure the service cost, since it does not reflect the degree of difficulty in providing the service. For example, a large buffer can yield a very small packet failure ratio ($\mathbf{f}$), but maybe with a large delay at the node ($\mathbf{d}$). In this case, the effective throughput can be as high as that provided by another service that offers very short $\mathbf{d}$. Usually, it is more difficult to provide a short delay service than long ones. The degree of this difficulty (ξ) can be measured in terms of the ratio of the amount of bandwidth to be over-provisioned by the network to the amount of bandwidth initially required by the flow, as discussed below. Note that even for the same service, ξ varies for flows having different traffic characteristics such as peak rates, which are described by the traffic specification $\mathbb{T}$.

Given an average amount of bandwidth to be allocated to a flow $\mathbf{r}(\mathbb{T}, \mathbb{S})$, ξ is given by

$$\xi = \frac{\mathbf{r}(\mathbb{T}, \mathbb{S})}{\psi}, \tag{6.5}$$

which is usually larger than 1 since some amount of over-provisioned bandwidth is usually needed for QoS guarantee, especially for irregular traffic such as variable bit rate (VBR) traffic. Then, Eq. (6.3) is written as follows:

$$\theta = (1 - \mathbf{f})\mathbf{r}(\mathbb{T}, \mathbb{S}). \tag{6.6}$$

Note that ξ here is more appropriate for measuring the difficulty in QoS provisioning than the difficult coefficient originally defined in [6], i.e., the term $\frac{c_h}{\bar{r}_i(h)}$

defined by Eq. (9) therein, where $\hat{r}_{i(h)}$ is the maximum average rate allowed for a flow described by $(\mathbb{T}, \mathbb{S})$ and requiring service i from node h. Actually, $\hat{r}_{i(h)}$ is calculated for a virtually aggregated flow since its calculation assumes that the node use its entire link capacity c_h to provide this service. Since c_h is usually much larger than the mean arrival rate of an individual flow, $\hat{r}_{i(h)}$ may be enlarged unnecessarily with respect to the real one required by this individual flow. This inaccuracy may be further affected by the CAC algorithm used to determine $\hat{r}_{i(h)}$.

Here ξ given by Eq. (6.5) avoids this problem by only using the mean bandwidth required by a particular flow specified by $(\mathbb{T}, \mathbb{S})$, i.e., $\mathbf{r}(\mathbb{T}, \mathbb{S})$ and its mean arrival rate ψ. Furthermore, $\mathbf{r}(\mathbb{T}, \mathbb{S})$ depends on ψ and other traffic parameters as well as QoS requirements $\mathbf{d}$ and $\mathbf{f}$. It can only be determined by CAC and is calculated for a service $\mathbb{S}$ by assuming that a single flow uses $\mathbb{S}$ without considering multiplexing gain in the case of several flows using the same service $\mathbb{S}$.

6.3.2 Cost for End-to-End Service

For a flow traveling along an $(n + 1)$-node route, there are several methods to calculate its end-to-end cost $\mathbb{C}$, for example, by summing the cost of each node along the route given by Eq. (6.6). However, this calculation is unfair to the user, since it may cause the user to have to pay for nothing if every packet is dropped over the last hop. Here we still need to follow the two points mentioned earlier. That is, the end-to-end effective throughput, i.e., $\psi \prod_{i=1}^{n+1}(1 - \mathbf{f}_i)$, should be taken as the base to calculate $\mathbb{C}$. Due to packet failure, the mean arrival rate at node j is reduced to

$$\psi_j = \psi \prod_{i=1}^{j-1}(1 - \mathbf{f}_i), \qquad (6.7)$$

which is used to calculate ξ at node j ($\psi_1 = \psi$). Since the difficult coefficient along a route is the sum of ξ of each node along this route, a calculation of $\mathbb{C}$ is calculated as follows:

$$\mathbb{C} = \psi \prod_{i=1}^{n+1}(1 - \mathbf{f}_i) \sum_{i=1}^{n+1} \frac{\mathbf{r}(\mathbb{T}_i, \mathbb{S}_i)}{\psi_i}. \qquad (6.8)$$

Given $\mathbb{C}$ for a flow lasting a t-time period, the overall cost is simply calculated by $\mathbb{C} \times t$. This linearity with t can provide a visibility for the user to estimate the overall cost, which can be used by rating functions to calculate the charge for the service provided for the user.

This cost model tries to reflect the user's expectation of using a service and the service provider's effort to provide this service as well as trade off between the expected QoS and the actual cost. Given the traffic characteristic of an application and service criterion, the related calculation can be carried out off-line without requiring packet counting. However, the fundamental part of this model is $\mathbf{r}(\mathbb{T}, \mathbb{S})$, which largely depends on the efficiency of CAC. Therefore, this model may cause unfairness to the user, since it is possible to shift some cost to the user due to the inefficiency of the adopted CAC algorithm. Furthermore, traffic multiplexing gain is not taken into account to calculate $\mathbf{r}(\mathbb{T}, \mathbb{S})$, probably resulting in an overestimation of the real cost.

6.4 Example of Average Bandwidth Calculation

As mentioned above, we need to calculate the average amount of bandwidth to be allocated to a flow with the traffic specified by $\mathbb{T}$ and using service $\mathbb{S}$, $\mathbf{r}(\mathbb{T}, \mathbb{S})$, with Eqs. (6.6) and (6.8). This calculation is determined by the adopted CAC algorithm. Here an example is discussed using a stochastically bounded traffic model. This model is called exponentially bounded burstiness (EBB) [7] and is described by

$$\mathbb{P}\{A[s,t] \geq \rho(t-s) + \sigma\} \leq \Gamma e^{-\alpha\sigma} \tag{6.9}$$

for all $\sigma > 0$, where α (bounding decay parameter), Γ, $t > s \geq 0$, and $\rho > 0$ all are constants against time t, and ρ is the upper average rate of traffic arrival rate function $A(t)$. Note that a flow aggregated from two EBB flows is still of EBB. With this model, a traffic controller can be used at the ingress node of a network to regulate traffic according to the traffic bounding function, e.g., $\Gamma e^{-\alpha\sigma}$ here. In this case, traffic can be specified by $\mathbb{T} = (\rho, \alpha, \Gamma)$.

6.4.1 A Preliminary Per-Hop CAC

Here, an estimation of packet failure ratio ($\mathbf{f}$) follows the method of "analyzing queue length in an infinite buffer to estimate loss in a finite buffer" [8]. That is, we consider a lossless queue first, in which loss due to buffer overflow does not occur. Then the failure probability for a packet with delay bound $\mathbf{d}$ is estimated by the probability for its delay to exceed $\mathbf{d}$ as follows:

$$\mathbf{f} \approx \mathbb{P}\{\text{packet delay } (D) \text{ in a lossless queue} > \mathbf{d}\}. \tag{6.10}$$

The following stochastic delay bound from the earliest deadline first (EDF)-schedulable condition for EBB [9] is then adopted; i.e., at any time t, for any $\mathbf{d} > \mathbf{d}^k$ with flow group k,

$$\mathbb{P}\{D^k(t) \geq \mathbf{d}\} \leq \tilde{\Gamma} e^{-\tilde{\alpha} r \mathbf{d}}, \tag{6.11}$$

where $\frac{1}{\tilde{\alpha}} = \sum_{j \in \mathcal{N}} \frac{1}{\alpha^j}$ and

$$\tilde{\Gamma} = \frac{e^{-\tilde{\alpha}(\sum_{j \in \mathcal{N}} \rho_j \mathbf{d}^j - \mathbf{d}^k \sum_{j \in \mathcal{N}} \rho^j - L_{\max})}}{1 - e^{-\tilde{\alpha}(r - \sum_{j \in \mathcal{N}} \rho^j)}} \sum_{j \in \mathcal{N}} \Gamma^j, \tag{6.12}$$

where $\mathcal{N} = \{\rho^j, \Gamma^j, \alpha^j, \mathbf{d}^j\}$ ($j = 1, 2, \ldots, |\mathcal{N}|$) denotes a set of EBB flow groups, and $L_{\max}$ is the maximum packet length. Replacing $\mathbf{d}$ with $\mathbf{d}^k$ and taking the equality in inequality (6.11), we can obtain

$$\mathbf{f}^k \approx \mathbb{P}\{D^k(t) \geq \mathbf{d}^k\} \approx \tilde{\Gamma} e^{-\tilde{\alpha} r \mathbf{d}^k}, \tag{6.13}$$

which is used to approximate $\mathbf{f}$ for a given $\mathbf{d}$ and $\mathbb{T}$.

6.4.2 Average Bandwidth Estimation

As mentioned earlier, the average amount of bandwidth to be allocated to a flow with traffic specified by $\mathbb{T}$ and using service $\mathbb{S}$, $\mathbf{r}(\mathbb{T}, \mathbb{S})$, is only for one flow. So we only need to consider one group here, i.e., $|\mathcal{N}| = 1$. In this case, $\tilde{\alpha} = \alpha$ and the flow group subscript is ignored, so Eq. (6.12) can be simplified as

$$\tilde{\Gamma} = \frac{\Gamma e^{\alpha L_{\max}}}{1 - e^{-\alpha(r-\rho)}}. \tag{6.14}$$

Note that r here is equivalent to $\mathbf{r}(\mathbb{T}, \mathbb{S})$. We can also see that ρ is equivalent to the mean packet arrival rate ψ discussed in Sect. 6.3.2. Then from Eqs. (6.13) and (6.14), we can obtain an approximation as follows:

$$\left[1 - e^{-\alpha[\mathbf{r}(\mathbb{T}, \mathbb{S}) - \psi]}\right] e^{\alpha[\mathbf{r}(\mathbb{T}, \mathbb{S})\mathbf{d} - L_{\max}]} \approx \frac{\Gamma}{\mathbf{f}}. \tag{6.15}$$

Since $\mathbf{r}(\mathbb{T}, \mathbb{S}) \geq \psi$ due to the over-provisioned bandwidth for QoS guarantee, we have

$$0 \leq e^{-\alpha[\mathbf{r}(\mathbb{T}, \mathbb{S}) - \psi]} \leq 1. \tag{6.16}$$

From Eq. (6.15), we have

$$e^{\alpha[\mathbf{r}(\mathbb{T}, \mathbb{S})\mathbf{d} - L_{\max}]} \geq \frac{\Gamma}{\mathbf{f}}, \tag{6.17}$$

which yields a bound of $\mathbf{r}(\mathbb{T}, \mathbb{S})$ as follows:

$$\mathbf{r}(\mathbb{T}, \mathbb{S}) \geq \max\left\{\psi, \frac{L_{\max}}{\mathbf{d}} + \frac{1}{\alpha \mathbf{d}} \ln \frac{\Gamma}{\mathbf{f}}\right\}, \tag{6.18}$$

where $\frac{L_{\max}}{\mathbf{d}}$ indicates the peak service rate.

6.5 Numerical Discussion

To further understand the service cost model proposed in Sect. 6.4, we now discuss some numerical results for the following issues: (i) average bandwidth versus traffic

Table 6.3 Per-hop cost rate (θ) versus traffic characteristics $\mathbb{T} = (\psi, \alpha, \Gamma)$ and $\mathbb{S}$

Traffic $\mathbb{T}$	$\mathbb{T}_1 = (64$ kbps, $0, 0)$		$\mathbb{T}_2 = (2.4$ Mbps, $20, 0.001)$		$\mathbb{T}_3 = (2.4$ Mbps, $20, 0.01)$		$\mathbb{T}_4 = (40$ Mbps, $20, 0.01)$		$\mathbb{T}_5 = (40$ Mbps, $5, 0.01)$	
PHS	$\mathbb{S}^1$	$\mathbb{S}^2$	$\mathbb{S}^1$	$\mathbb{S}^2$	$\mathbb{S}^1$	$\mathbb{S}^2$	$\mathbb{S}^1$	$\mathbb{S}^2$	$\mathbb{S}^1$	$\mathbb{S}^2$
Node	$L_{\max} = 500$ bytes									
1	64	64	11.9	4.69	23.4	6.99	40	40	92.5	40
2	64	64	18.3	9.42	47.1	15.2	47	40	185	60.1
3	64	64	14.5	10.7	107	19.9	107	40	417	78.6
4	64	64	2.5	10.8	108	22.3	108	40	419	88
Node	$L_{\max} = 1000$ bytes									
1	64	64	12.7	4.85	24.2	7.15	40	40	93.3	40
2	64	64	20.3	9.82	49.1	15.6	49.1	40	187	60.5
3	64	64	21.1	11.3	113	20.5	113	40	424	79.2
4	64	64	2.58	11.6	116	23.1	116	40	427	88.8

CBR for $\mathbb{T}_1$, VBR for $\mathbb{T}_2 \sim \mathbb{T}_5$. Units for θ are the same as for ψ in $\mathbb{T}$

characteristics and services, i.e., $\mathbf{r}(\mathbb{T}, \mathbb{S})$ versus $\mathbb{T}$ and $\mathbb{S}$, (ii) per-hop service (PHS) cost (θ) versus $\mathbb{T}$ and $\mathbb{S}$, (iii) end-to-end service (ETES) cost ($\mathbb{C}$) versus $\mathbb{T}$ and ETES, and (iv) QoS provisioning versus route lengths. If unspecified otherwise, the following units are used: Mbps for ψ, $\mathbf{r}(\mathbb{T}, \mathbb{S})$, θ, and $\mathbb{C}$, ms for $\mathbf{d}$, and byte for L. Three types of traffic are investigated: constant bit rate (CBR) voice with $\psi = 64$ kbps, real-time VBR video with $\psi = 2.4$ Mbps, and non-real-time VBR data with $\psi = 40$ Mbps [10]. For CBR, we simply set $\Gamma = 0$ and there is no need to set α. However, it is not straightforward to determine Γ and α for VBR. Here, they are set artificially only for discussing $\mathbf{r}(\mathbb{T}, \mathbb{S})$. Their detailed settings are listed in Table 6.3. Since non-real-time VBR is generally more bursty than real-time VBR, here the difference between them is mainly reflected by α since the more bursty traffic, the larger α should be.

6.5.1 Bandwidth Versus Traffic and Service

The average amount of bandwidth to be allocated to a flow, $\mathbf{r}(\mathbb{T}, \mathbb{S})$, is the key to the cost determination. The larger $\mathbf{r}(\mathbb{T}, \mathbb{S})$, the higher the cost. Here we first investigate how $\mathbb{T}$, $\mathbb{S}$ and the maximum packet length $L_{\max}$ affect $\mathbf{r}(\mathbb{T}, \mathbb{S})$. The numerical solution of $\mathbf{r}(\mathbb{T}, \mathbb{S})$ from Eq. (6.15) is obtained as follows. Given $\mathbb{T} = (\psi, \alpha, \Gamma)$ and $\mathbb{S} = (\mathbf{f}, \mathbf{d})$, the right-hand side of Eq. (6.15) is a constant, and the differentiation of the left-hand side against $\mathbf{r}(\mathbb{T}, \mathbb{S})$ satisfies

$$\alpha e^{-\alpha[L_{\max} - \mathbf{r}(\mathbb{T}, \mathbb{S})\mathbf{d} + \mathbf{r} - \psi]}\left\{1 + \mathbf{d}\left(e^{\alpha[\mathbf{r}(\mathbb{T}, \mathbb{S}) - \psi]} - 1\right)\right\} > 0. \tag{6.19}$$

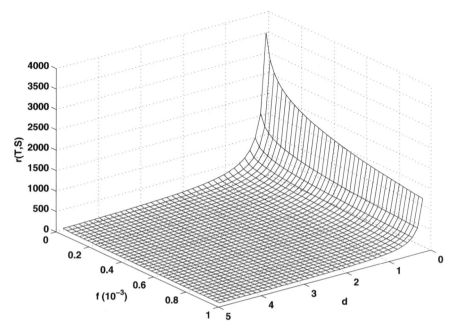

Fig. 6.1 $\mathbf{r}(\mathbb{T}, \mathbb{S})$ versus **d** (ms) and **f**: $\psi = 2.4$ Mbps, $L_{\max} = 1000$ bytes, $\Gamma = 0.01$, and $\alpha = 20$

Thus $\mathbf{r}(\mathbb{T}, \mathbb{S})$ can be solved numerically by stepwise increasing $\mathbf{r}(\mathbb{T}, \mathbb{S})$ from an initial value given by Eq. (6.18). To reduce the power calculation in Eq. (6.15), here mbit is used as the unit for L in the calculation.

Figures 6.1, 6.2 and 6.3 plot $\mathbf{r}(\mathbb{T}, \mathbb{S})$ against $\mathbb{S}$ and $\mathbb{T}$, respectively. As illustrated in Fig. 6.1, the more stringent $\mathbb{S}$ with smaller **d** and **f**, the more bandwidth is needed, resulting in large $\mathbf{r}(\mathbb{T}, \mathbb{S})$, especially when both **d** and **f** approach zero. We also find that $\mathbf{r}(\mathbb{T}, \mathbb{S})$ increases faster as **f** decreases than as **d** decreases until **d** reaches a certain point, before which $\mathbf{r}(\mathbb{T}, \mathbb{S})$ is mainly affected by **f**.

As illustrated in Fig. 6.2, $\mathbf{r}(\mathbb{T}, \mathbb{S})$ is very sensitive to traffic characteristics, especially to bounding decay parameter α. The larger α, the faster the bounding decades, resulting in looser bounding requirements of QoS. Thus a smaller $\mathbf{r}(\mathbb{T}, \mathbb{S})$ is sufficient to satisfy QoS requirements. The sensitivity of $\mathbf{r}(\mathbb{T}, \mathbb{S})$ to Γ decreases as Γ increases. As illustrated in Fig. 6.3, $\mathbf{r}(\mathbb{T}, \mathbb{S})$ increases almost linearly with $L_{\max}$ and ψ. Regarding ψ particularly, after it increases slowly to a certain value (e.g., $\psi \approx 23$ Mbps ~ 26 Mbps here), its increase becomes very fast, but $\mathbf{r}(\mathbb{T}, \mathbb{S})$ becomes less sensitive to $L_{\max}$, because the difficulty in providing a service in this case is mainly determined by ψ.

6.5.2 Per-Hop Service Cost Versus Traffic and Service

Here the per-hop cost rate (θ) is calculated by using Eqs. (6.6) and (6.15) for each PHS listed in Table 6.1 and different traffic sources. For CBR, we can get

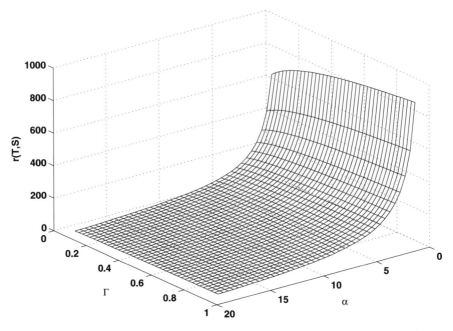

Fig. 6.2 $r(\mathbb{T}, \mathbb{S})$ versus Γ and α: $\psi = 2.4$ Mbps, $L_{max} = 1000$ bytes, $\mathbf{f} = 1.25 \times 10^{-4}$, and $\mathbf{d} = 10$ ms

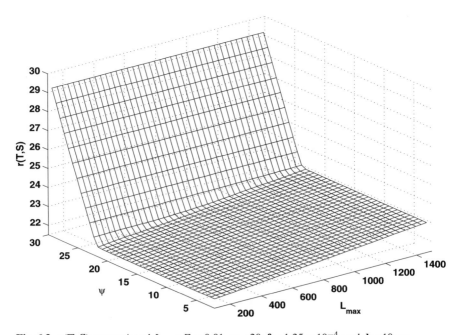

Fig. 6.3 $r(\mathbb{T}, \mathbb{S})$ versus ψ and L_{max}: $\Gamma = 0.01$, $\alpha = 20$, $\mathbf{f} = 1.25 \times 10^{-4}$, and $\mathbf{d} = 10$ ms

Table 6.4 End-to-end cost ($\mathbb{C}$) versus traffic characteristics ($\mathbb{T}$) for different end-to-end services

ETES index	$\mathbb{C}$ (Mbps) $\mathbb{T}_1$	$\mathbb{C}$ for $L_{max} = 500$ bytes				$\mathbb{C}$ for $L_{max} = 1500$ bytes				Final selection
		$\mathbb{T}_2$	$\mathbb{T}_3$	$\mathbb{T}_4$	$\mathbb{T}_5$	$\mathbb{T}_2$	$\mathbb{T}_3$	$\mathbb{T}_4$	$\mathbb{T}_5$	
1	0.255	57	872	888	3398	71.4	932	947	3457	✓
2	0.257	118	366	382	1437	135	383	399	1455	
3	0.256	50.6	278	305	1086	54.7	295	320	1102	✓
4	0.256	65.4	141	172	557	70.6	146	175	561	✓
5	0.255	42	653	693	2544	51.6	698	736	2589	
6	0.256	88.3	263	303	1036	100	276	314	1048	
7	0.256	37	196	253	765	39.1	208	263	777	✓
8	0.256	46.8	90.4	160	357	50.8	93.4	160	360	✓
9	0.255	45.9	778	811	3045	58.2	832	865	3099	
10	0.256	101.1	318	351	1263	116	333	366	1278	
11	0.256	40.1	238	284	943	43.3	253	298	958	✓
12	0.256	53.3	114	168	461	57.5	118	170	465	✓
13	0.256	32.2	579	637	2268	40.3	620	677	2309	
14	0.256	74.1	225	283	897	84.6	236	293	908	
15	0.256	27.7	164	241	652	29.1	174	250	662	✓
16	0.256	37.4	67.9	160	281	39.5	70	160	283	✓

$\mathbf{r}(\mathbb{T}, \mathbb{S}) = \psi$ as expected from (6.15), which is independent of the other parameters. As illustrated in Table 6.3, there is no difference between the settings of θ for different nodes and services since $\mathbf{f}$ is quite small, and the same for $L_{max} = 500$ bytes and 1000 bytes, respectively.

For VBR, it is not straightforward to find how $\mathbf{r}(\mathbb{T}, \mathbb{S})$ varies against $\mathbb{S}$ and $\mathbb{T}$ since they all affect $\mathbf{r}(\mathbb{T}, \mathbb{S})$ together. Given a VBR traffic source, its θ further depends on selected services. As shown in Table 6.3, for traffic $\mathbb{T}_2$, the θ given for nodes $1 \sim 3$ for $\mathbb{S}^1$ is higher than that for $\mathbb{S}^2$ except for node 4, mainly because a much lower $\mathbf{d}$ is provided by $\mathbb{S}^1$. Regarding the exception of node 4 with $\mathbb{T}_2$, although a longer $\mathbf{d}$ is provided by $\mathbb{S}^2$, its $\mathbf{f}$ is much lower than that provided by $\mathbb{S}^1$, which actually is the major factor in determining $\mathbf{r}(\mathbb{T}, \mathbb{S})$ for the traffic in this case. Regarding L_{max}, $\mathbf{r}(\mathbb{T}, \mathbb{S})$ does increase with it but slowly, as shown in the table; this can be explained by Fig. 6.3 discussed in Sect. 6.5.1.

6.5.3 End-to-End Cost Versus Traffic and Service

Table 6.4 lists the end-to-end cost $\mathbb{C}$ for the end-to-end services (ETES) provided in Table 6.2. We find that the 1st ETES provides the shortest end-to-end delay (i.e., 16.25 ms) while the 16th ETES provides the longest delay (i.e., 92.5 ms) as listed in Table 6.2. But they almost just reverse each other in terms of maximum end-to-end packet failure ratio **F**. Therefore, the former causes the highest $\mathbb{C}$ while the latter leads to the lowest for traffic sources $\mathbb{T}_2 \sim \mathbb{T}_5$ as listed in Table 6.2. Similar to PHS, for $\mathbb{T}_2$, the 2nd ETES has the highest $\mathbb{C}$ while the 13th ETES has the lowest one. For CBR $\mathbb{T}_1$, there is not much difference in $\mathbb{C}$ given by the different ETESs, and its $\mathbb{C}$ is independent of L_{max}, which is similar to the PHSs. For VBR, $\mathbb{C}$ increases slowly with L_{max}.

Although there are in total 16 ETESs available for selection, the difference between them in terms of end-to-end delay bound **D** and packet failure ratio **F** is not always as large as indicated in Table 6.2; however, the difference in their $\mathbb{C}$ is big such as between ETES pairs (2, 3), (4, 5) and so on until (14, 15) as indicated in Table 6.4. In this case, we can refine the selection of ETES sets according to $\mathbb{C}$ as follows: only those with smaller $\mathbb{C}$ are selected, resulting in a final ETES set selected as ticked in the table. Given a set of ETESs, the user can select a service able to provide the end-to-end QoS close to the application QoS requirement at the lowest cost. Whether or not the user's request can be granted by the network is still subject to the overall traffic load requiring the same type of service. If a selected service cannot be granted, the user can try to select other services with either higher or lower end-to-end QoS at different costs. This variety of end-to-end service options cannot be provided by per-class services such as DiffServ.

6.5.4 Difficulty in QoS Provisioning Versus Route Lengths

As discussed earlier, when an application runs along different routes, the difficulty in providing the same end-to-end QoS is also different. The more nodes a route has, the more difficult the end-to-end QoS provisioning is. Tables 6.5 and 6.6 list four routes, i.e., Route$_1$–Route$_4$, each of which is a combination of three nodes of the four nodes listed in Table 6.1. The ETES and $\mathbb{C}$ corresponding to traffic $\mathbb{T}_3$ for these three-node routes are also listed in Tables 6.5 and 6.6. Each node can provide two per-hop services (PHSs), i.e., $\mathbb{S}^1$ and $\mathbb{S}^2$, as listed in Table 6.1.

As shown in Table 6.3, for $\mathbb{T}_3$, PHS $\mathbb{S}^1$ costs much more than $\mathbb{S}^2$. An application should avoid using $\mathbb{S}^1$ if its end-to-end QoS can be satisfied by other PHSs. However, for an end-to-end delay bound of 20 ms over the four-node route, only the 1st ETES which uses $\mathbb{S}^1$ can support this delay requirement, as shown in Table 6.2, but at a cost of $\mathbb{C} = 872$, as indicated in Table 6.4. With a three-node route such as Route$_4$ listed in Table 6.6, there are cheaper options available (such as the 2nd ETES with $\mathbb{C} = 308$ Mbps and the 3rd ETES with $\mathbb{C} = 229$ Mbps), which can use $\mathbb{S}^2$ to provide the same level end-to-end delay as provided by the 1st ETES over the four-node route, but at a much lower cost.

When an application runs over shorter routes, its cost can be reduced not only because of reduced route lengths but also due to using low-cost PHSs. Since the three-node Route$_4$ does not go through node 1, the PHS cost of node 1, i.e., 23.4 Mbps corresponding to $\mathbb{S}^1$ as listed in Table 6.3, should be deducted from that of the original four-node route, i.e., $872 - 23.4 = 848.6$ (Mbps). This resultant cost is still much

Table 6.5 ETESs and $\mathbb{C}$ over three-node routes for $\mathbb{T}_3$ and $L_{max} = 500$ bytes: Route$_1$ and Route$_2$

ETES index	Combination of PHSs			Route$_1$: $N_1 \rightarrow N_2 \rightarrow N_3$			Route$_2$: $N_1 \rightarrow N_2 \rightarrow N_4$		
				D (ms)	**F** (10^{-3})	$\mathbb{C}$ (Mbps)	**D** (ms)	**F** (10^{-3})	$\mathbb{C}$ (Mbps)
1	$\mathbb{S}^1$	$\mathbb{S}^1$	$\mathbb{S}^1$	15.3	1.1	234	15	1.6	235
2	$\mathbb{S}^1$	$\mathbb{S}^1$	$\mathbb{S}^2$	26.5	0.4	105	24	0.5	109
3	$\mathbb{S}^1$	$\mathbb{S}^2$	$\mathbb{S}^1$	31.3	0.9	162	31	1.4	163
4	$\mathbb{S}^1$	$\mathbb{S}^2$	$\mathbb{S}^2$	42.5	0.2	62	40	0.2	66
5	$\mathbb{S}^2$	$\mathbb{S}^1$	$\mathbb{S}^1$	55.3	1	198	55	1.5	200
6	$\mathbb{S}^2$	$\mathbb{S}^1$	$\mathbb{S}^2$	66.5	0.3	81	64	0.4	85
7	$\mathbb{S}^2$	$\mathbb{S}^2$	$\mathbb{S}^1$	71.3	0.8	133	71	1.3	134
8	$\mathbb{S}^2$	$\mathbb{S}^2$	$\mathbb{S}^2$	82.5	0.1	43	80	0.2	45

Table 6.6 ETESs and $\mathbb{C}$ over three-node routes for $\mathbb{T}_3$ and $L_{max} = 500$ bytes: Route$_3$ and Route$_4$

ETES index	Combination of PHSs			Route$_3$: $N_1 \rightarrow N_3 \rightarrow N_4$			Route$_4$: $N_2 \rightarrow N_3 \rightarrow N_4$		
				D (ms)	**F** (10^{-3})	$\mathbb{C}$ (Mbps)	**D** (ms)	**F** (10^{-3})	$\mathbb{C}$ (Mbps)
1	$\mathbb{S}^1$	$\mathbb{S}^1$	$\mathbb{S}^1$	12.3	2.1	621	6.25	2.2	764
2	$\mathbb{S}^1$	$\mathbb{S}^1$	$\mathbb{S}^2$	21.3	1	241	15.3	1.1	308
3	$\mathbb{S}^1$	$\mathbb{S}^2$	$\mathbb{S}^1$	23.5	1.4	175	17.5	1.6	229
4	$\mathbb{S}^1$	$\mathbb{S}^2$	$\mathbb{S}^2$	32.5	0.3	72	26.5	0.4	106
5	$\mathbb{S}^2$	$\mathbb{S}^1$	$\mathbb{S}^1$	52.3	2	550	22.3	2	567
6	$\mathbb{S}^2$	$\mathbb{S}^1$	$\mathbb{S}^2$	61.3	0.9	205	31.3	0.9	216
7	$\mathbb{S}^2$	$\mathbb{S}^2$	$\mathbb{S}^1$	63.5	1.3	145	33.5	1.3	155
8	$\mathbb{S}^2$	$\mathbb{S}^2$	$\mathbb{S}^2$	72.5	0.2	51	42.5	0.2	60

higher than those along the three-node Route$_4$, i.e., 308 and 229 (Mbps) respectively for the 2nd and 3rd ETESs as indicated in Table 6.6. A similar phenomenon is also found for the other three-node routes here. Thus, if an application requires a voice-level PHS over a long route, a data-level PHS may be sufficient to provide the same-level end-to-end QoS over a short route. Such options are not provided by per-class services, since once it is classified, a packet is treated identically by every node all the way from source to destination.

6.6 Conclusion

This chapter further discusses a granular service cost model for DQS. The numerical examples show that the flexible per-hop service (PHS) can allow applications to select an end-to-end QoS service that can satisfy their QoS requirements at low cost. Given the end-to-end delay bound of an application, nodes can adjust PHSs according to the length of the route over which this application runs so that cost-effective PHSs can be selected. But these features are not provided by existing QoS provisioning approaches such as per-class QoS service like DiffServ.

Note that the proposed cost model is CAC dependent; the efficiency of the CAC algorithms will affect the calculated cost. The discussion in this chapter is based on a preliminary CAC algorithm with some simplification. More studies are needed to obtain more realistic CAC algorithms as well as the corresponding cost model for DQS.

References

1. Marbach, P.: Pricing differentiated services networks: bursty traffic. In: Proc. IEEE INFO-COM, Anchorage, Alaska, USA, vol. 2, pp. 650–658 (2001)
2. Mitra, D., Ramakrishnan, K.G., Wang, Q.: Combined economic modeling and traffic engineering: joint optimization of pricing and routing in multi-service networks. In: Proc. Int. Traffic Congress (ITC)-17, Salvador da Bahia, Brazil (2002)
3. Jiang, H., Jordan, S.: A pricing model for high speed networks with guaranteed quality of service. In: Proc. IEEE INFOCOM, San Francisco, USA, vol. 2, pp. 888–895 (1996)
4. Wang, X., Schulzrinne, H.: Pricing network resource for adaptive applications in a differentiated services network. In: Proc. IEEE INFOCOM, Anchorage, Alaska, USA, vol. 2, pp. 943–952 (2001)
5. DaSilva, L.A.: Pricing for QoS-enabled networks: a survey. IEEE Commun. Surv. Tutor. **3**, 2–8 (2000)
6. Jiang, S.M.: Granular differentiated queueing services for QoS: structure and cost model. Comput. Commun. Rev. **35**(2), 13–22 (2005)
7. Yaron, O., Sidi, M.: Performance and stability of communicatio networks via robust exponential bounds. IEEE/ACM Trans. Netw. **1**(3), 372–385 (1993)
8. Anick, D., Mitra, D., Sondhi, M.M.: Stochastic theory of a data-handling system with multiple sources. Bell Syst. Tech. J. **16**(8), 1871–1894 (1982)
9. Biton, E., Orda, A.: QoS provision with EDF scheduling, stochastic burtiness and stochastic guarantees. In: Proc. Int. Traffic Congress (ITC)-18, Berlin, Germany, vol. 5b, pp. 1061–1070 (2003)
10. Kramer, G.: Interleaved polling with adaptive cycle time (IPACT): a dynamic bandwidth distribution scheme in an optical access network. Photonic Netw. Commun. **4**(1), 89–107 (2002)

Chapter 7
Quantitative End-to-End Arguments: Performance Analysis

Abstract Reliable end-to-end transmission is one of the most important network services. Traditionally, its design follows the famous end-to-end arguments, which basically suggest putting the application-level functions at the network edge rather than inside the network as much as possible to simplify network design and implementation. However, in certain new types of networks such as multi-hop wireless ad hoc networks and all-optical networks, moving some functions from the network edge into the network is often considered in order to improve network performance, but at the expense of an increased implementation complexity. Therefore, an important issue is to estimate both the performance gain and implementation complexity resulting from a function displacement. To this end, this chapter analytically studies some typical reliable end-to-end transmission approaches by formulating some performance quantities that can be used to make a quantitative comparison between these approaches.

7.1 Introduction

Reliable end-to-end transmission ensures that a node receives what has been sent to it correctly. This transmission is a network service of utmost importance, since the major application in the Internet is that of data applications that require reliable end-to-end transmission. Traditionally, the protocol design of this service follows the famous end-to-end arguments [1], which as a whole strongly suggest the following design principle for simplicity: putting the application-level functions at the network edge rather than inside a network as much as possible.

Recently, some new end-to-end transmission schemes have been proposed for some new types of networks; these schemes basically shift certain functions from the network edge into the network in order to improve network performance. For example, a hop-by-hop congestion control has been proposed for multi-hop wireless ad hoc networks to improve the TCP performance [2–4]. With this kind of congestion control, the upstream node of a link coordinates the congestion control at its downstream node. Another example is for bandwidth-abundant networks that do not adopt the capacity over-provisioning [5] approach such as all-optical networks [6]. In this kind of network, data loss may occur frequently due to not only congestion but also collision because of poor optical computing and buffering capabilities available at network nodes. This fact forces sophisticated per-hop computing and buffering functions to be shifted to domain edges. Since TCP treats each packet loss as a congestive loss caused by a congestion, it may unnecessarily slow down packet forwarding speed, leading to a waste of network bandwidth. Therefore, splitting an end-to-end transmission into several domain-by-domain transmissions is proposed so that the reliable transmission across a domain can be carried out by its ingress and egress nodes. This type of proposal can be found for optical burst switching (OBS)-based networks [7–9].

A function displacement for reliable end-to-end transmission will increase implementation complexity. Thus an important question is whether such function displacement is cost-effective. To answer this question, at least two issues should be addressed: the performance gain to be offered and the additional implementation complexity to be caused by a function displacement. Neither of these issues has been addressed adequately in the literature. Therefore, this chapter tries to formulate some performance quantities for some typical reliable end-to-end transmission approaches, and the estimation of implementation complexity will be discussed in Chap. 8.

The remainder of this chapter is organized as follows. Section 7.2 discusses three basic reliable end-to-end transmission approaches and their hybrids. Performance indicators are formulated for the three basic approaches in Sect. 7.3 and for their hybrids in Sect. 7.4. The formulas are simplified for a special case in Sect. 7.5. This chapter is summarized in Sect. 7.6.

7.2 Reliable End-to-End Transmission

The major differences between the reliable end-to-end transmission schemes reported in the literature include (i) the placement of relevant functions, (ii) networking units (e.g., endpoints, routers, and switches) involved in reliable end-to-end transmission provisioning, and (iii) implementation particulars. The basic functions used to provide a reliable end-to-end transmission include reliability control and congestion control, which are often used jointly. Here the congestion control tries to reduce or avoid packet loss while reliability control tries to ensure that the receiver will receive what has been sent to it. This function is often realized through packet retransmission. The major networking units involved in an end-to-end transmission usually include the source and destination nodes as well as relaying units such as routers and switches. Networking units may be further grouped into domains according to their geographic locations and administrative autonomies.

Two schemes identical in terms of points (i), (ii) above should further differentiate each other in point (iii). For congestion control such as those used in TCP and its variants, implementation details may include whether a rate-based or window-based control is used by the source node [10] or whether active queue management (AQM) [11] is used by the router. Although these details may further differentiate their performance, the most important factors are points (i), (ii), since they have a greater effect than point (iii) on both network performance and implementation complexity.

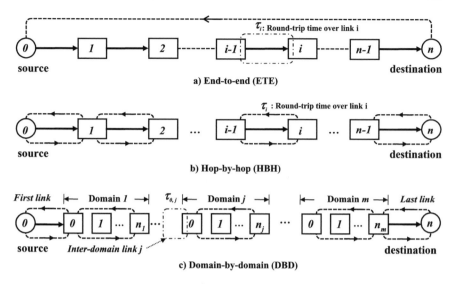

Fig. 7.1 Basic reliable end-to-end transmission approaches

Table 7.1 Networking units involved in typical reliable end-to-end transmission approaches

	Basic approaches			Hybrid approaches	
	ETE	HBH	DBD	ETE+HBH	ETE+DBD
∞-retransmission	src, dst	src, router, dst	igr, egr	src, dst	src, dst
K-retransmission	–	–	–	src, router, dst	igr, egr, idl
Congestion control	src, dst	src, router, dst	igr, egr	src, router, dst	igr, egr, idl
Example	TCP Reno	Credit-ABR	Split-TCP	Semi-TCP	OBS TCP

∞/K = infinity/limited number, dst = destination, src = source, igr = domain ingress, egr = domain egress, idl = inter-domain link (only applicable for ETE+DBD variant A)

In this sense, we classify different reliable end-to-end schemes according to points (i), (ii) as end-to-end (ETE), hop-by-hop (HBH), and domain-by-domain (DBD) as well as their hybrids: ETE plus HBH (ETE+HBH) and ETE plus DBD (ETE+DBD). They are summarized in Table 7.1 with more discussion given below.

7.2.1 Basic Reliable End-to-End Transmission Approaches

We first discuss three basic approaches: end-to-end (ETE), hop-by-hop (HBH), and domain-by-domain (DBD), as illustrated in Fig. 7.1.

7.2.1.1 End-to-End

With the end-to-end approach (ETE), only the source and destination nodes are involved in reliable end-to-end transmission provisioning, as illustrated in Fig. 7.1(a). The information on network congestion is fed back by the destination node to the source node no matter where the congestion occurs. It is usually assumed that once the congestion takes place, every packet arriving at the congested node is lost. Therefore, if the source node thinks that a congestion has occurred, it reduces the traffic load injected into the network and arranges the retransmission of the lost packets. TCP is just such an example, typically including TCP Tahoe and TCP Reno [12].

7.2.1.2 Hop-by-Hop

As illustrated in Fig. 7.1(b), with the hop-by-hop approach (HBH), every node along the route between the source and destination nodes is involved in reliable transmission provisioning. Here it is the pair of nodes of each link that ensures the reliable transmission over the link. If a packet is not received by the downstream node of the link, this packet will be retransmitted by the upstream node of this link until it has been received successfully. Similarly as for congestion control over the link, the upstream node is involved in congestion control at the downstream node of this link. Obviously, HBH can react fast to congestion but at the expense of high implementation complexity, since every node must be involved in the reliable transmission provisioning. A typical example is the credit-based flow control proposed for the asynchronous transfer mode (ATM) available bit rate (ABR) service [13], which requires every switch of an ATM connection to control flow on its connected links.

7.2.1.3 Domain-by-Domain

Actually, both ETE and HBH are two extreme cases for reliable end-to-end transmission provisioning. To trade off between performance gain and implementation complexity, with the domain-by-domain approach (DBD), a reliable transmission task is partitioned to domains along the route as illustrated in Fig. 7.1(c). The ingress and egress nodes of a domain ensure the reliable transmission across the domain itself by applying ETE therein so that the nodes within the domain are not involved, resulting in reduced implementation complexity. But HBH is still used here for inter-domain reliable transmission since only a link is used for the inter-domain connection. For example, a Split-TCP is proposed for a hybrid network consisting of different types of sub-networks such as wireless networks [14] and optical networks [9], in which a TCP connection is split over different types of sub-networks.

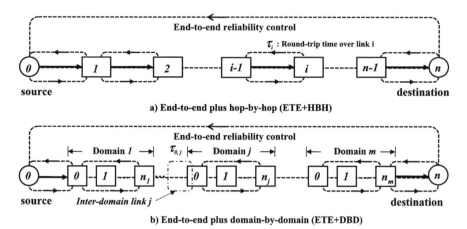

Fig. 7.2 Hybrids of ETE, HBH, and DBD

7.2.2 *Hybrid Reliable Transmission Approaches*

Although one perceives that HBH and DBD can outperform ETE, it is complex to fully implement the former two. To provide reliable end-to-end transmission with an undefined number of retransmissions up to infinity, a large buffer is needed at every intermediate node for HBH and at each domain edge for DBD, especially when intermediate nodes are farther away from the traffic source and have much transient traffic. Therefore, to trade off between the implementation complexity caused and the performance gain offered by a function displacement, hybrids of ETE, HBH, and DBD are proposed according to the following.

- To reduce buffer sizes, an intermediate node is allowed to provide only a limited number of retransmissions for a lost packet (K), while an infinite number of retransmissions are only provided by the source and destination nodes to assure reliable end-to-end transmission.
- To release congestion as quickly as possible, the node closer to a congested node should take an immediate action to control the congestion, i.e., the upstream node of the congested link with HBH and the ingress node of a congested domain with DBD.

Two types of hybrid approaches are discussed below.

7.2.2.1 End-to-End Plus Hop-by-Hop

As illustrated in Fig. 7.2(a), with the hybrid of the end-to-end and hop-by-hop approaches (ETE+HBH), the upstream node of a link will try maximally K retransmissions if a sent packet is not acknowledged positively by the downstream node of the link. If the packet is acknowledged positively or K retransmissions have been carried out, the packet is removed from the buffer at the upstream node. End-to-end transmission reliability is ultimately guaranteed by the retransmission between source and destination exactly as done by ETE. In the case of congestion, the upstream node reduces its traffic load toward the downstream congested node to release the congestion therein as done by HBH. For TCP, a scheme called Semi-TCP [15] is proposed for IEEE 802.11 based multi-hop wireless ad hoc networks, in which the medium access control (MAC)-level retransmission is used as the K-retransmission and RTS/CTS is slightly modified to provide a hop-by-hop congestion control [16]. In this case, congestion control is decoupled from TCP while end-to-end transmission reliability is still guaranteed by TCP.

7.2.2.2 End-to-End Plus Domain-by-Domain

Similar to ETE+HBH, as illustrated in Fig. 7.2(b), with the hybrid of the end-to-end and domain-by-domain approaches (ETE+DBD), the ingress node of a domain will try maximally K retransmissions if a sent packet is not acknowledged positively by the egress node of this domain. If the packet is acknowledged positively or K retransmissions have been carried out, the packet is removed from the buffer at the domain ingress node. End-to-end transmission reliability is ultimately guaranteed by the retransmission between source and destination. If congestion occurs inside the domain, the ingress and egress nodes of this domain act immediately to release this congestion. For example, reference [7] suggests that the ingress node of an OBS network retransmit lost bursts over this network, while TCP provides reliable end-to-end transmission but without being involved in the congestion control inside the OBS network.

According to whether retransmissions will be carried out for a packet lost on the inter-domain link between two adjacent domains, ETE+DBD can have two variants, as discussed below. With variant A (ETE+DBD.A), up to K retransmissions will be carried out for each lost packet, and with variant B (ETE+DBD.B), no retransmission is carried out for lost packets over the inter-domain link.

7.3 Analysis of Basic Approaches

There are many analytical works on reliable transmission schemes in the literature which primarily focus on specific schemes designed for particular networks; they cannot really be used to compare the reliable end-to-end transmission approaches discussed above. For example, many references such as [17, 18] take TCP and its variants as the solution to reliable end-to-end transmission, implicitly excluding other possible solutions like HBH and DBD as well as ETE+HBH and ETE+DBD. Actually, many proposals other than TCP have also been reported in the literature and may continue to appear in the future, particularly for some new types of networks such as multi-hop wireless networks and all-optical networks. Therefore, it is important to have a quantitative overview of their performance, and this section formulates some basic performance indicators.

As mentioned earlier, two elements are essential for reliable end-to-end transmission: retransmission of lost packets and congestion control to reduce or avoid packet loss. Therefore, the following issues are important: (i) how much network resource and time are needed to successfully send a packet to its destination and (ii) how fast a congestion can be released. Thus, transmission cost (C), transmission completion time (T), and congestion reaction time (A) are discussed below for the three basic approaches. We assume that no loss will happen at the source node and to ACK packets. This analysis will be extended to the hybrid approaches in Sect. 7.4.

The notation listed below is used in the discussion. Refer also to Fig. 7.1 for their definitions. Subscript i ($i = 0, 1, 2, \ldots, n$) is used to indicate a parameter for node i, and subscript pair (i, j) is associated with parameters for node i in domain j, when applicable. Similarly, subscripts e, h, and d are associated with performance indicators for ETE, HBH, and DBD, respectively.

- L: data packet size in bits.
- p: probability for a packet loss to happen on a link with a node.
- τ: round-trip time over the link between a pair of nodes, including propagation delay, packet queueing delay, and packet transmission time.
- m: number of domains of a route.
- n: number of links (or hops) of a route between source and destination.
- n': number of links (or hops) of a route between the ingress and egress nodes of a domain.

Both p and τ are important performance indicators of network protocols and algorithms such as MAC protocols, scheduling algorithms, congestion control schemes, and routing protocols. Therefore, the formulas to be derived below are expressed as a function of p and τ so that they can be used jointly with other analytical results of p and τ for a particular protocol and algorithm reported in the literature.

7.3.1 Transmission Cost

The transmission cost (C) for a successfully transmitted packet is defined as the total network resource (in bits) consumed by all failed transmission trials and the final successful transmission that are carried out by all the nodes along the route between source and destination. This cost only considers those for transmitting and retransmitting a packet without taking into account encapsulation overheads, which can be easily considered by multiplying a constant coefficient for a given protocol. We now derive the formula of C for ETE, HBH, and DBD.

7.3.1.1 Cost with ETE

For a route consisting of n hops as illustrated in Fig. 7.1(a), a packet loss occurs at node i with probability p_i as defined. Then the probability for a packet to successfully go through this route is given by

$$g_e = \prod_{i=1}^{n}(1 - p_i).\tag{7.1}$$

Then the probability for r retransmissions to be carried out for a successful end-to-end packet transmission over this route is $(1 - g_e)^r g_e$. The retransmission overhead for a packet loss depends on the whereabouts of a loss occurrence as discussed below.

A retransmission is triggered by the source node (i.e., node 0) once a packet is lost over a route. The probability for a packet to be lost along this route is $1 - g_e$, and that for it to be lost at node i is $p_i \prod_{k=1}^{i-1}(1 - p_k)$. Note that $p_0 = 0$ since no loss occurs at the source node as assumed. Then the probability for a packet to be lost over the route and this loss to happen at node i is given by $\frac{1}{1-g_e}[p_i \prod_{k=1}^{i-1}(1 - p_k)]$. Therefore, the average overhead per retransmission, $\bar{L}_e$, is calculated by

$$\bar{L}_e = \frac{L}{1 - g_e}\sum_{i=1}^{n} i p_i \prod_{k=1}^{i-1}(1 - p_k),\tag{7.2}$$

since once a packet is lost at node i, the transmission from node 0 to node $i - 1$ with total $i \times L$ bits is just wasted; particularly when $i = 1$, $\prod_{k=1}^{i-1}(1 - p_k) = 1$. The same setting is applicable to Eqs. (7.8), (7.15), and (7.25) to be discussed later.

For the final successful transmission, the cost is nL bits since each node from node 0 to node $n - 1$ has to transmit once the same L-bit long packet. Then, the total transmission cost for a successful packet transmission along this route, $\mathbf{C}_e$, is given by

$$\mathbf{C}_e = \bar{L}_e \sum_{r=0}^{\infty} r(1 - g_e)^r g_e + nL$$

$$= \bar{L}_e\left(\frac{1}{g_e} - 1\right) + nL.\tag{7.3}$$

7.3.1.2 Cost with HBH

As illustrated in Fig. 7.1(b), with HBH, a retransmission is only carried out by the upstream node of a link for a packet lost at the downstream node. Thus, the number of bits wasted per packet loss over a link is just L. Suppose that a packet is lost at node i. The probability for r_{i-1} retransmissions to be carried out by its upstream node $i - 1$ for a successful transmission over this link is $p_i^{r_{i-1}}(1 - p_i)$, with a total overhead of $r_{i-1} \times L$ bits. Similar to the $\mathbf{C}_e$ calculated above, the average overhead required for this successful transmission over this link, $\mathbf{C}_i$, is calculated by

$$\mathbf{C}_i = L \sum_{r_{i-1}=0}^{\infty} r_{i-1} p_i^{r_{i-1}} (1 - p_i) + L$$

$$= \frac{L}{1 - p_i}. \tag{7.4}$$

There are in total n links along the route, so the cost for a successful end-to-end packet transmission over this route, $\mathbf{C}_h$, is given by

$$\mathbf{C}_h = \sum_{i=1}^{n} \mathbf{C}_i$$

$$= L \sum_{i=1}^{n} \frac{1}{1 - p_i}. \tag{7.5}$$

7.3.1.3 Cost with DBD

Consider a route consisting of m domains and total n hops. For domain j, there are n_j hops as illustrated in Fig. 7.1(c). It is easy to show that $\sum_{j=1}^{m} n_j + m + 1 = n$. Since a domain adopts ETE for the reliable transmission across the domain as discussed in Sect. 7.2.1.3, Eq. (7.3) can be used to calculate the transmission cost for domain j ($n_j > 0$), $\mathbf{C}_{d,j}$, as follows:

$$\mathbf{C}_{d,j} = \bar{L}_j \left(\frac{1}{g_j} - 1 \right) + n_j L, \tag{7.6}$$

with

$$g_j = \prod_{i=1}^{n_j} (1 - p_{i,j}), \tag{7.7}$$

where $p_{i,j}$ is the probability for a packet to be lost at node i in domain j, and $\bar{L}_j$ indicates the average waste transmission for a packet lost inside domain j and can be calculated with Eq. (7.2) by replacing n, g_e, p_i, and p_k therein with n_j, g_i, $p_{i,j}$, and $p_{k,j}$, respectively. That is,

$$\bar{L}_j = \frac{L}{1 - g_i} \sum_{i=1}^{n_j} i p_{i,j} \prod_{k=0}^{i-1} (1 - p_{k,j}). \tag{7.8}$$

Here we need to further take into account the average cost over each inter-domain link along the whole route. The transmission over an inter-domain link is just a special case of HBH with $n = 1$. Therefore, for the link between domain $j - 1$ and domain j, from Eq. (7.5), we have $\frac{L}{1-p_{0,j}}$ as the cost for this 1-hop inter-domain link, where $p_{0,j}$ indicates the packet loss probability at the ingress of domain j. The same method can be used for the link between the source node and the ingress node of domain 1 (it is called first link henceforth) as well as the link between the egress node of domain m and the destination node (it is called last link henceforth). All the domains and inter-domain links as well as the first and last links together are considered the same way for HBH in the cost calculation. That is, Eq. (7.5) can be used to calculate the transmission cost, $\mathbf{C}_d$, as follows:

$$\mathbf{C}_d = \sum_{j=1}^{m} \left(\mathbf{C}_{d,j} + \frac{L}{1 - p_{0,j}} \right) + \frac{L}{1 - p_n}, \tag{7.9}$$

where the last item is the cost corresponding to the last link.

When there is only one node in each domain, i.e., $n_j = 0$ for $j = 1, 2, \ldots, m$, DBD is just equivalent to HBH. In this case, it is unnecessary to take into account $\mathbf{C}_{d,j}$ in Eq. (7.9), and we can easily have $\mathbf{C}_d = \mathbf{C}_h$ as expected. However, we cannot expect $\mathbf{C}_d = \mathbf{C}_e$ by letting $m = 1$, because the unique domain with $m = 1$ does not include the source and destination nodes, while ETE has to take into account every node. The same holds for the formula of $\mathbf{T}$ to be discussed below.

7.3.2 Transmission Completion Time

The completion time ($\mathbf{T}$) is the time used to successfully complete an end-to-end packet transmission. Here, a completed transmission means that the source node has received a positive ACK on the packet sent by it. An alternative definition of complete transmission is from the destination's point of view; i.e., if a packet is successfully received, then this packet transmission is completed. However, in practice if the source node is not acknowledged positively on a sent packet, it will retransmit the same packet even if this packet has already been received by the destination node. Therefore, this definition is not adopted here. The derivation of $\mathbf{T}$ is similar to that of $\mathbf{C}$ discussed above.

7.3.2.1 Completion Time with ETE

If a packet is not acknowledged positively within a round-trip time between source and destination after its transmission, this packet should be retransmitted. This also means that the source node needs to take at least a round-trip time to trigger retransmission for a packet lost anywhere along the route after it has been sent out. The minimum round-trip time between the source and destination nodes is $\sum_{i=1}^{n} \tau_i$.

Therefore, we have $\mathbf{T}_e$ as follows:

$$\mathbf{T}_e = \sum_{r=0}^{\infty}\left[r \sum_{i=1}^{n} \tau_i (1 - g_e)^r g_e \right] + \sum_{i=1}^{n} \tau_i$$

$$= \frac{1}{g_e} \sum_{i=1}^{n} \tau_i. \tag{7.10}$$

7.3.2.2 Completion Time with HBH

A retransmission is triggered if a packet is not acknowledged within a round-trip time over the link between a pair of nodes, i.e., the upstream sending node and the downstream receiving node. $\mathbf{T}_h$ in this case can be calculated with Eq. (7.5) by replacing L therein with τ_i, i.e.,

$$\mathbf{T}_h = \sum_{i=1}^{n} \frac{\tau_i}{1 - p_i}. \tag{7.11}$$

7.3.2.3 Completion Time with DBD

The calculation of the completion time for DBD, $\mathbf{T}_d$, is similar to that of $\mathbf{C}_d$ discussed in Sect. 7.3.1.3. That is, for domain j, the average completion time, $\mathbf{T}_{d,j}$, is given by

$$\mathbf{T}_{d,j} = \frac{1}{g_j} \sum_{i=1}^{n_j} \tau_{i,j}, \tag{7.12}$$

where $\tau_{i,j}$ is the round-trip time between node $i - 1$ and node i in domain j. $\mathbf{T}$ for an inter-domain link is $\frac{\tau_j}{1-p_{0,j}}$, where τ_j denotes the round-trip time over the inter-domain link between domain $j - 1$ and domain j. Similar to Eq. (7.9) for $\mathbf{C}_d$, $\mathbf{T}_d$ is given by

$$\mathbf{T}_d = \sum_{j=1}^{m} \left(\mathbf{T}_{d,j} + \frac{\tau_j}{1 - p_{0,j}} \right) + \frac{\tau_n}{1 - p_n}, \tag{7.13}$$

where the last item is the transmission completion time for the last link illustrated in Fig. 7.1(c).

7.3.3 Congestion Reaction Time

Here congestion refers to a buffer status that causes packet losses. That is, once a packet experiences a congestion, it is lost too. Therefore, the packet loss probability is just equal to the congestion probability. The congestion reaction time ($\mathbf{A}$) is a time interval between when a congestion happens and when a congestion release action arrives at the congested node, which actually is the minimum delay for a congestion to be relieved. Obviously, when $p = 0$, there is no need for this reaction, i.e., $\mathbf{A} = 0$. Therefore, in the following discussion, we always assume $p > 0$.

7.3.3.1 Reaction Time with ETE

In this case, no matter where a congestion occurs, the information on the congestion status has to be relayed by the destination node to the source node as illustrated in Fig. 7.1(a). So, the minimum reaction time in this case, $\mathbf{A}_e$, is just a round-trip time over the link between node 0 and node n, i.e.,

$$\mathbf{A}_e = \sum_{j=1}^{n} \tau_j. \tag{7.14}$$

7.3.3.2 Reaction Time with HBH

In this case, it is the upstream node $i - 1$ that reacts to a congestion at its downstream node i with a minimum reaction delay of τ_i. Since a congestion may occur at different nodes along a route with probability $1 - g_e$, similar to $\bar{L}_e$ given by Eq. (7.2), we have the average minimum reaction time for this case, $\mathbf{A}_h$, as follows:

$$\mathbf{A}_h = \frac{1}{1 - g_e} \sum_{j=1}^{n} \left[\tau_j p_j \prod_{i=1}^{j-1} (1 - p_i) \right]. \tag{7.15}$$

7.3.3.3 Reaction Time with DBD

In this case, the reaction time to a congestion over an inter-domain link is different from that to a congestion within a domain as discussed below. The probability for a congestion to occur at the ingress node of domain j, i.e., node$_{0,j}$, is given by

$$\xi'_j = p_{0,j} \prod_{k=1}^{j-1} \prod_{i=0}^{n_k} (1 - p_{i,k}), \tag{7.16}$$

and the reaction time is just τ_j. At the destination node (i.e., node$_n$), ξ'_n is given by $p_n \prod_{k=1}^{m} \prod_{i=0}^{n_k} (1 - p_{i,k})$, and the reaction time is equal to τ_n.

The probability for a congestion to occur within domain j is given by

$$\xi_j = \left[1 - \prod_{i=1}^{n_j} (1 - p_{i,j}) \right] \prod_{k=1}^{j-1} \prod_{i=0}^{n_k} (1 - p_{i,k})(1 - p_{0,j}), \tag{7.17}$$

where the second production indicates the probability for no congestion to happen all the way from domain 1 down to the ingress node of domain j. Since domain j adopts ETE for the reliable transmission across it, we have

$$\mathbf{A}_{d,j} = \sum_{i=1}^{n_j} \tau_{i,j}, \tag{7.18}$$

where $\tau_{i,j}$ is the round-trip time over the link between node $i-1$ and node i in domain j.

Similar to the HBH discussed above, since a congestion may take place in different nodes along a route, the average reaction time to a congestion in this case, $\mathbf{A}_d$, is given by

$$\mathbf{A}_d = \frac{1}{1-g_d}\left[\sum_{j=1}^{m}\left(\tau_j\xi'_j + \mathbf{A}_{d,j}\xi_j\right) + \tau_n\xi'_n\right], \tag{7.19}$$

where

$$g_d = (1-p_n)\prod_{j=1}^{m}\prod_{i=0}^{n_j}(1-p_{i,j}), \tag{7.20}$$

and τ_j denotes the round-trip time over the inter-domain link between domain $j-1$ and domain j, and the denominator $(1-g_d)$ is the probability for a congestion to happen along the whole route.

7.4   Analysis of Hybrid Approaches

This section further analyzes the hybrids of ETE, HBH, and DBD, i.e., ETE+HBH and ETE+DBD; the subscripts eh and ed, respectively, are used to denote them. Since the congestion control is still performed hop by hop for ETE+HBH and domain by domain for ETE+DBD as defined earlier, the congestion reaction times for HBH ($\mathbf{A}_e$) and DBD ($\mathbf{A}_d$) are still applicable for ETE+HBH and ETE+DBD, respectively, i.e., $\mathbf{A}_{eh} = \mathbf{A}_e$ and $\mathbf{A}_{ed} = \mathbf{A}_d$. Therefore, in the following, we focus on $\mathbf{C}_{eh}$ and $\mathbf{T}_{eh}$ as well as $\mathbf{C}_{ed}$ and $\mathbf{T}_{ed}$.

7.4.1   End-to-End Plus Hop-by-Hop

With up to K_i ($K_i \geq 0$) retransmissions to be carried out by node i to send a packet to its downstream node $i+1$ in the case of a packet loss, the probability for a failed transmission to occur over this link with K_i retransmissions having been performed is $p_{i+1}^{1+K_i}$. In this case, the end-to-end successful transmission probability (g_{eh}) is given by

$$g_{eh} = \prod_{i=0}^{n-1}(1 - p_{i+1}^{1+K_i}).$$ (7.21)

Since ETE is used to ensure reliable end-to-end transmission, similar to the derivation of Eq. (7.2), here we also have to calculate the average cost per packet loss ($\bar{L}_{eh}$). The only difference between ETE and ETE+HBH is the number of waste transmissions per packet loss. With ETE, this number is just equal to j for a loss at node j ($j = 1, 2, \ldots, n$) since each node from node 0 to node $j - 1$ just transmits the packet once. With ETE+HBH, this number is denoted by W_j, whose calculation consists of two parts: the successful transmissions from node 0 to node $j - 2$ and the failed transmissions over the link between node $j - 1$ and node j after K_{j-1} retransmissions. For the first part, the average number of transmissions for a successful transmission over the link between node i and node $i + 1$ is used, which is denoted by t_i. For the second part, a total of $1 + K_{j-1}$ transmissions have been carried out by node $j - 1$. Therefore,

$$W_j = \sum_{i=0}^{j-2} t_i + 1 + K_{j-1},$$ (7.22)

and particularly for $j = 1$, $W_1 = 1 + K_0$.

Now we calculate t_i, which is similar to the calculation of $\bar{L}_e$. The probability for a successful transmission over the link between node i and node $i + 1$ with K_i retransmissions is equal to $1 - p_{i+1}^{K_i+1}$. To have r trials for a successful transmission with the maximum number of trials up to $K_i + 1$, all the $(r - 1)$ previous trials must fail while the r-th trial succeeds. Whether node i retransmits a packet depends on the congestion status at node $i + 1$; then we have

$$t_i = \frac{1}{1 - p_{i+1}^{K_i+1}} \sum_{r=1}^{K_i+1} r p_{i+1}^{r-1}(1 - p_{i+1}),$$ (7.23)

where the right-hand side is given by $f(p_{i+1}, K_i)$, which is defined by

$$f(\varepsilon, \kappa) \triangleq \frac{1}{1 - \varepsilon} - \frac{(\kappa + 1)\varepsilon^{\kappa+1}}{1 - \varepsilon^{\kappa+1}}.$$ (7.24)

Then following Eq. (7.2), we can find the average cost per packet loss for ETE+HBH ($\bar{L}_{eh}$) as follows:

$$\bar{L}_{eh} = \frac{L}{1 - g_{eh}} \sum_{j=1}^{n} W_j p_j^{1+K_{j-1}} \prod_{k=1}^{j-1}(1 - p_k^{1+K_{k-1}}),$$ (7.25)

and following the derivation of Eq. (7.3) by replacing g_e, $\bar{L}_e$, and nL with g_{eh}, $\bar{L}_{eh}$, and $L\sum_{i=0}^{n-1} t_i$, we have the transmission cost in this case ($\mathbf{C}_{eh}$) as follows:

$$\mathbf{C}_{eh} = \bar{L}_{eh}\left(\frac{1}{g_{eh}} - 1\right) + L\sum_{i=0}^{n-1} t_i. \tag{7.26}$$

Similarly, replacing τ_i in Eq. (7.10) with $t_i \tau_{i+1}$, we have the transmission completion time ($\mathbf{T}_{eh}$) as follows:

$$\mathbf{T}_{eh} = \frac{1}{g_{eh}}\sum_{i=0}^{n-1} t_i \tau_{i+1}. \tag{7.27}$$

In particular, $\forall i$, if $K_i = 0$, then $t_i = 1$, which means that ETE+HBH is just equivalent to ETE. In this case, $W_j = j$ so $g_e = g_{eh}$ and $\bar{L}_e = \bar{L}_{eh}$. It can be easily manifested that both $\mathbf{C}_{eh} = \mathbf{C}_e$ and $\mathbf{T}_{eh} = \mathbf{T}_e$ as expected. Similarly, $\forall i$, when $K_i = \infty$, we can obtain $t_i = \frac{1}{1-p_{i+1}}$ and $g_{eh} = 1$, so $\mathbf{C}_{eh} = \mathbf{C}_h$ and $\mathbf{T}_{eh} = \mathbf{T}_h$ as expected.

7.4.2 End-to-End Plus Domain-by-Domain

The calculation in this case is similar to that for ETE+HBH discussed above; i.e., we need to determine the average waste per packet loss ($\bar{L}_{ed}$) caused by domain-by-domain retransmission and then follow Eq. (7.3) for ETE to calculate the final cost. As discussed in Sect. 7.2.2.2, ETE+DBD has two variants: variant A with retransmission over inter-domain links and variant B without retransmission over these links.

7.4.2.1 ETE+DBD Variant A

In this case, within domain j, the probability for a packet to be lost with one transmission is $1 - g_j$, where g_j is given by Eq. (7.7). With up to K_j retransmissions to be carried out by domain j for each packet, the average number of transmissions to be carried out by domain j for a successful packet transmission is given by

$$t_j = f(1 - g_j, K_j), \tag{7.28}$$

and the probability for a packet to be lost within this domain is given by

$$s_j = (1 - g_j)^{1+K_j}, \tag{7.29}$$

which excludes the loss at its ingress. This part will be discussed later for inter-domain links. Given t_j, $t_j - 1$ transmissions failed, each of these leads to an average waste transmission given by $\bar{L}_j$ from Eq. (7.8), while only one transmission succeeds at a cost of $n_j L$ bits since in this case every node except the domain egress node has to transmit the same packet once.

For the inter-domain link between domain $j - 1$ and domain j, a packet loss may occur at the ingress of domain j with probability $p_{0,j}$. With up to K'_{j-1} retransmissions to be carried out by the egress node of domain $j - 1$ to the ingress node of domain j, the packet loss probability over this inter-domain link is given by

$$s'_j = p_{0,j}^{1+K'_{j-1}}, \tag{7.30}$$

where $j = 1$ corresponds to the first link and $j = m + 1$ to the last link with $p_{0,m+1} = p_n$. Let t'_j denote the average number of trials per successful transmission over this inter-domain link. We can obtain

$$t'_j = f(p_{0,j+1}, K'_j), \tag{7.31}$$

and each transmission trial consumes L bits, resulting in a total cost of $t'_j L$.

The probability for a packet traveling from node 0 to be lost at the ingress of domain j after $K'_j + 1$ trials is given by $s'_j \prod_{i=1}^{j-1} (1 - s'_i)(1 - s_i)$, and the cost over the link between domain $j - 1$ and domain j is equal to $(K'_{j-1} + 1)L$. Then the average waste caused by this loss, ω'_j, is given by

$$\omega'_j = \sum_{k=1}^{j-1} \left[(t_k - 1)\bar{L}_k + t'_k L + n_k L \right] + (K'_{j-1} + 1)L. \tag{7.32}$$

Similarly, the probability for a packet traveling from node 0 to be lost within domain j is equal to $s_j(1 - s'_j) \prod_{i=1}^{j-1} (1 - s'_i)(1 - s_i)$, and the average waste caused by such a loss, ω_j, is calculated by

$$\omega_j = \sum_{k=1}^{j-1} \left[(t_k - 1)\bar{L}_k + t'_k L + n_k L \right] + t'_j L + (K_j + 1)\bar{L}_j, \tag{7.33}$$

where $(K_j + 1)\bar{L}_j$ denotes the cost for a packet loss within domain j after $K_j + 1$ transmissions and $t_j L$ for the cost over the link between domain $j - 1$ and domain j. Then, the average waste caused by a packet loss ($\bar{L}_{ed.a}$) is calculated by

$$\bar{L}_{ed.a} = \frac{1}{1 - g_{ed.a}} \left\{ \sum_{j=1}^{m+1} \omega'_j s'_j \prod_{i=1}^{j-1} (1 - s'_i)(1 - s_i) \right.$$
$$\left. + \sum_{j=1}^{m} \omega_j s_j (1 - s'_j) \prod_{i=1}^{j-1} (1 - s'_i)(1 - s_i) \right\}. \tag{7.34}$$

Similar to ETE+HBH, we obtain the successful end-to-end packet transmission probability here as follows:

$$g_{ed.a} = \prod_{j=1}^{m} [(1 - s_j)(1 - s_j')](1 - s_{m+1}'), \tag{7.35}$$

where $\prod_{j=1}^{m}(1 - s_j)$ corresponds to all the domains, $\prod_{j=1}^{m}(1 - s_j')$ to the first link plus the inter-domain links, and $(1 - s_{m+1}')$ to the last link.

In this case, the amount of transmission resource in bits consumed for the successful end-to-end transmission is given by $L[\sum_{j=1}^{m}(n_j t_j + t_j') + t_{m+1}']$. Then following Eq. (7.3), we have $\mathbf{C}_{ed.a}$ as follows:

$$\mathbf{C}_{ed.a} = \bar{L}_{ed.a} \left(\frac{1}{g_{ed.a}} - 1 \right) + L \left[\sum_{j=1}^{m}(n_j t_j + t_j') + t_{m+1}' \right]. \tag{7.36}$$

Similarly, following Eq. (7.10), we have $\mathbf{T}_{ed.a}$ as follows:

$$\mathbf{T}_{ed.a} = \frac{1}{g_{ed.a}} \left[\sum_{j=1}^{m} \left(t_j' \tau_{0,j} + t_j \sum_{i=1}^{n_j} \tau_{i,j} \right) + t_{m+1}' \tau_n \right], \tag{7.37}$$

where $\tau_{0,j}$ denotes the round-trip time of the link between the egress node of domain $j - 1$ and the ingress node of domain j.

Now we check the equivalence between ETE+DBD and ETE+HBH in the special case discussed below. If $\forall j, n_j = 0$, it means that there is only one node per domain. Then we have

$$s_j = p_j^{1+K_j}, \tag{7.38}$$

$g_{ed.a} = g_{eh}$, $\bar{L}_k = L$, and $n = 2m + 1$. With a rearrangement of the subscripts in Eqs. (7.34)–(7.37), we can manifest that $\bar{L}_{ed.a} = \bar{L}_{eh}$, leading to both $\mathbf{C}_{ed} = \mathbf{C}_{eh}$ and $\mathbf{T}_{ed} = \mathbf{T}_{eh}$ as expected. Similarly, if $\forall j, K_j = 0$, then $s_j = 1 - g_j$ and $s_j' = p_{0,j}$, and thus $g_{ed.a} = g_e$.

Regarding $\bar{L}_{ed.a}$, $t_j = t_j' = 1$ in this case, we then have

$$\omega_j' = L \sum_{k=1}^{j-1}(n_k + 1) + L.$$

The average transmission waste per packet loss over link j indicated by the first summation in Eq. (7.34) is in the same form as that used for $\bar{L}_e$ given by Eq. (7.2). Similarly, for the second summation in Eq. (7.34) for the average transmission waste per packet loss inside the domains, we have

$$\omega_j = L \sum_{k=1}^{j-1}(n_k + 1) + L + \bar{L}_j,$$

and so

$$\omega_j s_j = L\left\{\left[\sum_{k=1}^{j-1}(n_k+1)+1\right](1-g_j)+\sum_{i=1}^{n_j}ip_{i,j}\prod_{k=0}^{i-1}(1-p_{k,j})\right\}.$$

Since

$$1-g_j = \sum_{i=1}^{n_j}p_{i,j}\prod_{k=0}^{i-1}(1-p_{k,j}) \quad \text{and}$$

$$\omega_j s_j = L\left\{\sum_{i=1}^{n_j}\left[\sum_{k=1}^{j-1}(n_k+1)+1+i\right]p_{i,j}\prod_{k=0}^{i-1}(1-p_{k,j})\right\},$$

we also have the same form as that used for $\bar{L}_e$ given by Eq. (7.2). There are in total $\sum_{j=1}^{m}n_j+m+1=n$ items. Then with a rearrangement of notation, we have $\bar{L}_{ed.a}=\bar{L}_e$, leading to $\mathbf{C}_{ed}=\mathbf{C}_e$ and $\mathbf{T}_{ed}=\mathbf{T}_e$ as expected.

7.4.2.2 ETE+DBD Variant B

In this case, if a packet loss occurs over the inter-domain links including the first and last links, no retransmission is triggered by the egress node of its immediately upstream domain. This is the only difference between ETE+DBD.B here and ETE+DBD.A discussed above, i.e., $K'_j = 0$ here. Therefore, here $t'_j = 1$ and $s'_j = p_{0,j}$ for $j = 1, 2, \ldots, m+1$, and the formulas for ETE+DBD.A derived above can be used for the calculation of ETE+DBD.B by taking the above parameter settings.

7.5 Simplified Formulas in a Special Case

Here we further simplify the formulas discussed in the preceding sections for a special case, in which, $\forall i, j, p_i = p_j = p_{i,j} = p, \tau_i = \tau_j = \tau_{i,j} = \tau, K_i = K_j = K, K'_i = K'_j = K'$, and $n_i = n_j = n'$. In this case, we have $mn'+m+1=n$, and the formulas for $\mathbf{C}$, $\mathbf{T}$, and $\mathbf{A}$ discussed earlier can be further simplified. The subscripts e, h, d, eh, ed.a, and ed.b stand for ETE, HBH, DBD, ETE+HBH, and ETE+DBD variants A and B, respectively.

7.5.1 End-to-End (ETE)

Here $\bar{L}_e$ from Eq. (7.2) is given by $\mathbf{F}_0(n)$, which is defined by

$$\mathbf{F}_0(x) = L\left[\frac{1}{p}-\frac{x(1-p)^x}{1-(1-p)^x}\right], \tag{7.39}$$

and $\mathbf{C}_e$ from Eq. (7.3) is given by $\mathbf{F}_1(n)$, which is defined by

$$\mathbf{F}_1(x) = \frac{L}{p}\left[\frac{1}{(1-p)^x} - 1\right]. \tag{7.40}$$

Similarly, $\mathbf{T}_e$ from Eq. (7.10) is given by

$$\mathbf{T}_e = \frac{n\tau}{(1-p)^n}, \tag{7.41}$$

and $\mathbf{A}_e$ from Eq. (7.14) is equal to $n\tau$.

7.5.2 Hop-by-Hop (HBH)

In this case, $\mathbf{C}_h$ from Eq. (7.5) is given by $\mathbf{F}_2(L)$, which is defined by

$$\mathbf{F}_2(x) = \frac{nx}{1-p}. \tag{7.42}$$

Similarly, $\mathbf{T}_h$ from Eq. (7.11) is given by $\mathbf{F}_2(\tau)$, and $\mathbf{A}_h$ from Eq. (7.15) is just equal to τ.

7.5.3 Domain-by-Domain (DBD)

Similar to $\mathbf{C}_e$, here $\mathbf{C}_{d,j}$ from Eq. (7.6) is simplified into $\mathbf{F}_1(n')$, and $\mathbf{C}_d$ from Eq. (7.9) is given by

$$\mathbf{C}_d = m\mathbf{F}_1(n') + \frac{m+1}{1-p}. \tag{7.43}$$

Similarly, $\mathbf{T}_d$ from Eq. (7.13) is given by

$$\mathbf{T}_d = \tau\left[\frac{mn'}{(1-p)^{n'}} + \frac{m+1}{1-p}\right], \tag{7.44}$$

and when $p \neq 0$, $\mathbf{A}_d$ from Eq. (7.19) is equal to

$$\mathbf{A}_d = \frac{(1-\varepsilon^m)\tau}{1-(1-p)\varepsilon^m}\left[n' - \frac{p(n'-1)}{1-\varepsilon} + p\varepsilon^m\right], \tag{7.45}$$

where $\varepsilon = (1-p)^{n'+1}$.

7.5.4 End-to-End Plus Hop-by-Hop (ETE+HBH)

Here t_i from Eq. (7.23) is denoted by t. Following Eq. (7.24) for $f()$, we have

$$t = \frac{1}{1-p} - (K+1)\left(\frac{1}{1-p^{K+1}} - 1\right), \qquad (7.46)$$

and $\bar{L}_{eh}$ from Eq. (7.25) can be simplified as

$$\bar{L}_{eh} = (K+1)L + tL\left[\frac{1}{p^{K+1}} - \frac{n(1-p^{K+1})^n}{1-(1-p^{K+1})^n} - 1\right]. \qquad (7.47)$$

Therefore, $\mathbf{C}_{eh}$ from Eq. (7.26) is given by

$$\mathbf{C}_{eh} = \bar{L}_{eh}\left[\frac{1}{(1-p^{K+1})^n} - 1\right] + nLt, \qquad (7.48)$$

and $\mathbf{T}_{eh}$ from Eq. (7.27) is simplified as

$$\mathbf{T}_{eh} = \frac{n\tau}{(1-p)(1-p^{K+1})^{n-1}}. \qquad (7.49)$$

7.5.5 End-to-End Plus Domain-by-Domain (ETE+DBD)

For ETE+DBD.A, $g = (1-p)^{n'}$, $s = (1-g)^{K+1}$, $s' = p^{K'+1}$, $t = f(1-g, K)$, $t' = f(p, K')$, and $\bar{L} = \mathbf{F}_0(n')$. Let

$$a = (t-1)\bar{L} + (t'+n')L \quad \text{and}$$
$$b = (1-s)(1-s').$$

Then $g_{ed.a}$ from Eq. (7.35) is given by

$$g_{ed.a} = b^m(1-s'),$$

ω'_j from Eq. (7.32) is given by

$$\omega'_j = (j-1)a + (K'+1)L,$$

and ω_j from Eq. (7.33) is given by

$$\omega_j = (j-1)a + t'L + (K+1)\bar{L}.$$

Then $\bar{L}_{ed.a}$ from Eq. (7.34) in this case is rewritten as follows:

$$\bar{L}_{ed.a} = \left[1 - b^m(1-s')\right]^{-1}\left\{s'\sum_{j=1}^{m+1}[(j-1)a + (K'+1)L]b^{j-1}\right.$$

$$+ s(1 - s') \sum_{j=1}^{m} \left[(j-1)a + t'L + (K+1)\bar{L} \right] b^{j-1} \Big\}$$

$$= (1-b)^{-1} \left[1 - b^m(1-s') \right]^{-1} \left\{ s' \left[ab\beta(m) + (K'+1)(1 - b^{m+1})L \right] \right.$$
$$\left. + s(1-s') \left[ab\beta(m-1) + [t'L + (K+1)\bar{L}](1 - b^m) \right] \right\}, \qquad (7.50)$$

where

$$\beta(x) = \frac{1 - b^x}{1 - b} - x b^x.$$

If $b = 1$, it means that no loss occurs along the route, thus $\bar{L}_{ed.a} = nL$.
$\mathbf{C}_{ed.a}$ from Eq. (7.36) in this case is given by

$$\mathbf{C}_{ed.a} = \bar{L}_{ed.a} \left[\frac{1}{b^m(1-s')} - 1 \right] + L \left[m(n't + t') + t' \right]. \qquad (7.51)$$

Similarly, $\mathbf{T}_{ed.a}$ from Eq. (7.37) in this case is given by

$$\mathbf{T}_{ed.a} = \frac{\tau}{b^m(1-s')} \left[m(t' + tn') + t' \right]. \qquad (7.52)$$

For ETE+DBD.B, $K' = 0$, $t' = 1$, and $s' = p$. $\mathbf{C}_{ed.b}$ as well as $\mathbf{T}_{ed.b}$ can be calculated using Eqs. (7.50), (7.51), and (7.52), respectively, with the above parameter settings.

7.6 Conclusion

This chapter discusses some performance indicators for three reliable end-to-end transmission approaches and their hybrids: ETE, HBH, DBD, ETE+HBH, and ETE+DBD. The formulas derived here can be used jointly with other results such as packet loss probability and queueing delay to estimate the performance gain to be offered by each approach, which may be useful for network design. An estimation of their implementation complexity will be discussed in Chap. 8, and a numerical discussion will be given in Chap. 9 with a comparison of these approaches in both performance and implementation complexity.

References

1. Saltzer, J.H., Reed, D.P., Clark, D.D.: End-to-end arguments in system design. ACM Trans. Comput. Syst. **2**(4), 277–288 (1984)
2. Sadeghi, B., Yamdad, A., Fujiwara, A., Yang, L.: A simple and efficient hop-by-hop congestion control protocol for wireless mesh networks. In: Proc. Annual Int. Wireless Internet Conf. (WICON), Boston, USA (2006)

3. Yi, Y., Shakkottai, S.: Hop-by-hop congestion control over a wireless multi-hop network. IEEE/ACM Trans. Netw. **15**(1), 133–144 (2007)
4. Scheuermann, B., Locherta, C., Mauve, M.: Implicit hop-by-hop congestion control in wireless multihop networks. Ad Hoc Netw. **6**, 260–288 (2008)
5. Menth, M., Martin, R., Charzinski, J.: Capacity overprovisioning for networks with resilience requirements. In: Proc. ACM SIGCOMM, Pisa, Italy (2006)
6. Gladisch, A., Braun, R.P., Breuer, D., Ehrhardt, A., Foisel, H.M., Jaeger, M., Leppla, R., Schneiders, M., Vorbeck, S., Weiershausen, W., Westphal, F.J.: Evolution of terrestrial optical system and core network architecture. Proc. IEEE **94**(5), 869–891 (2006)
7. Zhang, Q., Vokkarane, V.M., Wang, Y., Jue, J.P.: Analysis of TCP over optical burst-switched networks with burst retransmission. In: Proc. IEEE Global Tele. Conf. (GLOBOCOM), Missouri, USA, vol. 4, pp. 1978–1983 (2005)
8. Luo, J.T., Huang, J., Chang, H., Qiu, S.F., Guo, X.J., Zhang, Z.Z.: ROBS: A novel architecture of Reliable Optical Burst Switching with congestion control. J. High Speed Netw. **16**(2), 123–131 (2007)
9. Padmanabhan, D., Bikram, R., Vokkarane, V.M.: TCP over optical burst switching (OBS): to split or not to split? In: Proc. IEEE Conf. Comp. Commun. Net. (ICCCN), St. Thomas, US Virgin Islands, pp. 1–6 (2008)
10. Sundaresan, K., Anantharaman, V., Hsieh, H.Y., Sivakumar, R.: ATP: A Reliable Transport Protocol for Ad Hoc Networks. IEEE Trans. Mob. Comput. **4**(6), 588–603 (2005)
11. Braden, B., Clark, D., Crowcroft, J., Davie, B., Deering, S., Estrin, D., Floyd, S., Jacobson, V.: Recommendations on queue management and congestion avoidance in the Internet. RFC 2309, Internet Engineering Task Force (1998)
12. Fall, K., Floyd, S.: Simulation-based comparisons of Tahoe, Reno and SACK TCP. Comput. Commun. Rev. **26**(3), 5–21 (1996)
13. Kung, N.T., Morris, R.: Credit-based flow control for ATM networks. IEEE Netw. **9**(2), 40–48 (1995)
14. Bakre, A., Badrinath, B.R.: I-TCP: indirect TCP for mobile hosts. In: Proc. IEEE Int. Conf. Dist. Computing Systems, Vancouver, British Columbia, Canada, pp. 136–143 (1995)
15. Jiang, S.M., Zuo, Q., Wei, G.: Decoupling congestion control from TCP for multi-hop wireless networks: semi-TCP. In: Proc. ACM MobiCom Workshop on Challenged Networks (CHANTS), Beijing, China (2009)
16. Lee, J.S., Lee, M.J., Taori, R., Lee, S.W.: Congestion control for wireless mesh networks. Jun. 2005, pending USA patent No. 60/686459
17. Canton, A.F., Chahed, T.: End-to-end reliability in UMTS: TCP over ARQ. In: Proc. IEEE Global Tele. Conf. (GLOBOCOM), San Antonio TX, USA, vol. 6, pp. 3473–3477 (2001)
18. Filali, F.: Link-layer fragmentation and retransmission impact on TCP performance in 802.11-based networks (2005). http://whitepapers.zdnet.com/abstract.aspx?docid=333439

Chapter 8
Quantitative End-to-End Arguments: Complexity Estimation

Abstract Chapter 7 analyzes the performance gains to be offered by a function displacement for reliable end-to-end transmission by formulating the performance indicators of three approaches and their hybrids. This chapter further discusses how to estimate the increased implementation complexity caused by a function displacement. The results reported in this chapter can be jointly used with the results provided in Chap. 7 to compare different reliable end-to-end transmission approaches in terms of both performance gain and implementation complexity.

8.1 Introduction

How to measure implementation complexity itself is a complicated issue, especially for a large system consisting of various subsystems, which may be further divided into smaller components. In the literature, computational complexity research [1] studies how much time and resources are needed to solve a particular problem, focusing on algorithm processing rather than its implementation. For example, [2] analyzes the complexity of virtual private networks. The network complexity study usually adopts entropy to measure the amount of information passed between a transmitter-receiver pair without addressing the implementation complexity [3]. Cyclomatic complexity [4] is often used to measure software complexity by counting the number of paths through a program. It is difficult to use this method to measure the complexity of a system composed of a large number of programs, especially if their source codes are not open to the public.

To compare the reliable end-to-end transmission approaches discussed in Chap. 7, a relative complexity approach is proposed here to measure the relative difference in implementation complexities of two systems under comparison by referring to a third system. This approach is used because designers are often interested in which design is the simplest or less complex in making a decision. The third system is usually a well-known system, such as TCP here.

The remainder of this chapter is organized as follows. Section 8.2 discusses the definition of relative complexity for implementation. An estimation of this complexity is formulated in Sect. 8.3 for the reliable end-to-end transmission approaches discussed in Chap. 7. In Sect. 8.4, these formulas are further simplified for the same special case as defined in Sect. 7.5. Finally, the chapter is concluded in Sect. 8.5.

S.M. Jiang, *Future Wireless and Optical Networks*,
Computer Communications and Networks,
DOI 10.1007/978-1-4471-2822-9_8, © Springer-Verlag London Limited 2012

8.2 Definition of Relative Complexity

Here we assume that a system, denoted by $\mathbf{S}$ henceforth, usually consists of multiple subsystems. A subsystem may be further divided into smaller components and so on until the complexity of each component can be determined. The complexity of a system can be measured by summarizing the complexity of each divided component; that is, $\mathbf{S} = \{\theta_1, \theta_2, \dots, \theta_i, \dots\}$, where θ_j denotes a component of $\mathbf{S}$. Note that θ_j may be identical to θ_i since the complexity of a system depends on the number of components and not only the number of component types. Then the complexity of $\mathbf{S}$ is the sum of the complexity of each component therein. That is,

$$|\mathbf{S}| = \sum_{\forall \theta_i \in \mathbf{S}} |\theta_j|, \tag{8.1}$$

where a pair of "|" is used as the operator for complexity calculation.

Let $\mathbf{S}_1$ and $\mathbf{S}_2$ denote two systems under comparison. Then the relative complexity of $\mathbf{S}_1$ over $\mathbf{S}_2$ with reference to a third system Ω is defined as follows:

$$\Lambda_{1/2}(\Omega) = \frac{|\mathbf{S}_1| - |\mathbf{S}_2|}{|\Omega|}. \tag{8.2}$$

As discussed later, this calculation can be projected to the calculation of ratio $\frac{|\theta_i|}{|\theta_j|}$, which can be further estimated by referring to the complexity of a simulation implementation if the real one is not available with the following approximation:

$$\frac{|\theta_i|}{|\theta_j|} \approx \frac{|\vartheta_i|}{|\vartheta_j|}, \tag{8.3}$$

where $|\vartheta_i|$ is the complexity of the counterpart of θ_i that is implemented in simulation. There are many good simulation tools with open sources available publicly such as NS2 [5] (a free tool) and OPNET [6] (a commercialized tool), which can be exploited here to estimate the implementation complexity. Furthermore, with $|\mathbf{S}_1| - |\mathbf{S}_2|$, the calculation of the complexity for the parts common to both $\mathbf{S}_1$ and $\mathbf{S}_2$ can be avoided, so the calculation can be further simplified. This is done because both systems may have the same components whose complexity is difficult to measure, such as hardware components.

A network is primarily composed of nodes and links. Here we focus on the implementation complexity of protocols by assuming that the same hardware, such as links, is used for each approach under comparison. Thus this part can be excluded from comparison as indicated by Eq. (8.2). Similarly, since the reliable end-to-end transmission approaches discussed earlier only differentiate themselves at layers 2, 3, and 4 (denoted by $\mathbb{L}_2$, $\mathbb{L}_3$, and $\mathbb{L}_4$ henceforth), it is unnecessary to discuss the other layers for comparison. In this case, a terminal is simply expressed by

$$\Theta^t = \{\mathbb{L}_2, \mathbb{L}_3, \mathbb{L}_4\}, \tag{8.4}$$

and a router by

$$\Theta^r = \{\mathbb{L}_2, \mathbb{L}_3\}. \tag{8.5}$$

The complexity of a node is determined by the complexity of each of its layers, i.e.,

$$|\Theta| = \sum |\mathbb{L}_\iota|. \tag{8.6}$$

A layer can be further divided into functions (denoted by θ henceforth), i.e., $\mathbb{L} = \{\theta_1, \theta_2 \ldots\}$ with $|\mathbb{L}| = \sum |\theta_k|$.

For a unicast reliable end-to-end transmission over the chain network topology as illustrated in Fig. 7.1, we have

$$\mathbf{S} = \{\Theta_0, \Theta_1, \ldots, \Theta_n\}, \tag{8.7}$$

where Θ_i may be either a terminal or a router. Then its complexity is calculated by

$$|\mathbf{S}| = \sum_{\forall \Theta_i} |\Theta_i| = \sum_{i=0}^{n} \sum_{\forall \theta_j \in \Theta_i} |\theta_j|. \tag{8.8}$$

8.3 Calculation of Relative Complexity

Here we first discuss how to calculate $|\mathbf{S}|$ for each of the reliable end-to-end transmission approaches discussed earlier. $|\mathbf{S}|$ will be used to calculate the relative complexity in Sect. 8.4.

The major functions of layers 2~4 used in the comparison are listed in Table 8.1, where θ_k^ι indicates function k in layer ι. The other functions not listed there are assumed to exist in each node for all approaches under comparison; thus they can be canceled out for simplicity. The same physical layer is assumed to be used in each approach under comparison.

8.3.1 Relative Complexity for ETE

In this case, as listed in Table 8.1, the major functions of layer 4 include θ_1^4 and θ_2^4; they are mainly θ_1^3 and θ_2^3 for layer 3. The major functions of layer 2 include θ_1^2, θ_2^2, and θ_3^2. Note that θ_3^2 is used only in shared-media networks such as wireless networks.

There are two types of nodes here: terminal (Θ^t) and router (Θ^r). Node 0 and node n are terminals, while the other nodes are routers. For a terminal, we only need to consider layers 2~4; for a router layers 2 and 3. This is because when a router is used as a relaying unit, the transient packets will not be passed to the transport layer. Therefore, the function collection for the terminal is as follows:

$$\Theta^t = \{\theta_1^4, \theta_2^4, \theta_1^3, \theta_2^3, \theta_1^2, \theta_2^2, [\theta_3^2]\}. \tag{8.9}$$

Table 8.1 Major functions in layers 2~4 under comparison

Layer	Function	Symbol
2	Error control	θ_1^2
2	Scheduling	θ_2^2
2	Medium access control (MAC)	θ_3^2
2	Infinite (∞) number of retransmissions at link level	θ_4^2
2	Congestion control at link level	θ_5^2
2	Definite (K) number of retransmissions at link level	θ_6^2
3	Network addressing	θ_1^3
3	Network routing	θ_2^3
3	Definite (K) number of retransmissions at network level	θ_3^3
3	Congestion control at network level	θ_4^3
4	End-to-end infinite (∞) number of retransmissions	θ_1^4
4	End-to-end congestion control	θ_2^4

Similarly for the router, we have

$$\Theta^r = \{\theta_1^3, \theta_2^3, \theta_1^2, \theta_2^2, [\theta_3^2]\}, \tag{8.10}$$

where $[\theta_3^2]$ indicates that θ_3^2 is required only in shared-media networks and is null for wired networks. Then the complexity of ETE is given by

$$|\mathbf{S}_e| = \sum_{i=0,n} |\Theta_i^t| + \sum_{i=1}^{n-1} |\Theta_i^r|, \tag{8.11}$$

where Θ_i is the function collection of node i.

8.3.2 Relative Complexity for HBH

The major functions in layer 4 for end-to-end (ETE) mentioned above are not used in hop-by-hop (HBH) here; instead, with HBH, each node must conduct link-level reliability control (θ_4^2) and congestion control (θ_5^2). There is only one type of node here, i.e., the router, which has been enhanced with θ_4^2 and θ_5^2. There is no difference between HBH and ETE in layer 3. Therefore, the function collection for HBH is given by

$$\Theta^{r+} = \{\theta_1^3, \theta_2^3, \theta_1^2, \theta_2^2, [\theta_3^2], \theta_4^2, \theta_5^2\}, \tag{8.12}$$

and its complexity is given by

$$|\mathbf{S}_h| = \sum_{i=0}^{n} |\Theta_i^{r+}|. \tag{8.13}$$

8.3.3 Relative Complexity for DBD

In this case, the type and function of a node are the same as those for ETE, but with a difference in the numbers of terminals and routers involved. The reason is that an end-to-end connection is split into segments over different domains, and the ingress and egress nodes of a domain are also treated as terminals in addition to nodes 0 and n that also exist in ETE. Thus the complexity of domain-by-domain (DBD) is given by

$$|\mathbf{S}_d| = \sum_{i=0,n} |\Theta_i^t| + \sum_{j=1}^{m} \left[\sum_{i=0,n_j} |\Theta_{i,j}^t| + \sum_{i=1}^{n_j-1} |\Theta_{i,j}^r| \right], \qquad (8.14)$$

where $\Theta_{i,j}$ indicates the function collection under comparison at node i in domain j.

8.3.4 Relative Complexity for ETE+HBH

Here, as shown in Table 7.1, the major differences between HBH and ETE+HBH are (i) the end-to-end reliability control (θ_1^4) is added into layer 4 at nodes 0 and n for ETE+HBH, and (ii) the K-retransmission (θ_6^2) here replaces the original ∞-retransmission (θ_4^2) for the hop-by-hop reliability control at every node here. Therefore, for nodes 0 and n, the function collections are given by

$$\Theta^{t'} = \{\theta_1^4, \theta_1^3, \theta_2^3, \theta_1^2, \theta_2^2, [\theta_3^2], \theta_5^2, \theta_6^2\}, \qquad (8.15)$$

and for the other nodes by

$$\Theta^{r'} = \{\theta_1^3, \theta_2^3, \theta_1^2, \theta_2^2, [\theta_3^2], \theta_5^2, \theta_6^2\}. \qquad (8.16)$$

Then the complexity of ETE+HBH is calculated by

$$|\mathbf{S}_{eh}| = \sum_{i=0,n} |\Theta_i^{t'}| + \sum_{i=1}^{n-1} |\Theta_i^{r'}|. \qquad (8.17)$$

8.3.5 Relative Complexity for ETE+DBD

In this case, between the ingress and egress nodes of a domain, only the K-retransmission is provided by layer 3 (θ_3^3) for reliability control across the domain instead of the original infinite number of retransmissions (θ_1^4). Similar to DBD, the ingress and egress nodes of the domain here also must provide congestion control across the domain in layer 3 (θ_4^3). Therefore, the function collection for both the ingress and egress nodes of a domain is

$$\Theta^{t^-} = \{\theta_1^3, \theta_2^3, \theta_3^3, \theta_4^3, \theta_1^2, \theta_2^2, [\theta_3^2]\}, \tag{8.18}$$

which holds for both variants A and B since the function for the retransmission over a domain can also be used over inter-domain links. Similar to ETE+HBH, nodes 0 and n also use the end-to-end reliability control (θ_1^4), so their function collections are as follows:

$$\Theta^{t^+} = \{\theta_1^4, \theta_1^3, \theta_2^3, [\theta_3^3], \theta_4^3, \theta_1^2, \theta_2^2, [\theta_3^2]\}, \tag{8.19}$$

where $[\theta_3^3]$ indicates that θ_3^3 is required only for variant A and null for variant B, which does not carry out retransmission over the inter-domain links. The function for the retransmission over a domain can also be used over inter-domain links, so there is no difference in the routers between ETE+DBD and DBD. Therefore, the complexity of ETE+DBD is calculated by

$$|S_{ed}| = \sum_{i=0,n} |\Theta_i^{t^+}| + \sum_{j=1}^{m} \left[\sum_{i=0,n_j} |\Theta_{i,j}^{t^-}| + \sum_{i=1}^{n_j-1} |\Theta_{i,j}^{r}| \right]. \tag{8.20}$$

8.4 Simplification in Our Special Case

Here we further simplify the formulas discussed in the preceding sections for the same special case defined in Sect. 7.5, with an additional assumption that the complexity of the same function at different nodes is identical.

8.4.1 End-to-End

From Eq. (8.11), we have

$$|S_e| = 2\Gamma(\Theta^t) + (n-1)\Gamma(\Theta^r)$$
$$= 2(|\theta_1^4| + |\theta_2^4|) + (n+1)(|\theta_1^3| + |\theta_2^3| + |\theta_1^2| + |\theta_2^2| + [|\theta_3^2|]), \tag{8.21}$$

where $[|\theta_3^2|] = 0$ for non-shared-media networks and $[|\theta_3^2|] = |\theta_3^2|$ for shared-media networks. Since, intuitively, ETE is the simplest among the approaches discussed above, it is used below as the reference for comparison.

8.4.2 Hop-by-Hop

From Eq. (8.13), we have

$$|S_h| = (n+1)\Gamma(\Theta^{r^+})$$
$$= (n+1)(|\theta_1^3| + |\theta_2^3| + |\theta_1^2| + |\theta_2^2| + [|\theta_3^2|] + |\theta_4^2| + |\theta_5^2|). \quad (8.22)$$

For the relative complexity of HBH over ETE, following Eqs. (8.2), (8.21), and (8.22), we have

$$\Lambda_{h/e}(\Omega) = \frac{(n+1)(|\theta_4^2| + |\theta_5^2|) - 2(|\theta_1^4| + |\theta_2^4|)}{|\Omega|}. \quad (8.23)$$

8.4.3 Domain-by-Domain

From Eq. (8.14), we have

$$|S_d| = 2\Gamma(\Theta^t) + m[2\Gamma(\Theta^t) + (n'-1)\Gamma(\Theta^r)]$$
$$= 2(m+1)(|\theta_1^4| + |\theta_2^4|) + (n+1)(|\theta_1^3| + |\theta_2^3| + |\theta_1^2| + |\theta_2^2| + [|\theta_3^2|]). \quad (8.24)$$

Similar to the HBH discussed above, we have

$$\Lambda_{d/e}(\Omega) = \frac{2m(|\theta_1^4| + |\theta_2^4|)}{|\Omega|}. \quad (8.25)$$

8.4.4 End-to-End Plus Hop-by-Hop

From Eq. (8.17), we have

$$|S_{eh}| = 2|\Theta^{t'}| + (n-1)|\Theta^{r'}|$$
$$= 2|\theta_1^4| + (n+1)(|\theta_1^3| + |\theta_2^3| + |\theta_1^2| + |\theta_2^2| + [|\theta_3^2|] + |\theta_5^2| + |\theta_6^2|). \quad (8.26)$$

Sightly different from the relative complexity for HBH over ETE, here θ_1^4 at nodes 0 and n is common to both HBH and ETE+HBH, so it can be excluded from the comparison. Thus the relative complexity for ETE+HBH over ETE is calculated by

$$\Lambda_{eh/e}(\Omega) = \frac{(n+1)(|\theta_5^2| + |\theta_6^2|) - 2|\theta_2^4|}{|\Omega|}. \quad (8.27)$$

8.4.5 End-to-End Plus Domain-by-Domain

From Eq. (8.20), we have

$$
\begin{aligned}
|\mathbf{S}_{ed}| &= 2\Gamma\left(\Theta^{t^+}\right) + m\left[2\Gamma\left(\Theta^{t^-}\right) + (n'-1)\Gamma\left(\Theta^r\right)\right] \\
&= 2\left(|\theta_1^4| + [|\theta_3^3|]\right) + 2m\left(|\theta_3^3| + |\theta_4^3|\right) \\
&\quad + (n+1)\left(|\theta_1^3| + |\theta_2^3| + |\theta_1^2| + |\theta_2^2| + [|\theta_3^2|]\right),
\end{aligned}
\tag{8.28}
$$

where $[|\theta_3^3|] = |\theta_3^3|$ for variant A and $[|\theta_3^3|] = 0$ for variant B. Similar to ETE+HBH, we have the following result for the relative complexity of ETE+DBD over ETE:

$$
\Lambda_{ed/e}(\Omega) = \frac{2[|\theta_3^3|] + 2m(|\theta_3^3| + |\theta_4^3|) - 2|\theta_2^4|}{|\Omega|}.
\tag{8.29}
$$

8.5 Conclusion

This chapter further discusses how to estimate implementation complexity for the reliable end-to-end transmission approaches discussed in Chap. 7. The formulas derived here can be used jointly with the results of the performance gain offered by each approach discussed in Chap. 7 to make a comprehensive comparison among them in terms of performance gain and increased implementation complexity. Some numerical results will be given in Chap. 9.

The major strength of the proposed estimation method is its applicability and scalability of complexity estimation through the use of relative measurement and a reference system. Its major weakness is its inaccuracy, which is caused by projecting a real system onto a simulated system for complexity estimation. However, a real system is often unavailable at its design and development stage.

References

1. Papadimitriou, C.H.: Computational complexity. In: Ralston, A., Reilly, E.D., Hemmendinger, D. (eds.) Encyclopedia of Computer Science, vol. 4 pp. 260–265. Wiley, New York (2003). ISBN 0-470-86412-5
2. Cohen, R., Kaempfer, G.: On the cost of virtual private networks. IEEE/ACM Trans. Netw. 8(6), 775–784 (2002)
3. Battini, D., Persona, A., Allesina, S.: Towards a use of network analysis: quantifying the complexity of supply chain networks. J. Electron. Cust. Relatsh. Manag. 1(1), 75–90 (2007)
4. Gill, G.K., Kemerer, C.F.: Cyclomatic complexity density and software maintenance productivity. IEEE Trans. Softw. Eng. 17(12), 1284–1288 (1991)
5. Network Simulator (NS-2). http://www.isi.edu/nsman/ns
6. MIL 3 Inc., OPNET. http://www.opnet.com

Chapter 9
Numerical Discussion of Quantitative End-to-End Arguments

Abstract Chapters 7 and 8 have analytically studied three reliable end-to-end transmission approaches and their hybrids by formulating some quantities for performance gain and implementation complexity. These formulas can be used jointly to make a quantitative comparison among these approaches in terms of the cost-effectiveness of a function displacement. Therefore, this chapter further provides some numerical examples for the comparison.

9.1 Introduction

As mentioned earlier, a function displacement for a reliable end-to-end transmission can improve the performance, but at the expense of increased implementation complexity. Chapters 7 and 8 have formulated several quantities for both performance gain and implementation complexity for three reliable end-to-end transmission approaches and their hybrids, i.e., ETE, HBH, DBD, ETE+HBH, and ETE+DBD.

This chapter further provides numerical examples of the special case defined in Sects. 7.5 and 8.4 with the following observations. (i) The performance gain offered by the congestion control function displacement can be remarkable, but at the expense of a large increase in implementation complexity. However, this complexity can be much reduced in shared-media networks since the medium access control (MAC) protocol in this kind of network can be slightly modified to provide an efficient hop-by-hop congestion control. (ii) A limited number of retransmissions carried out by intermediate nodes for lost packets may greatly improve reliable end-to-end transmission performance, but more retransmissions can hardly improve the performance further.

The remainder of this chapter is organized as follows. Section 9.2 discusses some comprehensive quantities used for numerical comparison, and the numerical results are discussed in Sect. 9.3. The chapter is concluded in Sect. 9.4.

9.2 Comprehensive Quantities for Comparison

In this section, an example of using NS2 to estimate the relative complexity of implementation (i.e., Λ) is discussed first, and then a per-bit throughput (denoted by Ψ henceforth) is defined for comparison.

S.M. Jiang, *Future Wireless and Optical Networks*,   133
Computer Communications and Networks,
DOI 10.1007/978-1-4471-2822-9_9, © Springer-Verlag London Limited 2012

9.2.1 Estimation of Relative Complexity

From Eqs. (8.23), (8.25), (8.27), and (8.29), we have to know $|\theta_1^4|$, $|\theta_2^4|$, $|\theta_3^3|$, $|\theta_4^3|$, $|\theta_5^2|$, and $|\theta_6^2|$ to estimate the relative complexity. The congestion control in domain-by-domain (DBD) (θ_4^3) can use the same one as used by end-to-end (ETE) (θ_2^4) since a TCP-like control can also be used by a domain for the congestion control therein. Therefore, we can have $|\theta_4^3| \approx |\theta_2^4|$. With ETE+DBD, the K-retransmission over a domain (θ_3^3) is similar to the ∞-retransmission used by ETE (θ_1^4) in terms of design but simpler because less buffer space is required by the K-retransmission. This complexity can be approximated by the ratio of their average retransmission numbers for a successful packet transmission. This number can be calculated by using Eq. (7.24) as follows: suppose θ_3^3 and θ_1^4 are used in a domain, and their average transmission times are calculated by

$$\varepsilon = 1 - (1 - p)^{n'}$$

for both, but K is set to ∞ for calculating θ_1^4 while K for θ_3^3. Then

$$\frac{|\theta_3^3|}{|\theta_1^4|} \approx \frac{f(\varepsilon, K)}{f(\varepsilon, \infty)} = f(\varepsilon, K)(1 - p)^{n'}. \tag{9.1}$$

Similarly, for the ∞-retransmission (θ_4^2) used by HBH and the K-retransmission (θ_6^2) used by ETE+HBH, we have

$$\frac{|\theta_6^2|}{|\theta_4^2|} \approx f(p, K)(1 - p). \tag{9.2}$$

Note that Eq. (7.24) also shows that with a large K or a small p,

$$f(p, K)(1 - p) \approx 1,$$

and similarly,

$$f(\varepsilon, K)(1 - p)^{n'} \approx 1$$

for a large K or a small ε. This, along with Eqs. (9.1) and (9.2), means that $|\theta_3^3| \approx |\theta_1^4|$ and $|\theta_6^2| \approx |\theta_4^2|$ in these cases.

With the above approximation, now we only need to calculate $|\theta_1^4|$, $|\theta_2^4|$, $|\theta_5^2|$, and $|\theta_6^2|$ as well as a reference system Ω, which is discussed below. Since TCP has been well implemented in NS2, TCP is used here as Ω, which mainly consists of θ_1^4 and θ_2^4, just like ETE. Since TCP only needs to be implemented at the source and destination nodes, we obtain an estimation of the complexity of Ω for an end-to-end connection as follows:

$$|\Omega| = 2|\text{TCP}|$$
$$\approx 2(|\theta_1^4| + |\theta_2^4|).$$

Table 9.1 Complexity (bytes) of TCP and MAC implemented in NS2

	TCP				IEEE 802.11 MAC			
File	TCP.h	TCP.cc	Cctl	Rctl	MAC.h	MAC.cc	Cctl	Rctl
Size	3894	37796	16250	1195	7689	34183	11001	1862
(bytes)	$\|\vartheta_1^4\| = 2856$		$\|\vartheta_2^4\| = 38834$		$\|\vartheta_5^2\| = 35811$		$\|\vartheta_6^2\| = 6061$	

Now we use the approximation given by Eq. (8.3) to estimate $|\theta_1^4|$, $|\theta_2^4|$, $|\theta_5^2|$, and $|\theta_6^2|$. The retransmission ($|\vartheta_1^4|$) and congestion control ($|\vartheta_2^4|$) of the TCP implementation in NS2 correspond to θ_1^4 and θ_2^4, respectively. Similarly, the IEEE 802.11 MAC is also well implemented in NS2. As discussed in [1, 2], the RTS/CTS of 802.11 (ϑ_5^2) can be slightly modified to provide a hop-by-hop congestion control (θ_5^2), while its MAC-level retransmission (ϑ_6^2) is equivalent to the link-level K-retransmission here (θ_6^2). Therefore, ϑ_5^2 and ϑ_6^2 correspond to θ_5^2 and θ_6^2, respectively. Then, with a simple manipulation, Eqs. (8.23), (8.25), (8.27), and (8.29) can be rewritten as follows:

$$\Lambda_{h/e}(\text{TCP}) \approx \frac{(n+1)}{2(|\vartheta_1^4| + |\vartheta_2^4|)} \left[\frac{|\vartheta_6^2|}{f(p, K)(1-p)} + |\vartheta_5^2| \right] - 1,$$

$$\Lambda_{d/e}(\text{TCP}) \approx m,$$

$$\Lambda_{eh/e}(\text{TCP}) \approx \frac{(n+1)(|\vartheta_5^2| + |\vartheta_6^2|) - 2|\vartheta_2^4|}{2(|\vartheta_1^4| + |\vartheta_2^4|)},$$

$$\Lambda_{ed/e}(\text{TCP}) \approx \frac{(m + [1])f(\varepsilon, K)(1-p)^{n'}|\vartheta_1^4| + (m-1)|\vartheta_2^4|}{|\vartheta_1^4| + |\vartheta_2^4|},$$

where $[1] = 1$ for ETE+DBD.A and $[1] = 0$ for ETE+DBD.B.

The implementation complexity of a simulated function is measured in terms of the size of its files in bytes by excluding the commentary parts. However, for the TCP in NS2, its congestion control (or simply Cctl) and transmission reliability control (or simply Rctl) are implemented in the same files (i.e., TCP.cc and TCP.h), and some programs are shared by both functions. Here we first identify the parts only dedicated to Cctl and Rctl in TCP.cc, respectively. Then the sizes of Rctl ($|\vartheta_1^4|$) and Cctl ($|\vartheta_2^4|$) are determined in the following way:

$$|\vartheta_1^4| = \frac{|\text{Rctl}|}{|\text{Rctl}| + |\text{Cctl}|} \times (|\text{TCP.cc}| + |\text{TCP.h}|), \qquad (9.3)$$

and

$$|\vartheta_2^4| = (|\text{TCP.cc}| + |\text{TCP.h}|) - |\vartheta_1^4|. \qquad (9.4)$$

The same method can be used to estimate the complexity of the MAC function (i.e., $|\vartheta_5^2|$ and $|\vartheta_6^2|$). The results are listed in Table 9.1.

9.2.2 Per-Bit Throughput

The throughput here is defined as the number of bits positively acknowledged by the destination node per time unit. Give an L-bit long packet, its transmission completion time is $\mathbf{T}$, so $\Psi = \frac{L}{\mathbf{T}}$, which however comes at a transmission cost $\mathbf{C}$. Therefore, the average throughput per bit consumed (called per-bit throughput henceforth) is given by

$$\psi \triangleq \frac{L}{\mathbf{T}} \Big/ \mathbf{C} = \frac{L}{\mathbf{TC}}, \tag{9.5}$$

which reflects the network resource efficiency in providing reliable end-to-end transmission. This quantity can be used jointly with transmission energy consumption models to further estimate energy efficiency for green networking research [3].

9.3 Numerical Discussion

According to the "small Internet world" reported in [4], the average length of the Internet at the domain level is less than 4 while that at the router level is shorter than 10. So we let $m = 3$ and $n' = 3$ by default, and hence $n = mn' + m + 1 = 13$.

Here we compare numerically the reliable end-to-end transmission approaches discussed in Sect. 7.5 in terms of transmission cost ($\mathbf{C}$), transmission completion time ($\mathbf{T}$), congestion reaction time ($\mathbf{A}$), per-bit throughput (Ψ), and relative complexity (Λ). For simplicity, the ratio of a performance indicator of an approach under comparison to that of ETE is depicted, i.e., $\frac{\mathbf{C}_x}{\mathbf{C}_e}$, $\frac{\mathbf{T}_x}{\mathbf{T}_e}$, $\frac{\mathbf{A}_x}{\mathbf{A}_e}$, and $\frac{\Psi_x}{\Psi_e}$ as well as $\Lambda_{x/e}$, where x stands for either HBH, DBD, ETE+HBH, or ETE+DBD, respectively. For Ψ, the ratio is given by

$$\frac{\Psi_x}{\Psi_e} = \frac{\mathbf{C}_e \mathbf{T}_e}{\mathbf{C}_x \mathbf{T}_x}, \tag{9.6}$$

which is independent of L. Here we first let $\alpha \triangleq \frac{p_x}{p_e} = 1$ and $\beta \triangleq \frac{\tau_x}{\tau_e} = 1$ by default, which means that packet loss probability over a link and link latency for different approaches are identical to each other. Other settings of these two parameters are further investigated in Sect. 9.3.5.

9.3.1 HBH Versus ETE

Figure 9.1 plots the ratio mentioned above against the packet loss probability over links (p), which shows that as p increases, both the transmission cost ($\mathbf{C}$) and completion time ($\mathbf{T}$) given by ETE quickly become larger than those by HBH, especially $\mathbf{T}$. The result is that the per-bit throughput (Ψ) of HBH is much larger than that of ETE. This happens because, with ETE, retransmission is carried out by the source

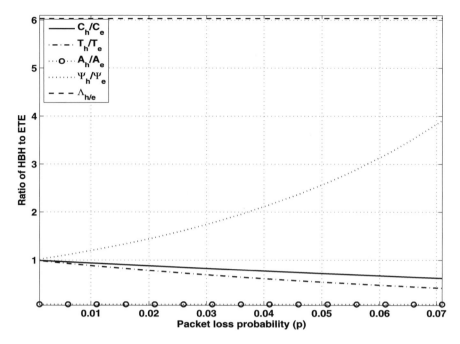

Fig. 9.1 Comparison between HBH and ETE against packet loss probability (p): $n = 13$

node, while with HBH it is carried out immediately by the upstream node of the link over which a loss occurs.

Regarding the congestion reaction time (**A**), since the congestion reaction takes at least a round-trip time over the end-to-end connection with ETE, but just a round-trip time over the link with HBH, we have $\mathbf{A}_e = n\tau$ and $\mathbf{A}_h = \tau$, and thus $\frac{\mathbf{A}_h}{\mathbf{A}_e} = \frac{1}{n}$ (see Sect. 7.5), which is a constant against p. As shown here for the relative complexity of HBH over ETE ($\Lambda_{h/e}$), $\Lambda_{h/e} \approx 6$, which means that the complexity of HBH is larger than that of ETE with a difference equal to six times TCP's complexity. Here Λ is almost insensitive to p due to the reason mentioned earlier for Eqs. (9.1) and (9.2). We find that the superiority of HBH over ETE even for small p is also remarkable, but at the expense of much higher complexity.

Figure 9.2, which plots the ratios against n, shows a similar phenomenon as illustrated in Fig. 9.1 for **C**, **T**, and Ψ. As mentioned above, $\frac{\mathbf{A}_h}{\mathbf{A}_e} = \frac{1}{n}$, which decreases quickly with n. But Λ goes oppositely, since the number of extra components required for HBH over ETE increases linearly with n. Thus both $\frac{\Psi_h}{\Psi_e}$ and $\Lambda_{h/e}$ are very sensitive to n.

9.3.2 DBD Versus ETE

Figure 9.3 shows phenomena similar to those reflected in Fig. 9.1, with an improvement in Ψ less than that given by HBH over ETE because HBH is the best in terms

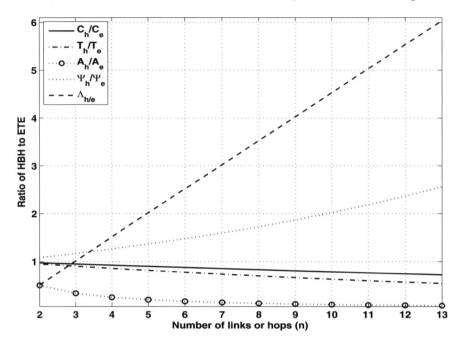

Fig. 9.2 Comparison between HBH and ETE against the number of links or hops of a route (n):
$p = 0.05$

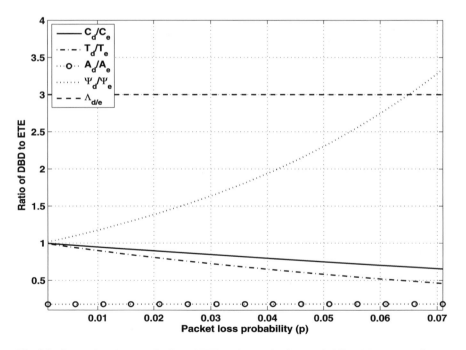

Fig. 9.3 Comparison between DBD and ETE against packet loss probability (p): $m = n = 3$

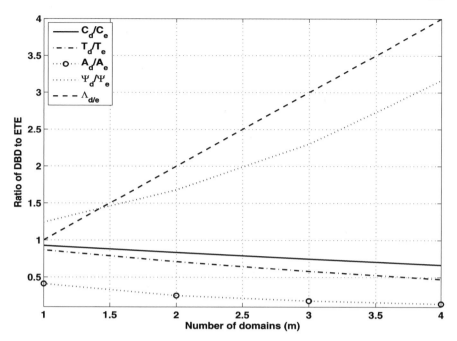

Fig. 9.4 Comparison between DBD and ETE against the number of domains of a route (m): $n = 3$ and $p = 0.05$

of performance; but this improvement is still remarkable. The Λ here is also lower and equal to 3, half of that given by HBH over ETE. This is because within a domain, the simplest ETE is adopted instead of the most complex HBH for the reliable transmission across the domain. As m increases, as illustrated in Fig. 9.4, both $\frac{\Psi_d}{\Psi_e}$ and $\Lambda_{d/e}$ increase with n but at a rate lower than that for HBH over ETE, which is illustrated in Fig. 9.2. These phenomena suggest that DBD is better than HBH for trading off between performance gain and implementation complexity.

Note that the above tradeoff mainly holds in wired networks, because the major difference in the implementation complexity is caused by the hop-by-hop congestion control (i.e., θ_5^2) of HBH. Actually, in wireless networks, particularly those based on IEEE 802.11, the RTS/CTS protocol used to solve the hidden terminal problem and a MAC retransmission scheme (i.e., θ_6^2) have already been implemented in the data link layer at every node. As discussed in Sect. 7.2.2.1, the RTS/CTS protocol can be slightly modified to provide the hop-by-hop congestion control. Then in this case, the complexity of θ_5^2 can be approximated by that of the RTS/CTS protocol, so $|\mathbf{S}_e|$ for ETE given by Eq. (8.21) now can be rewritten as follows:

$$|\mathbf{S}_e| \approx 2\left(\left|\theta_1^4\right| + \left|\theta_2^4\right|\right) + (n+1)\left(\left|\theta_1^3\right| + \left|\theta_2^3\right| + \left|\theta_1^2\right| + \left|\theta_2^2\right| + \left[\left|\theta_3^2\right|\right]\right) + \theta_5^2 + \theta_6^2.$$

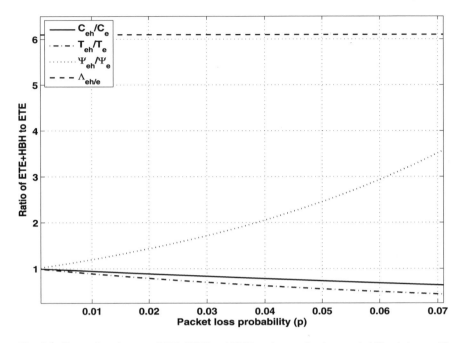

Fig. 9.5 Comparison between ETE+HBH and ETE against packet loss probability (p): $n = 13$ and $K = 1$

Then with the approximation discussed in Sect. 9.2.1, we have

$$\Lambda_{h/e}(\text{TCP}) \approx \frac{(n+1)|\vartheta_6^2|}{2(|\vartheta_1^4| + |\vartheta_2^4|)}\left[\frac{1}{f(p, K)(1 - p)} - 1\right] - 1 \approx -1,$$

which indicates that in this case, ETE is even more complex than HBH with a difference equal to a TCP implementation. This is because a set of TCP is still needed in the source and destination nodes with ETE, while it is not with HBH. This strongly suggests that, in a wireless network, congestion control function displacement to improve network performance is a good option.

9.3.3 ETE+HBH Versus ETE

Figures 9.5, 9.6 and 9.7 plot the ratios mentioned above for ETE+HBH over ETE. Since **A** here is the same as that for HBH, it is not discussed again. The phenomena depicted in Figs. 9.5 and 9.6 are similar to those reflected in Figs. 9.1 and 9.2 with a slightly different change rate, because a definite number of retransmissions (i.e., K) is adopted here instead of the infinite one used with HBH. It is quite interesting to find that, even with $K = 1$, the performance is greatly improved over ETE as illustrated in Fig. 9.7. This phenomenon suggests that a small buffer used for retransmission at intermediate nodes can greatly improve the end-to-end transmission

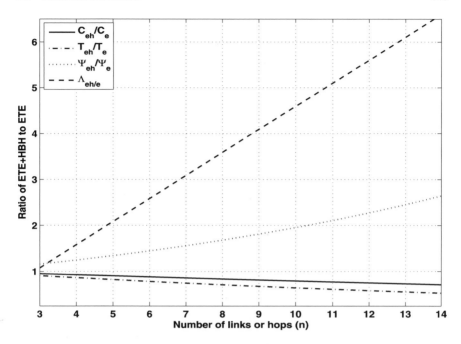

Fig. 9.6 Comparison between ETE+HBH and ETE against the number of links or hops of the route (n): $p = 0.05$ and $K = 1$

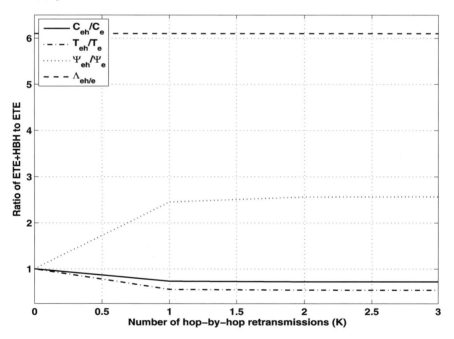

Fig. 9.7 Comparison between ETE+HBH and ETE against the maximum number of hop-by-hop retransmissions (K): $n = 13$ and $p = 0.05$

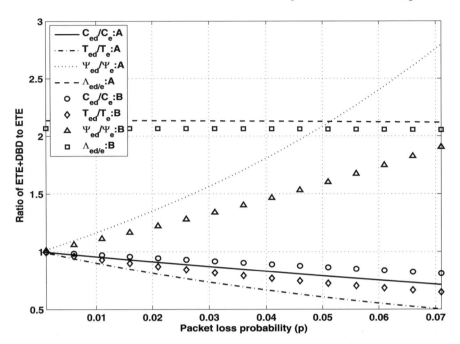

Fig. 9.8 Comparison between ETE+DBD (variants A and B) and ETE against packet loss probability (p): $m = n = 3$ and $K = 1$

reliability. But the fast convergence of the gain after $K > 2$ indicates that there is no need of using a large buffer at intermediate nodes.

9.3.4 ETE+DBD Versus ETE

As illustrated in Figs. 9.8, 9.9 and 9.10, the phenomena here are similar to those reflected in Figs. 9.5, 9.6 and 9.7. The major differences are that (i) the Ψ ratio here is smaller than that depicted in Figs. 9.5, 9.6 and 9.7, since HBH is more efficient than DBD, and (ii) ETE+DBD.A is more efficient than ETE+DBD.B (which are respectively depicted by circles, diamonds, triangles, and squares in these figures) as expected. This is because the former carries out retransmission over inter-domain links but the latter does not. Accordingly, ETE+DBD.A is slightly more complex than ETE+DBD.B.

9.3.5 Packet Loss Probability and Link Latency

The preceding comparison assumes that (i) the ratio of link packet loss probability given by approach x over that by ETE, i.e., $\gamma_1 \triangleq \frac{p_x}{p_e}$, is equal to 1, and (ii) the ratio

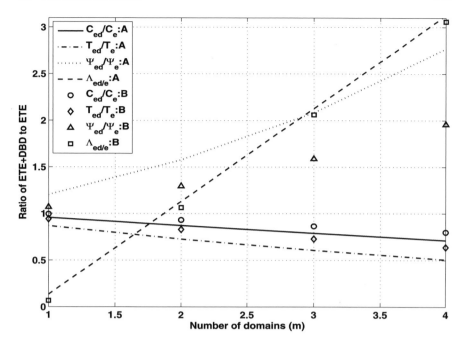

Fig. 9.9 Comparison between ETE+DBD (variants A and B) and ETE against the number of domains of a route (m): $p = 0.05$, $n = 3$ and $K = 1$

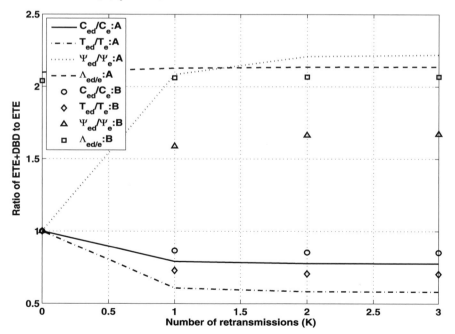

Fig. 9.10 Comparison between ETE+DBD (variants A and B) and ETE against the number of retransmissions over a domain or an inter-domain link (K): $m = n = 3$ and $p = 0.05$

of link round-trip time given by approach x over that by ETE, i.e., $\gamma_2 \triangleq \frac{\tau_x}{\tau_e}$, is equal to 1. This means that the two approaches under comparison experience an identical packet loss probability (p) and link round-trip (τ), which however may not be the case in practice, as discussed below.

Although the congestion reaction time with ETE $(\mathbf{A}_e)$ is the longest, this may cause ETE to inject less traffic into the network compared to the other approaches. This may further cause shorter packet queueing delay and lower packet loss ratio. Particularly in a shared-media network, a MAC protocol has to be installed as mentioned earlier, which contributes very much to queueing delay. For example, in a multi-hop wireless ad hoc network, the per-node throughput cannot exceed one-third of the channel capacity on average [5] and will further shrink as the number of contending nodes increases. But the determination of packet queueing delay and loss ratio is not further discussed here, since it requires more information on MAC and routing protocols as well as congestion control schemes and traffic models.

Since $\Lambda_{x/e}$ is rarely affected by γ_1 and γ_2, here we only investigate how $\frac{\psi_x}{\psi_e}$ is affected by them. We simply change the settings of γ_1 and γ_2 to check how the performance gain offered by non-ETE (i.e., HBH, DBD, ETE+HBH, and ETE+DBD) over ETE is affected by different γ_1 and γ_2 settings. For the special case discussed in Sect. 7.5, given γ_2, the term $\frac{\mathbf{T}_x}{\mathbf{T}_e}$ for $\frac{\psi_x}{\psi_e}$ in Eq. (9.6) is independent of each individual τ but the ratio γ_2. For example, for HBH over ETE,

$$\frac{\mathbf{T}_h}{\mathbf{T}_e} = \gamma_2(1 - p)^{n-1}. \tag{9.7}$$

Therefore, we do not discuss $\frac{\psi_x}{\psi_e}$ against individual τ but γ_2. However, given γ_1 and/or γ_2, $\frac{\psi_x}{\psi_e}$ is still dependent on each individual p besides ratio γ_1. So two p_e settings are investigated by increasing p_x larger than p_e following $p_x = \gamma_1 p_e$ with $\gamma_1 \geq 1$.

As illustrated in Fig. 9.11 against γ_1, when the packet loss probability given ETE (p_e) is very small, i.e., $p_e = 0.005$, if $p_x = p_e$ (i.e., $\gamma_1 = 1$), there is still some superiority given by non-ETE over ETE. However, as p_x continuously increases to exceed 1 with γ_1, which means that the packet loss probability given by non-ETE is larger than that by ETE, ETE becomes better and better, and the performance degradation of ETE+DBD.B is the fastest while that of HBH is the slowest. This is because no retransmission is carried out over inter-domain links with ETE+DBD.B, which affects severely the end-to-end transmission reliability, especially in the case of high p_x. When $p_e = 0.05$ as depicted in Fig. 9.12, the superiority given by non-ETE over ETE becomes much larger than that with $p_e = 0.005$, but it also degrades much faster as γ_1 increases. This indicates that the superiority given by non-ETE over ETE is very sensitive to the difference in their packet loss probabilities.

Regarding the effect of γ_2, when $p_e = 0.005$, packet loss occurs rarely, resulting in few retransmissions, which makes these approaches perform similarly in terms of transmission cost $\mathbf{C}$. As illustrated in Fig. 9.13, the per-bit throughput ratio is almost equal to 1 when $\tau_x = \tau_e$ (i.e., $\gamma_2 = 1$). In this case, this ratio mainly depends on the ratio of their transmission completion times as indicated by Eq. (9.6), i.e., $\frac{\mathbf{T}_x}{\mathbf{T}_e}$, because of the trivial difference in $\mathbf{C}$ with low p as mentioned above. Therefore,

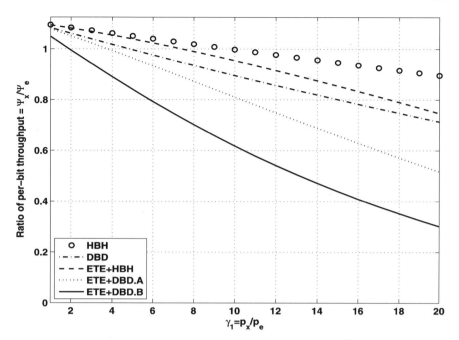

Fig. 9.11 Ratio of per-bit throughput given by non-ETE to that by ETE ($\frac{\Psi_x}{\Psi_e}$) against packet loss probability ratio ($\gamma_1 = \frac{p_x}{p_e}$) for $p_e = 0.005$: link round-trip time ratio ($\gamma_2 = \frac{\tau_x}{\tau_e} = 1$), $n = 13$, $m = 3$, $n' = 3$, $K = 1$

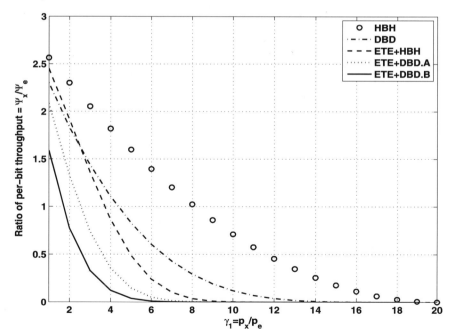

Fig. 9.12 The same setting as that of Fig. 9.11 but with $p_e = 0.05$

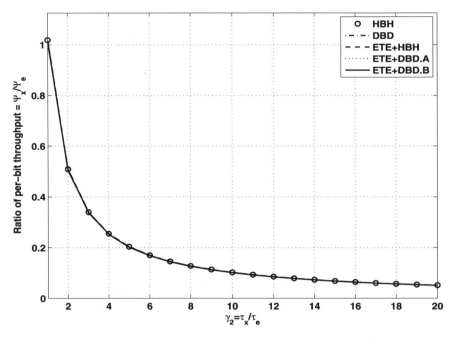

Fig. 9.13 Ratio of per-bit throughput given by non-ETE to that by ETE ($\frac{\Psi_x}{\Psi_e}$) against link round-trip time ratio ($\gamma_2 = \frac{\tau_x}{\tau_e}$) for $p_e = 0.005$: packet loss probability ratio ($\gamma_1 = \frac{p_x}{p_e} = 1$), $n = 13, m = 3, n' = 3, K = 1$

when τ_x becomes larger than τ_e as γ_2 increases to exceed 1, the superiority given by ETE over non-ETE becomes larger. However, for $p_e = 0.05$ as depicted in Fig. 9.14, the superiority given by non-ETE over ETE is still big, even when τ_x is close to τ_e, with some slight differences between different approaches. From the phenomena reflected in these figures against γ_1 and those against γ_2, we find that the effect of the difference in packet loss probability (p) is larger than that of link round-trip time (τ) on the performance gain for reliable end-to-end transmission.

9.4 Conclusion

This chapter provides some numerical results for the performance gain and implementation complexity of the reliable end-to-end transmission approaches discussed in Chap. 7. These results suggest that the performance gain offered by both HBH and DBD as well as their hybrids over ETE can be remarkable, but at the expense of increased implementation complexity due to the function displacement from higher layers to lower layers. However, this increased complexity can be much reduced in shared-media networks such as wireless networks, since MAC protocols therein can be slightly modified to provide the hop-by-hop congestion and reliability control functions. These results also show that a small number of retransmissions provided

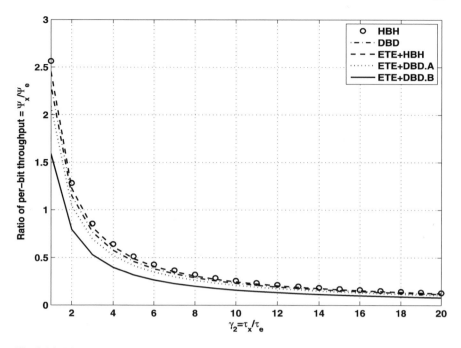

Fig. 9.14 The same setting as that of Fig. 9.13 but with $p_e = 0.05$

by intermediate nodes may greatly improve the performance of reliable end-to-end transmission.

References

1. Lee, J.S., Lee, M.J., Taori, R., Lee, S.W.: Congestion control for wireless mesh networks. Jun. 2005, pending USA patent No. 60/686459
2. Jiang, S.M., Zuo, Q., Wei, G.: Decoupling congestion control from TCP for multi-hop wireless networks: semi-TCP. In: Proc. ACM MobiCom Workshop on Challenged Networks (CHANTS), Beijing, China (2009)
3. Bianzino, A.P., Chaudet, C., Rossi, D., Rougier, J.L.: A survey of green networking research. IEEE Commun. Surv. Tutor. **PP**(99), 1–18 (2010)
4. Albert, R., Barabási, A.L.: Statistical mechanics of complex networks. Rev. Mod. Phys. **74**(1), 47–98 (2002)
5. Gerla, M., Tang, K., Bagrodia, R.: TCP performance in wireless multi-hop networks. In: Proc. IEEE WS. Mobile Computing Systems & App. (WMCSA), New Orleans, LA, USA, pp. 41–50 (1999)

Chapter 10
Decoupling Congestion Control from TCP: Semi-TCP

Abstract It is well known that the Transmission Control Protocol (TCP) performs poorly in multi-hop wireless networks. This problem also appears in bandwidth-abundant all-optical networks, in which data loss may occur frequently due to not only congestion but also collision because of the poor photonic computing and buffering capabilities available at all-optical nodes. This problem is due to the end-to-end nature of TCP, in which only the source and destination nodes are involved in congestion control. However, these nodes cannot learn exactly the congestion status in the network and often react slowly to congestion states, especially when a congested node is far away from the source node. Although much research has been conducted on this topic, the problem has not been solved completely. Inspired by findings from the quantitative end-to-end arguments discussed in Chaps. 7, 8 and 9, in this chapter a Semi-TCP approach is discussed to solve this problem. The basic idea of Semi-TCP is to decouple the congestion control function from TCP and shift it down to lower layers.

10.1 Introduction

The Transmission Control Protocol (TCP) is the most important transport protocol for the Internet. It was originally designed for wired networks to control transmission reliability, and later was enhanced with congestion control. Transmission reliability control is realized through packet retransmission, in which a source node will retransmit each packet that has not been acknowledged by the destination node. Congestion control is performed by the source node by sliding its congestion control window, which adjusts the amount of output traffic according to the congestion status inferred through the reception of ACK and the retransmission timeout. If a congestion is inferred, the congestion control window is shrunk; otherwise, it is increased upon the arrival of every positive ACK at the source node. Thus, TCP simplifies relaying units such as routers by excluding them from congestion and transmission reliability control. This is why TCP can run successfully over various types of networks [1].

Many studies and experiments show that TCP performs poorly in multi-hop wireless networks as the number of hops of the TCP connection increases [2, 3]. This happens because TCP cannot allow the source node to quickly learn the exact congestion situation in wireless networks. Consequently, no proper action can be taken immediately to either an ongoing or a released congestion. TCP performs dramatically worse as the round-trip time increases, and may not even work if the end-to-end connectivity is broken. This event may happen frequently in mobile networks. Moreover, some characteristics of wireless networks, such as unreliable radio channels, shared media, and terminal mobility, cause certain networking functions such as routing to perform poorly, which further degrades TCP performance.

This problem has been studied for more than a decade with many proposals published in the literature (see Sect. 10.2). Although these proposals vary in design and method, they share a similarity in their efforts to improve TCP's capability of judging congestion status in networks by using more efficient mechanisms. Typical mechanisms include negative acknowledgement (NACK) [4–6], Explicit Congestion Notification (ECN) [7, 8], and congestion measurement using probing or monitoring mechanisms [9, 10]. More discussions on this issue can be found in the literature, such as [11–14].

Although these proposals can improve TCP's performance, they do not solve these problems completely. Recently some proposals have applied a hop-by-hop congestion control to greatly improve performance in multi-hop wireless networks [15–19]. We think that (i) shifting congestion control down to lower layers is a promising solution to overcome TCP problems and (ii) it is necessary to further decouple congestion control from TCP in order to eliminate the constraint of its congestion control window on further performance improvement. In this case, only the transmission reliability control is retained in TCP, so the original TCP-ACK stream can still be maintained to keep the end-to-end semantic of TCP. Moreover, since the control efficiency does not rely on the availability of end-to-end connectivity in this case, this kind of TCP is more suitable than the original TCP for mobile networks. This kind of TCP is called Semi-TCP henceforth.

TCP also faces similar problems in bandwidth-abundant all-optical networks [20] without adopting capacity over-provisioning [21]. In this kind of network, data loss may occur frequently due to not only congestion but also collision caused by the poor photonic computing and buffering capabilities available at all-optical nodes. This fact forces sophisticated computing and buffering functions to be shifted to domain edges and an end-to-end transmission to be split into domain-by-domain transmissions. In this case, congestion control must be shifted down to lower layers and performed domain by domain.

The remainder of this chapter is organized as follows. Sections 10.2 and 10.3 give a brief survey of TCP enhancements for multi-hop wireless networks and all-optical networks, respectively. Section 10.4 discusses the principle of Semi-TCP for wireless and optical networks. The chapter is summarized in Sect. 10.5.

10.2 TCP in Multi-hop Wireless Networks

As mentioned earlier, TCP can work well in wired networks but not in multi-hop wireless networks. This section summarizes the major challenges that TCP faces in these kinds of networks and some enhancements to it.

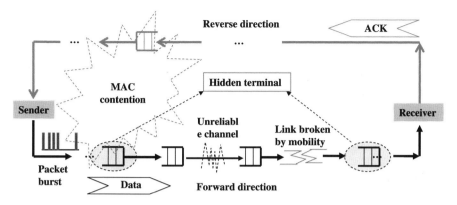

Fig. 10.1 Causes for non-congestive losses in multi-hop wireless networks

10.2.1 Major Challenges

Since the transport layer cannot know exactly the congestion status in the network layer, the source node can only infer congestion status based on the reception of ACK packets and the retransmission timeout. Inevitably this method may lead to misjudgements on the real situation. For example, a failure in the reception of an ACK packet in time may be due to a long queueing delay rather than a congestive loss. Even in the case of a congestion, this congestion may not occur in the direction from the source to destination nodes but probably in the opposite direction. This misjudgement can become severe in multi-hop wireless networks, leading to significant performance degradation.

As illustrated in Fig. 10.1, many failures in TCP segment reception are not caused by congestion but are due to other factors as described below.

- As mentioned earlier, the bit error rate (BER) of radio channels typically ranges from 10^{-2} to 10^{-5}. Such unreliable channels cause more data to be received in error in comparison with wired channels, whose BER usually ranges from 10^{-8} to 10^{-10}.
- A wireless medium is usually shared by multiple terminals in a vicinity, and signal collision due to simultaneous transmission from several terminals will also cause reception failure. Both packet bursts from the source node and ACK packets on the reverse path will intensify the medium access control (MAC) contention of the shared wireless media.
- Mobile terminals can move during a communication in progress and may leave the signal coverage. This may break currently engaged radio links and trigger rerouting. In this case, more time is needed to forward packets, which may cause some packets not to be received before the retransmission timeout.
- The congestion control window (cwnd) determines the number of TCP segments to be sent to the network. Its increment is largely affected by the round-trip time (RTT) over the TCP connection. The longer the RTT, the slower the increment. In multi-hop wireless networks, the RTT may be longer than expected due to link

Table 10.1 Possible causes for TCP segment reception failure in multi-hop wireless networks

Possible causes	Consequence	Judgement
Congestion	Packet loss	Correct
Unreliable channel	Packet corruption	Wrong
Terminal mobility	Packet overdue	Wrong
Hidden terminal	Packet collision	Wrong
MAC contention	Packet collision	Wrong
Delayed/lost ACK	Retransmission timeout	Wrong

unavailability caused by mobility, which may further cause unnecessary decrease in cwnd, resulting in low network throughput.

- The distribution of active nodes in the network determines how severe the hidden terminal problem will be. This problem will also cause non-congestive losses that the TCP source node cannot distinguish from congestive losses.
- A lost or delayed ACK packet on the reverse route from destination to source may also cause the source node to be unable to receive ACKs in time, which however cannot be distinguished by the source node.

Thus, TCPs often make a wrong judgement on the congestion status in the network as listed in Table 10.1, leading to unnecessary decrease of traffic loads injected into networks.

Even if an initial judgement on the congestion status along a path is correct, this judgement may become invalid due to changes in the path caused by an unpinned route and/or changed links due to terminal mobility. If the path is changed, all efforts to control the congestion along this path cannot make sense, since the congested node may no longer be part of the current path or may even become unreachable if some related radio links are broken.

There are many proposals in the literature to handle this problem, and these are described briefly in the following subsections.

10.2.2 Judgement on Congestion Status

Since misjudgement on the congestion status in the network is the major factor that degrades TCP performance in multi-hop wireless networks, many enhancements have been proposed, as discussed below.

10.2.2.1 Route Failure Notification

In multi-hop wireless networks, route failure may occur frequently due to either link failure (e.g., radio links are broken by terminal mobility) or nodal failure (e.g., exhausted battery or powered-off terminals). Packets traveling on a failed route may be lost since rerouting may make them overdue. Once such non-congestive losses take place, the network layer notifies the TCP source node so that it does not react to these non-congestive losses. Such proposals include TCP with Feedback (TCP-F) [22] and Explicit Link Failure Notification (ELFN) [23] as well TCP-BuS [24] schemes. TCP-BuS can also notify the TCP source node of the reestablishment of a failed route.

10.2.2.2 Detection and Notification of Congestion

Since there are so many types of non-congestive losses, instead of notifying every non-congestive loss, it should be much simpler to notify the TCP source node of congestive loss only. Upon receiving an Explicit Congestion Notification (ECN), the TCP source node reacts accordingly without need of inferring congestion status in the network. Such an example is the Ad Hoc TCP (ATCP) scheme [25]. To detect congestion, some probing mechanisms are required. This can be realized either by sending some probing packets, e.g., TCP-Peach [26] and TCP-Peach+ [27], or by using some specific devices such as TCP-Probing [28].

10.2.2.3 Heuristic Congestion Inference

Since the above two schemes require cooperation from the network layer to detect route failure or congestion status, they are criticized for the loss of the end-to-end semantic of TCP. Alternatively, some efforts have been made to enable the TCP source node to make more accurate judgements on the cause of packet losses through heuristic analysis of received ACK packets, such as fixed retransmission timeout (RTO) [29], or by letting an ACK packet carry more information for judgement, such as the detection of out-of-order and response (TCP-DOOR) [30] scheme. TCP Veno [31] tries to infer a packet loss by estimating the backlog accumulated along the communication route. The jitter-based TCP (JTCP) [32] tries to estimate the congestion level of the network according to the jitter ratio. The delayed congestion response TCP (TCP-DCR) [33] delays the response to the first duplicate ACK in order to have more time to make a judgement.

10.2.3 Hidden Terminal Problem

The hidden terminal problem in multi-hop wireless networks cannot be resolved by simply using the RTS/CTS protocol proposed by the IEEE 802.11 MAC, so some methods in the transport layer have been proposed to handle this problem. One example is TCP with adaptive pace (TCP-AP) [34], which allows the TCP source node to control the interval between consecutive TCP segment transmissions to be close to a 4-hop propagation delay with a joint use of the TCP congestion control window. The reason behind such design is due to the fact that two mutually hidden

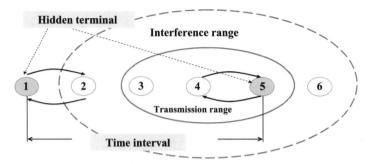

Fig. 10.2 Schematic principle of TCP-AP

terminals along a route in the multi-hop ad hoc network based on the IEEE 802.11 MAC is about 4 hops away as illustrated in Fig. 10.2, where node 1 is a hidden terminal of node 5, and vice versa. Thus with this pacing, the number of collisions caused by hidden terminals can be greatly reduced. Obviously, this pacing efficiency largely depends on the estimation accuracy for the 4-hop propagation delay, which however is dynamic by nature, especially in mobile environments and in the case of time-varying traffic loads.

10.2.4 Reducing MAC Contention

MAC contention degree affects TCP performance very much since it can cause non-congestive losses that will be mistaken by the TCP source node and congestive losses. This contention can be intensified by ACK transmission on the reverse route as well as the burstiness of TCP segments injected by the source node to the network layer. Some proposals to handle these issues are briefly described below.

10.2.4.1 Reducing ACK Transmission

Although the size of the ACK packet is much smaller than that of a data packet, it also has to go through the same MAC contention procedure as required for a data packet in order to win access to the wireless channel. As mentioned earlier, the wireless channel is a shared media, and in this case, it is shared by packet trans-missions in both forward and reverse directions. Therefore, reducing the number of ACK packets transmitted along the reverse route can alleviate the MAC contention over the forward route. One example is the delayed ACK [35], which delays sending ACKs until a certain number of data segments have been received so as to reduce the number of ACK packets to be sent per packet reception. Similarly, TCP with adap-tive delayed acknowledgement (TCP-ADA) [36] delays sending ACKs by a certain time period.

10.2.4.2 Disjointing Forward and Backward Routes

As mentioned above, the wireless channel is shared by both forward and reverse routes. Basically, the forward route is used to deliver data packets and the reverse one for ACK packets. The transmissions of data packets and ACK packets are almost synchronized due to the TCP operation so the MAC contention degree is high when the packet route and the ACK route go through the same intermediate nodes. If the backward route for ACK packets can go through intermediate nodes different from those that the forward route does for data packets, MAC contention can be alleviated. One such scheme, called contention-based path selection (COPAS), was proposed in [37]; it tries to disjoint the forward packet route and the backward ACK route through a routing protocol.

10.2.4.3 Smoothing Packet Burst

Since TCP uses the congestion control window to throttle the amount of data traffic to be injected into the network, packets may arrive at the lower layers in a burst, which intensifies MAC contention, leading to longer delays and more collisions. A rate-based flow control can smooth such burstiness by controlling the time interval between consecutive packets. Therefore, the Ad Hoc Transport Protocol (ATP) [38] proposes using a rate-based flow control to replace the window-based congestion control to reduce the MAC contention degree caused by packet bursts.

10.2.5 Decoupling of Reliability and Congestion Control

As mentioned earlier, in TCP, transmission reliability control and congestion control are coupled in such a way that congestion status is inferred based on the reception of ACK segments that are used for reliability control. Thus the frequency of ACK segments to be sent by the destination node affects the setting of the congestion control window at the source node. That is, the faster ACKs are sent, the larger the congestion window will be set, resulting in more data segments to be injected into the network by the source node. However, more ACKs from destination to source will intensify the MAC contention of wireless channels, which degrades the packet forwarding performance from source to destination, as mentioned above. Therefore, one solution to this problem is to just decouple congestion control from transmission reliability control. In this case, some other schemes have to be designed to infer the congestion status in the network. For example, TCP Westwood [39] and TCP Westwood+ [40] as well as TCP-Jersey [41] try to infer a TCP segment loss by monitoring the TCP segment rate acknowledged by ACKs.

Note that, although the reliability control function and congestion control function are decoupled with this proposal, they are still part of TCP. That is, in this case, the congestion control is still performed in the transport layer by inferring the congestion status in the network, even if the methods are different from the original one. This is significantly different from the Semi-TCP approach to be discussed in Sect. 10.4.

10.2.6 Hop-by-Hop Congestion Control

The hop-by-hop congestion control approach was originally proposed to achieve high performance in wired networks due to its fast and accurate reaction to the congestion status in the network. However, its implementation is complex, since every node along a path, i.e., the source node, routers, or switches as well as the destination node, must be involved in this type of control. Thus it is seldom deployed in practice. However, with MAC protocols installed in a shared-media wireless network, a node may have to detect activities of other nodes in the vicinity, and the nodes may even have to interact with each other. Some mechanisms for information capture and exchange between neighbors have been already implemented in wireless networks, for example, the RTS/CTS handshake protocol used by the IEEE 802.11 distributed coordination function (DCF) [42]. In this case, it can be relatively easy to implement a hop-by-hop congestion control with piggyback mechanisms without a big increase in system complexity.

There are also some cross-layer designed hop-by-hop congestion control schemes such as [16, 19, 43]. The proposal in [19] tries to distinguish between packet losses caused by radio link failure and those by congestion according to the information obtained from MAC and routing protocols. The schemes reported in [16, 43] try to provide congestion control by combining hop-by-hop and end-to-end congestion controls. An available bit rate (ABR)-like explicit rate-based control is proposed in [43], while [16] develops and formulates a congestion control scheme by considering MAC constraints in terms of channel access time in wireless ad hoc networks.

10.3 TCP over Optical Networks

Currently, most studies of TCP over optical networks primarily focus on optical burst switching (OBS) networks [44]. Thus this section first discusses TCP over OBS and then TCP over hybrid networks consisting of OBS and other types of networks.

10.3.1 TCP over Optical Burst Switching Networks

One of the earliest references addressing TCP performance over OBS is [45], which finds that deflection routing can significantly improve TCP throughput, but the congestion of the deflection route may greatly affect this improvement. Reference [46] points out analytically that a large number of wavelengths are needed for OBS networks to efficiently transport TCP traffic, since a wavelength is a light path that is independent of other paths using different wavelengths.

An important factor that affects TCP performance is burst losses caused by congestion within OBS networks. However, nodes inside the OBS network cannot handle this issue due to their limited photonic computing and buffering capabilities. So reference [47] proposes a burst retransmission scheme in the OBS layer, in which the ingress and egress nodes of the OBS network retransmit bursts lost inside the network. However, this scheme does not handle congestion control problems inside the OBS network. Therefore, a congestion control function is further added in the OBS layer in addition to the burst retransmission as proposed in [48].

Due to contention resolution and avoidance schemes used in OBS networks, the delivery of some bursts may be delayed, resulting in changes in their arrival sequence. Out-of-order bursts may cause all related TCP source nodes to halve their congestion control windows, resulting in low network throughput. Therefore, reference [49] discusses how to quantify the impact of burst reordering on TCP throughput, and an optical burst reordering model is also developed in [50]. A source-ordering mechanism is proposed to greatly improve TCP throughput in [51]. Similar to wireless networks, the burstiness of burst arrivals also greatly impacts the performance of TCP in OBS networks, since the same light path may contend for the same optical carrier at the same node. Therefore, a pacing mechanism with intentional delay is proposed in [52] to smooth transmission bursts, which can greatly improve TCP performance even with small buffers.

10.3.2 TCP over Hybrid Networks

For a hybrid network consisting of OBS and other types of networks, a possible solution for TCP over this hybrid network is the Split-TCP, which splits an end-to-end TCP connection into several segments, each of which can perform more efficiently than the end-to-end TCP. Such a scheme was proposed in [53, 54] for OBS networks. However, this scheme does not follow well the end-to-end semantic of the conventional TCP and requires the OBS edge nodes to possess powerful computing and buffering capabilities, resulting in an increased complexity of edge nodes. Therefore, a Semi-Split-TCP was proposed in [55] to handle this problem. The basic idea of this enhancement is to use agents at the OBS network edge to hook TCP packets from the network layer and acknowledge the TCP source node with a spoofed ACK.

10.4 Semi-TCP

As discussed above and especially analyzed in Chaps. 7, 8 and 9, hop-by-hop congestion control is much more efficient than end-to-end congestion control. Particularly in shared-media networks, the complexity of implementing a hop-by-hop congestion control is low, since this control can be realized through a piggyback on

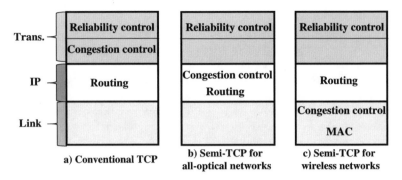

Fig. 10.3 Possible displacement of congestion control function with Semi-TCP

implemented MAC protocols. Since in this case, congestion control is implemented below the transport layer, i.e., either in the network layer (i.e., IP here) or data link layer as illustrated in Fig. 10.3, the same function of the conventional TCP becomes redundant and can be removed from it. At the same time, only the transmission reliability control is retained in the transport layer to guarantee the end-to-end transmission reliability. This kind of TCP is called Semi-TCP. With Semi-TCP, no congestion control window is used to regulate packet sending in the transport layer at the source node, so the impact of the round-trip time on end-to-end throughput is small.

10.4.1 Major Features of Semi-TCP

Decoupling the congestion control function from TCP and shifting it down to lower layers can provide the following benefits: (i) improved congestion control efficiency with more accurate judgement on and faster action to congestion status in the network, and (ii) elimination of the impact of the correlation between the congestion control window and the number of TCP ACKs sent by the destination mentioned earlier on end-to-end throughput. Each of these benefits is discussed in detail below.

10.4.1.1 Accurate and Fast Reaction to Congestion

As discussed in Sect. 10.2.1, TCP often makes wrong judgements on congestion status in multi-hop wireless networks. This causes the source node to unnecessarily decrease its congestion control window, resulting in reduced network throughput. On the other hand, TCP's slow reaction to ongoing congestion, especially in the case of long round-trip times (RTTs), wastes network bandwidth, as discussed below.

Once a congestion occurs, wherever it is, a minimum reaction time, i.e., the time interval between when a congestion occurs to when a correction action arrives at the congested node, is at least one RTT over the TCP connection. The reason is that the source node infers the congestion status in a network based on the reception of ACKs sent by the destination node, as mentioned earlier. Similarly, it will take at least another RTT for the source node to learn whether a congestion state has been released, and more time will be used by the source node to restore its normal congestion control window due to the slow start mechanism adopted by TCP.

Note that there are some proposals that suggest decoupling the congestion control and the transmission reliability control of TCP, as discussed in Sect. 10.2.5. But this is not sufficient since they do not change the fact that the transport layer does not have enough instant information on the congestion status in the network and cannot react rapidly to an ongoing congestion. Decoupling congestion control from TCP and shifting it down to lower layers can solve these problems completely, since the lower layers can know exactly what is happening in the network and react to a congestion status immediately.

10.4.1.2 More Space for Further Performance Improvement

As mentioned earlier, TCP applies the congestion control window to control the amount of traffic to be injected to the network layer based on the reception of ACKs that are returned by the destination node. In this case, the RTT between source and destination greatly affects TCP throughput. The RTT mainly includes packet queueing delay, transmission time, and propagation delay, and increases with the path length. According to [56], in the wired-line network, the maximum sending rate for a TCP connection over a single cycle of the steady-state model is bounded by

$$\bar{\lambda} \leq \frac{1.5 L_{\max}}{R} \sqrt{\frac{2}{3p}}, \tag{10.1}$$

where R is the minimum RTT, p is the steady-state link dropping rate, and $L_{\max}$ is the maximum TCP segment size.

For a TCP connection consisting of n links, each of which has an RTT of τ with a packet dropping rate of p, R can be estimated by $n\tau$, and the probability for a packet to reach the destination node is given by $(1 - p)^n$. Then with inequality (10.1), the goodput is bounded by

$$\bar{\mu} \leq \frac{L_{\max}}{n\tau} \sqrt{\frac{3}{2p}} (1 - p)^n, \tag{10.2}$$

which indicates that the goodput decreases rapidly with n, especially in the case of large p. This is because in this case n is the dominant factor that affects the goodput. This phenomenon is depicted in Fig. 10.4 based on the calculation with inequality (10.2), and has also been observed empirically as reported in the literature, e.g., [57].

10.4.2 Semi-TCP for Multi-Hop Wireless Networks

Since a MAC protocol has to be installed in the data link layer in a shared-media wireless network, it is reasonable to exploit the MAC protocol to provide a hop-

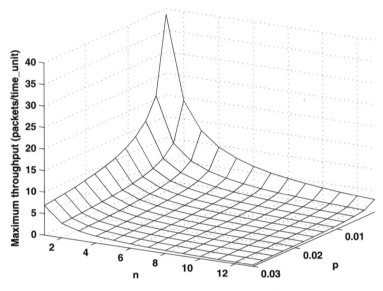

Fig. 10.4 Maximum throughput of TCP in packets/time unit (here $\frac{L_{\max}}{\tau} = 1$) versus p and n

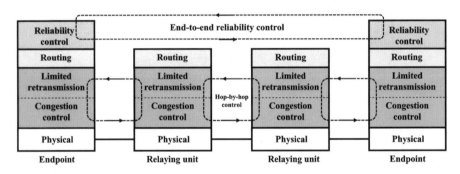

Fig. 10.5 Function stack of Semi-TCP for multi-hop wireless networks

by-hop congestion control. In this case, the decoupled congestion control function should be shifted to the data link layer in order to be performed hop by hop as illustrated in Fig. 10.5. Actually, this Semi-TCP is an instance of the ETE+HBH approach discussed in Chap. 7. In this case, the upstream node can take an action on the congestion occurring at its downstream node in a link RTT rather than an end-to-end RTT with TCP.

Take the IEEE 802.11 DCF [42] as an example. Due to the hidden terminal problem, an RTS/CTS handshake protocol has been adopted and standardized. Basically, the RTS/CTS protocol asks a node to send an RTS packet first to the receiver, which will send back a CTS if it is clear to receive. It is not difficult to find that this RTS/CTS exchange can be slightly modified by including congestion information at the receiver so that a hop-by-hop congestion control can be realized. Actually, this is just the basic idea of the hop-by-hop congestion control scheme discussed in [58], and IEEE 802.11s also tries to consolidate this function into the standard under discussion [17].

There are also some hop-by-hop congestion control schemes implemented in the data link layer such as [15], which changes MAC parameters such as CWmin and CWmax of IEEE 802.11e to carry congestion control information. In [18], an implicit hop-by-hop congestion control is discussed, in which the information on congestion status and control is obtained by observing transmission activities of its neighboring nodes rather than through explicit information exchange between them. With a hop-by-hop congestion control, the congestion control efficiency will not rely on route availability. Thus, Semi-TCP is more suitable than TCP in highly mobile networks such as opportunistic networks, since it is difficult to maintain route connectivity in these kinds of networks.

10.4.3 Semi-TCP for All-Optical Networks

Unlike wireless networks, the all-optical network is not a shared-media network, and the all-optical node has poor buffering and processing capabilities. Thus it is impossible for all-optical nodes to provide hop-by-hop congestion control. In this case, congestion control needs to be shifted to the network layer rather than the data link layer. For the same reason, sophisticated networking functions should be shifted from all-optical nodes to network edges as much as possible.

As mentioned in Chap. 7, the Internet is usually divided into domains, which can be considered as the basic building block of all-optical networks. A domain consists of ingress and egress nodes as well as intermediate all-optical nodes located inside the domain. Both ingress and egress nodes are assumed to have powerful electronic computing and buffering capabilities. Therefore with Semi-TCP as illustrated in Fig. 10.6, a TCP-like congestion control scheme is used to control congestion across a domain with domain ingress and egress nodes acting as virtual endpoints of the TCP connection. In this case, all-optical nodes inside a domain are not involved in congestion control. But a limited number of retransmissions can be carried out by ingress and egress nodes of a domain to recover packets lost in this domain as much as possible. However, the end-to-end transmission reliability between the source and destination nodes is ultimately assured by the end-to-end reliability control performed by source and destination with an unlimited number of retransmissions. Actually, this Semi-TCP is an instance of the ETE+DBD approach discussed in Chap. 7, and a simulation study of this Semi-TCP can be found in [59].

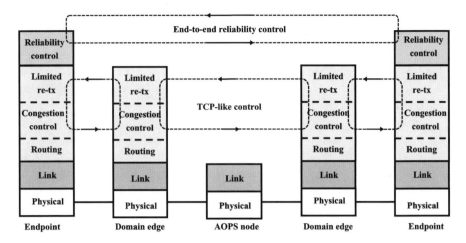

Fig. 10.6 Function stack of Semi-TCP for all-optical networks

10.4.4 Interoperability of Semi-TCP with TCP

With Semi-TCP, the transport layer primarily focuses on the end-to-end transmission reliability control, and the congestion control is shifted to either the network layer or data link layer. Actually, the initial TCP also only provided transmission reliability control without any congestion control. A big issue raised by Semi-TCP is its interoperability with conventional TCP. To trade off between interoperability and complexity as well as performance, the implementation of Semi-TCP can be either implicit or explicit.

With an explicit implementation, the original TCP is reimplemented by removing the congestion control function along with the congestion window as well as simplifying the ACK mechanism to reduce the number of ACKs sent on the reverse route. In this case, the interconnection with the conventional TCP can follow the Split-TCP mode [60]; that is, at the border between the conventional TCP and Semi-TCP networks, a gateway is implemented for necessary conversion between them.

An implicit implementation tries to keep the implemented TCP intact by adding a sublayer between the transport layer and the lower layer. This sublayer tries to animate TCP ACK behavior at the source node so that TCP can adjust its congestion control window as usual according to spoofed TCP ACKs. This is similar to the Semi-Split TCP [55] mentioned earlier. This implementation can provide a good interoperability with TCP but at the expense of high system complexity and possible performance inefficiency, because some components of conventional TCP such as the congestion control window and ACK scheme will limit the performance improvement offered by the congestion control scheme implemented in lower layers.

10.5 Conclusion

The congestion control implemented in lower layers is much more efficient than the end-to-end control of conventional TCP because it is able to overcome the mis-judgement on congestion status and slow actions to the congestion status in the network, Thus, the Semi-TCP approach is discussed in this chapter. It decouples the congestion control function from TCP and shifts this function to either the network layer or data link layer. Compared with many other proposals that only modify TCP, Semi-TCP may not be the best solution in terms of end-to-end interoperability with conventional TCP. However, since TCP faces many problems in multi-hop wireless networks, while the hop-by-hop congestion control can be easily implemented in wireless networks, it is worth exploiting Semi-TCP to achieve higher performance. For all-optical networks, Semi-TCP can also help handle the problem caused by the poor optical buffering capability of all-optical nodes for congestion control.

References

1. Clark, D.: The design philosophy of the DARPA Internet protocols. In: SIGCOMM '88: Symposium Proceedings on Communications Architectures and Protocols, pp. 106–114 (1988)
2. Fu, Z., Zerfos, P., Luo, H., Lu, S.W., Zhang, L.X., Gerla, M.: The impact of multihop wireless channel on TCP throughput and loss. IEEE Trans. Mob. Comput. **4**(2), 209–221 (2005)
3. Kawadia, V., Kumar, P.R.: Experimental investigations into TCP performance over wireless multihop networks. In: Proc. 2005 ACM SIGCOMM Workshop on Experimental Approaches to Wireless Network Design and Analysis, New York, USA, pp. 29–34 (2005)
4. Balakrishnan, H., Sehan, S., Katz, R.H.: Improving reliable transport and handoff performance in cellular wireless networks. Wirel. Netw. **1**(4), 469–481 (1995)
5. Vangala, S., Mehta, M.: The TCP SACK-aware-snoop protocol for TCP over wireless networks. In: Proc. IEEE Veh. Tech. Conf. (VTC) – Fall, Orlando, FL, USA, vol. 4, pp. 2624–2628 (2003)
6. Sun, F.L., Li, V.O.K., Liew, S.C.: Design of SNACK mechanism for wireless TCP with new snoop. In: Proc. IEEE Wireless Commun. & Networking Conf. (WCNC), Atlanta, Georgia, USA, vol. 5, pp. 1046–1051 (2004)
7. Floyd, S.: TCP and explicit congestion notification. Comput. Commun. Rev. **24**(5), 10–23 (1994)
8. Ramakrishnan, K., Floyd, S.: A proposal to add explicit congestion notification (ECN) to IP. IETF RFC 2481 (1999)
9. Tsaoussidis, V., Badr, H.: TCP-probing: towards an error control scheme with energy and throughput performance gains. In: Proc. IEEE Int. Conf. Net. Protocols (ICNP), Osaka, Japan, pp. 12–21 (2000)
10. Gerla, M., Sanadidi, M.Y., Wang, R., Zanella, A., Casetti, C., Mascolo, S.: TCP Westwood: congestion window control using bandwidth estimation. In: Proc. IEEE Global Tele. Conf. (GLOBOCOM), San Antonio, TX, USA, vol. 3, pp. 1698–1702 (2001)
11. Chlamtac, I., Conti, M., Liu, J.: Mobile ad hoc networking: imperatives and challenges. Ad Hoc Netw. **1**(1), 13–64 (2003)
12. Hanbali, A.A., Altman, E., Nain, P.: A survey of TCP over ad hoc networks. IEEE Commun. Surv. Tutor. **7**(3), 22–36 (2005)
13. Leung, K.C., Li, V.O.K.: Transmission control protocol (TCP) in wireless networks: issues, approaches, and challenges. IEEE Commun. Surv. Tutor. **8**(4), 64–79 (2006)
14. Sardar, B., Saha, D.: Survey of TCP enhancements for last-hop wireless networks. IEEE Commun. Surv. Tutor. **8**(3), 20–34 (2006)

15. Sadeghi, B., Yamdad, A., Fujiwara, A., Yang, L.: A simple and efficient hop-by-hop congestion control protocol for wireless mesh networks. In: Proc. Annual Int. Wireless Internet Conf. (WICON), Boston, USA (2006)

16. Yi, Y., Shakkottai, S.: Hop-by-hop congestion control over a wireless multi-hop network. IEEE/ACM Trans. Netw. **15**(1), 133–144 (2007)

17. Camp, J.D., Knightly, E.W.: The IEEE 802.11s extended service set mesh networking standard (2007). http://networks.rice.edu/papers/mesh80211s.pdf

18. Scheuermann, B., Locherta, C., Mauve, M.: Implicit hop-by-hop congestion control in wireless multihop networks. Ad Hoc Netw. **6**, 260–288 (2008)

19. Wang, X.Y., Perkins, D.: Cross-layer hop-by-hop congestion control in mobile ad hoc networks. In: Proc. IEEE Wireless Commun. & Networking Conf. (WCNC), Las Vegas, USA (2008)

20. Gladisch, A., Braun, R.P., Breuer, D., Ehrhardt, A., Foisel, H.M., Jaeger, M., Leppla, R., Schneiders, M., Vorbeck, S., Weiershausen, W., Westphal, F.J.: Evolution of terrestrial optical system and core network architecture. Proc. IEEE **94**(5), 869–891 (2006)

21. Menth, M., Martin, R., Charzinski, J.: Capacity overprovisioning for networks with resilience requirements. In: Proc. ACM SIGCOMM, Pisa, Italy (2006)

22. Chandran, K., Raghunathan, S., Venkatesan, S., Prakash, R.: A feedback-based scheme for improving TCP performance in ad hoc wireless networks. IEEE Pers. Commun. Mag. **8**(1), 34–39 (2001)

23. Holland, S.G., Vaidya, N.: Analysis of TCP performance on mobile ad hoc network on wireless. Wirel. Netw. **8**(2–3), 275–288 (2002)

24. Kim, D., Toh, C., Choi, Y.: TCP-BuS: improving TCP performance in wireless ad hoc networks. J. Commun. Netw. **3**(2), 175–186 (2001)

25. Liu, J., Singh, S.: ATCP: TCP for mobile ad hoc networks. IEEE J. Sel. Areas Commun. **19**(7), 1300–1315 (2001)

26. Akyildiz, I.F., Morabito, G., Palazzo, S.: TCP-peach: a new congestion control scheme for satellite IP networks. IEEE/ACM Trans. Netw. **9**(3), 307–321 (2001)

27. Akyildiz, I.F., Zhang, X., Fang, J.: TCP-peach+: enhancement of TCP-peach for satellite IP networks. IEEE Commun. Lett. **6**(7), 303–305 (2002)

28. Lahanas, A., Tsaoussidis, V.: Improving TCP performance over networks with wireless components using probing devices. Int. J. Commun. Syst. **15**(6), 495–511 (2002)

29. Dyer, T., Boppana, R.: A comparison of TCP performance over three routing protocols for mobile ad hoc networks. In: Proc. ACM Int. Symp. Mobile Ad Hoc Networking and Computing (MobiHoc), Long Beach, CA, USA, pp. 56–66 (2001)

30. Wang, F., Zhang, Y.: Improving TCP performance over mobile ad hoc networks with out-of-order detection and response. In: Proc. ACM Int. Symp. Mobile Ad Hoc Networking and Computing (MobiHoc), Lausanne, Switzerland, pp. 217–225 (2002)

31. Fu, C.P., Liew, S.C.: TCP Veno: TCP enhancement for transmission over wireless access networks. IEEE J. Sel. Areas Commun. **21**(2), 216–228 (2003)

32. Wu, E.H.K., Chen, M.Z.: TJTCP: jitter-based TCP for heterogeneous wireless networks. IEEE J. Sel. Areas Commun. **22**(4), 757–766 (2004)

33. Bhandarkar, S., Sadry, N.E., Reddy, A.L.N., Vaidya, N.H.: TCP-DCR: a novel protocol for tolerating wireless channel errors. IEEE Trans. Mob. Comput. **4**(5), 517–529 (2005)

34. ElRakabawy, S.M., Alexander, K., Christoph, L.: TCP with adaptive pacing for multihop wireless networks. In: Proc. ACM Int. Symp. Mobile Ad Hoc Networking and Computing (MobiHoc), New York, NY, USA, pp. 288–299 (2005)

35. Altman, E., Jimenez, T.: Novel delayed ACK techniques for improving TCP performance in multihop wireless networks. In: Proc. IEEE Int. Conf. on Personal Wireless Comm., Venice, Italy, pp. 237–242 (2003)

36. Singh, A.K., Kankipati, K.: DTCP-ADA: TCP with adaptive delayed acknowledgement for mobile ad hoc networks. In: Proc. IEEE Wireless Commun. & Networking Conf. (WCNC), Atlanta, Georgia, USA, vol. 3, pp. 1685–1690 (2004)

37. Cordeiro, C., Das, S., Agrawal, D.: COPAS: dynamic contention-balancing to enhance the performance of TCP over multi-hop wireless networks, Miami, USA, pp. 382–387 (2003)

38. Sundaresan, K., Anantharaman, V., Hsieh, H.Y., Sivakumar, R.: ATP: a reliable transport protocol for ad hoc networks. IEEE Trans. Mob. Comput. **4**(6), 588–603 (2005)
39. Casetti, C., Gerla, M., Mascolo, S., Sanadidi, M.Y., Wang, R.: TCP Westwood: end-to-end congestion control for wired/wireless networks. Wirel. Netw. **8**(5), 467–479 (2002)
40. Mascolo, S., Grieco, L.A., Ferorelli, R., Camarda, P., Piscitelli, G.: Performance evaluation of Westwood+ TCP congestion control. Perform. Eval. **55**(1–2), 93–111 (2004)
41. Xu, K., Tian, Y., Ansari, N.: TCP-Jersey for wireless IP communications. IEEE J. Sel. Areas Commun. **22**(4), 747–756 (2004)
42. IEEE Std 802.11: Medium Access Control (MAC) Sub Layer and 3 Physical Layer Specifications (1997)
43. Chen, K., Nahrstedt, K., Vaidya, N.: The utility of explicit rate-based flow control in mobile ad hoc networks. In: Proc. IEEE Wireless Commun. & Networking Conf. (WCNC), Atlanta, Georgia, USA, vol. 3, pp. 1921–1926 (2004)
44. Qiao, Q.M., Yeo, M.: Optical burst switching (OBS) – a new paradigm for an optical Internet. J. High Speed Netw. **8**(1), 69–84 (1999)
45. He, J.Y., Gary Chan, S.H.: TCP and UDP performance for Internet over optical packet-switched networks. In: Proc. IEEE Int. Conf. Commun. (ICC), Anchorage, Alaska, USA, vol. 1, pp. 1350–1354 (2003)
46. Cameron, C., Vu, H.L., Choi, J., Bilgrami, S., Zukerman, M., Kang, M.H.: TCP over OBS – fixed-point load and loss. Opt. Express **13**(23), 9167–9174 (2005)
47. Zhang, Q., Vokkarane, V.M., Wang, Y., Jue, J.P.: Analysis of TCP over optical burst-switched networks with burst retransmission. In: Proc. IEEE Global Tele. Conf. (GLOBOCOM), Missouri, USA, vol. 4, pp. 1978–1983 (2005)
48. Luo, J.T., Huang, J., Chang, H., Qiu, S.F., Guo, X.J., Zhang, Z.Z.: ROBS: A novel architecture of Reliable Optical Burst Switching with congestion control. J. High Speed Netw. **16**(2), 123–131 (2007)
49. Perelló, J., Gunreben, S., Spadaro, S.: A quantitative evaluation of reordering in OBS networks and its impact on TCP performance. In: Proc. Int. Conf. Optical Network Design and Modeling, Vilanova i la Geltru, Spain, pp. 1–6 (2008)
50. Gunreben, S.: An optical burst reordering model for time-based and random selection assembly strategies. Perform. Eval. **68**(3), 237–255 (2010)
51. Komatireddy, B., Charbonneau, N., Vokkarane, V.M.: Source-ordering for improved TCP performance over load-balanced optical burst-switched (OBS) networks. Photonic Netw. Commun. **19**(1), 1–8 (2010)
52. Cai, Y., Wolf, T., Gong, W.B.: Delaying transmissions in data communication networks to improve transport-layer performance. IEEE J. Sel. Areas Commun. **29**(5), 916–927 (2011)
53. Padmanabhan, D., Bikram, R., Vokkarane, V.M.: TCP over optical burst switching (OBS): to split or not to split? In: Proc. IEEE Conf. Comp. Commun. Net. (ICCCN), St. Thomas, US Virgin Islands, pp. 1–6 (2008)
54. Bikram, R.R.C., Vokkarane, V.M.: TCP over optical burst switching: to split or not to split? J. Lightwave Technol. **27**(22), 5208–5219 (2009)
55. Xie, F., Jiang, N., Ho, Y.H., Hua, K.A.: Semi-split TCP: maintaining end-to-end semantics for split TCP. In: Proc. IEEE Conf. Local Computer Net. (LCN), Dublin, Ireland, pp. 301–314 (2007)
56. Floyd, S., Fall, K.: Promoting the use of end-to-end congestion control. IEEE/ACM Trans. Netw. **7**(4), 458–472 (1999)
57. Xu, S., Saadawi, T.: Does the IEEE 802.11 MAC protocol work well in multihop wireless ad hoc networks? IEEE Commun. Mag. **39**(4), 130–137 (2001)
58. Zhai, H.Q., Wang, J.F., Fang, Y.G.: Distributed packet scheduling for multihop flows in ad hoc networks. In: Proc. IEEE Wireless Commun. & Networking Conf. (WCNC), Atlanta, Georgia, USA, vol. 2, pp. 1081–1086 (2004)
59. Guo, B.Y., C Mao, H., Jiang, S.M., Guan, Q.S., Deng, X.F.: Domain-by-domain implementation of semi-TCP in all-optical networks. Jinan, China (2011)
60. Bakre, A., Badrinath, B.R.: I-TCP: indirect TCP for mobile hosts. In: Proc. IEEE Int. Conf. Dist. Computing Systems, Vancouver, British Columbia, Canada, pp. 136–143 (1995)

Chapter 11
Enabling Simultaneous MAC Transmission with MIMO: Logical MIMO

Abstract The multiple-input-multiple-output (MIMO) antenna technology has been extensively applied in the physical layer to improve transmission bit rates of individual terminals. This is due to MIMO's support of simultaneous transmissions at the same frequency. However, it is difficult to implement multiple antennas at a small-sized terminal, yet it is essential to realize MIMO. Although virtual MIMO solves this problem, it requires inter-node cooperative communication, which has to be addressed carefully. This chapter discusses how to use MIMO in the data link layer to enable medium access control (MAC) to provide simultaneous transmissions at the same frequency from different nodes. This kind of MIMO aims at improving network throughput rather than the transmission bit rates of individual nodes. Furthermore, it requires neither multiple antennas installed per terminal nor inter-node cooperative communication, resulting in an easier implementation. This chapter analyzes the MAC schemes based on the above three types of MIMO for uplink sharing in centralized wireless networks.

11.1 Introduction

The multiple-input-multiple-output (MIMO) antenna technology has proved capable of greatly improving radio channel capacity. Spatial diversities allow signals transmitted simultaneously from multiple transmit antennas at the same frequency to be successfully decoded if the same number or more of receive antennas are installed at the receiver. However, it is difficult to implement MIMO at a small-sized terminal due to many issues, which mainly include the limited number of antennas that can be installed at the transmitter and receiver, the availability of channel state information (CSI), and the spatial diversities of signal propagation paths.

Traditionally, MIMO has been extensively applied in the physical layer to increase transmission bit rates [1–3]. This increase is almost proportional to the number of antennas installed at the transmitter and receiver. Henceforth, this type of MIMO is called physical MIMO (phyMIMO) in our discussion. However, it is difficult to install an antenna array in a compact terminal to realize phyMIMO since theoretically the dimension of an antenna must be at least half of a wavelength. It is also difficult to have sufficient spatial diversities with a highly dense antenna array. Thus virtual MIMO (virMIMO) was proposed [4], which uses multiple one-antenna terminals to form a cooperative communication group [5]. In this case, a sending node distributes a transmission task to the group members, each of which then functions as one antenna to form a transmit antenna array as required by phyMIMO to transmit its assignment simultaneously at the same frequency. Although virMIMO avoids the necessity of installing multiple antennas in a compact terminal, the issue of realizing inter-node cooperative communication must be addressed carefully [6].

Actually, both phyMIMO and virMIMO share a similarity in terms of improving the communication capabilities of individual terminals by increasing the per-terminal transmission bit rate. However, as mentioned earlier, a wireless network is a shared-media network, in which a medium access control (MAC) protocol is needed to arbitrate terminals to share communication media. In many cases, except with the code division multiple access (CDMA) technology, only one transmission at one frequency is allowed at one time since concurrent transmissions may collide at the same receiver, causing transmission failure. Thus at one time, only one terminal in the network can transmit at its transmission bit rate; the other terminals have to wait at least until the currently transmitting terminal has completed its transmission or released the occupied channel. This MAC overhead may severely impact the overall network throughput.

Section 11.2 discusses how to exploit MIMO to enable MAC to provide simultaneous transmissions at the same frequency from different one-antenna terminals in order to shorten the MAC overhead. This MIMO is called logical MIMO (logMIMO). A comparison of logMIMO, phyMIMO, and virMIMO is conducted in Sect. 11.3, along with a brief survey of related works. A performance analysis of the phyMIMO- and logMIMO-based MAC schemes is given in Sect. 11.4, and the chapter is summarized in Sect. 11.5.

11.2 Logical MIMO

The principle of MIMO with an $\mathbf{m} \times \mathbf{m}$ transmit-receive antenna array can be mathematically described by

$$\mathbf{r} = \mathbb{H}\mathbf{s} + \mathbb{N}, \tag{11.1}$$

where $\mathbf{r}$, $\mathbf{s}$, and $\mathbb{N}$ are an $\mathbf{m}$-dimension vector, respectively indicating the received signal, source signal, and noise. Here $\mathbb{H}$ is an $\mathbf{m} \times \mathbf{m}$ matrix representing the channel state information (CSI) [1]. The source signal vector $\mathbf{s}$ to be decoded by the receiver is just a set of solutions to this equation array if $\mathbb{H}$ and $\mathbb{N}$ are known. This is why MIMO can support simultaneous transmissions at the same frequency without using beamforming or space division with directional antennas.

Logical MIMO (logMIMO) suggests exploiting the above MIMO capability to provide MAC simultaneous transmissions for uplink sharing in a centralized wireless network such as cellular networks. That is, a common uplink channel can be used by a number of terminals up to $\mathbf{m}$ to send data simultaneously, where $\mathbf{m}$ is the number of antennas installed at the receiver. In a centralized network, a central unit like an access point (AP) in wireless local area networks (WLANs) or a base station

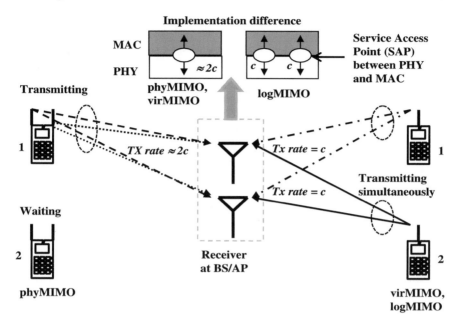

Fig. 11.1 Uplink sharing with 2 × 2 antennas for phyMIMO, virMIMO, and logMIMO (PHY = physical layer)

in wireless cellular networks is used to coordinate communication as illustrated in Fig. 11.1, where c denotes the transmission bit rate of a single-input-single-output (SISO) channel. In this kind of network, the uplink channel from the terminals to the central unit is shared by the terminals covered by the central unit, and the downlink channel from the central unit to the terminals is fully controlled by the central unit.

It is relatively easy to implement multiple antennas at the central unit, which can also coordinate the uplink sharing. To this end, a terminal needs to submit a request first to the central unit to apply for channel access. Upon receiving a request from a terminal, the central unit grants the request if there is a free data slot access available, and notifies the requesting terminals of the allocation result through the downlink channel. This procedure can also allow the central unit to learn in advance the number of simultaneous senders in order to decode the received signal with MIMO.

For the implementation, the uplink channel needs to be divided into a request channel and a data channel as illustrated in Fig. 11.2. The request channel is used by the terminals to submit requests for using the data channel to transmit to the central unit. The data channel is further divided into slots. Similarly, the downlink channel is divided into a broadcast channel and a data channel. The former is used by the central unit to notify the requesting terminals of the allocation result, while the latter is used by the central unit to transmit to terminals.

Since it is difficult for the central unit to learn in advance how many terminals are going to contend for the request channel for request submission, only one transmission is allowed to use the request channel at one time. Thus the request channel

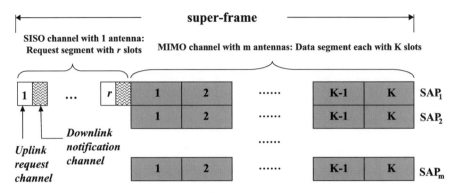

Fig. 11.2 Super-frame structure for the logical MIMO

is still a SISO channel and cannot allow simultaneous transmissions at the same frequency from multiple terminals. In this case, a contention-based MAC such as ALOHA or carrier sensing multiple access (CSMA) should be used to control access to the request channel.

The request submitted by a terminal to the central unit for a data slot allocated for the transmission in the uplink channel can be made either with or without a reservation. Without a reservation, only one slot is allocated per request; with a reservation, a slot per frame is reserved periodically until the terminal releases the reservation. For both types of requests, we assume that a requesting terminal can know the result of its request almost immediately by arranging the downlink notification channel to immediately follow the uplink request channel.

11.3 Typical MIMO-Based MAC Schemes

This section first makes a comparison among three MIMO-based MAC schemes and then conducts a brief survey of some related works.

11.3.1 Comparison of Three MIMO-Based MAC Schemes

Table 11.1 summarizes the major characteristics of MAC schemes based on phyMIMO, virMIMO, and logMIMO; more detailed discussions are given below.

The major advantage of the phyMIMO MAC is its high per-terminal transmission bit rate, which is roughly proportional to the number of receive antennas ($\mathbf{m}$) if the number of transmit antennas is not smaller than $\mathbf{m}$ as depicted in Fig. 11.1. However, this kind of MAC allows only one terminal to transmit at this high rate at one time; other terminals have to wait until the occupied channel is released, resulting in a longer MAC overhead. This kind of MAC also requires that at least $\mathbf{m}$ antennas be implemented in the transmitting terminal like compact mobile terminals.

Table 11.1 Comparison of phyMIMO, virMIMO, and logMIMO for MAC schemes

Attributes (per node)	phyMIMO	virMIMO	logMIMO
Number of receive antennas	**m**	**m**	**m**
Number of transmit antennas	**m**	1	1
Transmission bit rate	$\approx \mathbf{m}c$	c	c
Concurrent transmissions per slot	1	**m**	**m**
MAC overhead	large	small	small
Inter-node cooperation	no	yes	no
Power control	no	yes	yes
MAC awareness of MIMO	no	no	yes
Spatial diversity	small	large	large
Implementation complexity	high	medium	low

m = number of antennas or cooperative one-antenna terminals

Both the virMIMO and logMIMO MAC schemes offer only a lower transmission bit rate, which is equal to the rate of a SISO channel as indicated in Fig. 11.1, i.e., c. However, both schemes require only one antenna per transmitting terminal, and **m** one-antenna terminals can transmit to the central unit simultaneously at the same frequency, resulting in a smaller MAC overhead and a lower terminal complexity. Furthermore, for both, the distance between transmit antennas is actually the distance between terminals, which is usually spaciously distributed. Thus this inter-antenna distance is much longer than that at the phyMIMO terminal, where antennas are compacted. This factor leads to different spatial diversities, which further influences the MIMO channel capacity, as will be discussed later. Unlike phyMIMO, with virMIMO and logMIMO, the signals received by the central unit come from different terminals, so power control at transmitting terminals is needed to avoid the capture effect at the central unit.

Apparently, logMIMO is identical to virMIMO in terms of their support of concurrent transmissions at the same frequency from multiple one-antenna terminals. But they are still basically different. First, their objectives are different, i.e., logMIMO aims at increasing per-terminal throughput by reducing the MAC overhead, while similar to phyMIMO, virMIMO tries to enhance the communication capability of an individual terminal through cooperative communication. Second, virMIMO requires inter-terminal cooperation, by which the transmission task of a sending terminal is distributed to other terminals in the group, which virtually functions as one antenna as used in phyMIMO. But logMIMO does not need such inter-terminal cooperation; thus logMIMO is simpler than virMIMO for the implementation at terminals. Third, the MAC layer of the central unit with virMIMO is not aware of the MIMO used by the lower layer, since the signals received from different one-antenna terminals are processed for the same destinations. This is similar to phyMIMO. With logMIMO, the signals received from multiple terminals correspond to different destinations, and accordingly the MAC layer needs to process signals from up to **m** terminals simultaneously. To this end, **m** service access points (SAPs) must be implemented between the MAC layer and the physical layer, each of which corresponds to one terminal as illustrated in Fig. 11.1.

11.3.2 Related Works

Similar to logMIMO, the space division multiple access (SDMA) scheme can also allow simultaneous transmissions from up to **m** one-antenna transmitting terminals [7]. But unlike logMIMO, SDMA is "on the ground of a node's physical location or spatial separation" [8], and usually must use beamforming with directional antennas [9, 10], which is not needed by logMIMO. A combination of MIMO and SDMA is also proposed in [11] to efficiently suppress successive group interference in the case of multiple antennas per transmitter. Another type of supporting simultaneous transmission from multiple one-antenna transmitting terminals is based on virMIMO, particularly used for small-sized wireless terminals such as a sensor, which is usually too small to implement multiple antennas therein to realize phyMIMO. Several virMIMO-based MAC schemes using cooperative communication have been proposed for the transmission from sensors to the sink, such as [12–14].

Many phyMIMO-based MAC schemes have been proposed for mobile ad hoc networks (MANETs) for different objectives. These schemes are different from those based on virMIMO and logMIMO since multiple antennas are necessarily implemented at both senders and receivers to realize phyMIMO. In [15], a method is proposed to use the knowledge of the MIMO arrays at different nodes to design a transmit-receive beamformer for the desired nodes while nulling other ongoing communication in order to save energy and achieve spatial reuse gain. Reference [16] proposes a MAC scheme to enable mutually interfering links to operate simultaneously. It uses multiple receive antennas to receive and differentiate the signals transmitted simultaneously from independent transmitters, but at the expense of a large amount of control information exchanged between neighboring nodes. A weighting method is proposed in [17] to form a beamformer as follows: each antenna transmits the same signal after applying its own weight to the signal while the received signals from all antennas are individually weighted and summed. The design and implementation of a MIMO MAC protocol are reported in [18].

Many cross-layer designed phyMIMO MAC schemes have also been proposed for MANETs. In [19], a MAC scheme was proposed using MIMO spatial multiplexing to solve the hidden terminal problem, using half of the transmit antennas for transmission and all of the receive antennas for receiving in order to differentiate flows transmitted simultaneously from the two independent nodes. In [20], space-time coding (STC) and MIMO techniques are employed jointly to solve the asymmetry in gain problem appearing in wireless networks using beamforming for broadcast. Reference [21] studies an RTS/CTS-based MAC scheme, which fully exploits the spatial diversity of MIMO to combat fading in mobile environments and characterizes the optimal hop distance for routing in MANETs. In [22], a MAC scheme is proposed to solve the hidden and exposed terminal problems caused by multiple antennas in MIMO-based orthogonal frequency division multiplexing (OFDM) ad hoc networks. Although the above-mentioned MIMO MAC schemes try to address some particular problems in MANETs, they are not designed to enable simultaneous MAC transmissions at the same frequency from multiple one-antenna terminals.

11.4 Analysis of MIMO-Based MAC for Uplink Sharing

This section analyzes the performance of MAC schemes based on phyMIMO and logMIMO with the following notation:

- l: size of the request packet in bits
- L: size of the data packet in bits
- r: number of request slots available per frame
- **K**: number of data slots available per frame
- c: transmission bit rate of a SISO channel
- C: transmission bit rate with MIMO
- f: frame duration in time
- **b**: backoff time, which is the time interval by which a terminal defers its MAC contention action
- s: maximum simultaneous transmissions allowed by a data slot in the MAC layer
- k: total number of data slots reserved by a request. In particular, $k = 1$ indicates a request just for one packet transmission without a reservation for future transmission, and $k > 1$ indicates a request with a reservation for a burst, with which the terminal can get a data slot from k frames periodically
- **m**: number of antennas installed at the receiver for phyMIMO or one-antenna terminals for virMIMO and logMIMO
- **n**: number of transmit antennas per terminal with phyMIMO or number of one-antenna terminals covered by one central unit with virMIMO and logMIMO
- v: mean packet arrival rate at a terminal without reservation ($k = 1$), or mean burst arrival rate with reservation ($k > 1$)
- **p**: MAC persistent probability for a terminal to continue its MAC contention
- λ: wavelength of transmission signal
- R: MIMO channel capacity in bps/Hz
- T: MAC overhead, which is the time interval between when a packet ($k = 1$) or burst ($k > 1$) arrives at a terminal and when the terminal starts to transmit it (see Fig. 11.4)
- G: network throughput, which here is defined as the number of packets successfully sent by all terminals covered by one central unit per time unit
- χ: fraction of time that the server is busy in a queueing system, which indicates the probability for a terminal to be active in MAC competition
- S: average MAC service time for a packet ($k = 1$) or burst ($k > 1$).

  The following assumptions are adopted in the analysis.

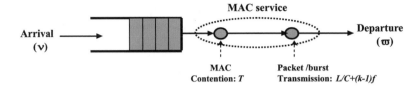

Fig. 11.3 A queueing model for MAC analysis

- **p**-persistent MAC contention policy: for either packet transmission or request submission, a terminal contends for the channel with probability **p**, and does not with probability $1 - \mathbf{p}$ in order to reduce collision. In the latter case, a terminal defers its MAC contention action by a random backoff time and then decides again whether to contend for the channel at the end of this period.
- Durable MAC behavior: once a terminal has data to transmit or a request to submit, it will contend for the channel with the above **p**-persistent policy until it succeeds.
- The transmission bit rate of each terminal covered by the same network is identical, i.e., c for the network with logMIMO and $\mathbb{C}_{phy}$ (see Sect. 12.2.1) for the network with phyMIMO.

The first assumption can cause packet transmission and request submission from different terminals to be almost uncorrelated to each other, which can simplify the analysis.

As mentioned earlier, the difference between the virMIMO and logMIMO MAC schemes mainly lies in their implementation and operation rather than their performance. Therefore, if the overhead for inter-terminal cooperative communication required by virMIMO can be ignored, the following result of the logMIMO MAC can be used to approximate that of the virMIMO MAC in terms of the overall network throughput. For more analysis of virMIMO, also refer to the relevant references such as [23, 24].

11.4.1 Analytical Model

A queueing system (illustrated in Fig. 11.3) is adopted here to analyze the MAC performance of a terminal using either phyMIMO or logMIMO. This system consists of an infinity buffer, which corresponds to the link layer buffer, and one server, which corresponds to the link transmitter. A client arriving at the queue can be either a single packet or a burst at a mean arrival rate of v. The MAC without a reservation is used to transmit a packet per request (i.e., $k = 1$), while the MAC with a reservation is used to transmit multiple packets (i.e., a burst) per request (i.e., $k > 1$). The server is further divided into two parts: MAC contention and packet transmission. Accordingly, the average MAC service time per packet (S) consists of the MAC overhead and transmission time of a packet with $k = 1$ or a burst with $k > 1$, i.e.,

$$S = \frac{L}{C} + (k - 1)f. \tag{11.2}$$

Therefore, the mean MAC service rate is given as follows:

$$\varpi = \frac{1}{T + \frac{L}{C} + (k - 1)f}. \tag{11.3}$$

Whether a terminal tries to contend for the channel depends on (i) the queue occupancy and (ii) the terminal's decision following the **p**-persistent MAC contention policy mentioned earlier. The former triggers a MAC contention process, while the latter decides when a terminal should contend again. The queue occupancy can be reflected by the probability for the queue not to be idle, which is measured by the fraction of time that the server is busy according to the queueing theory, i.e.,

$$\chi \triangleq \frac{\nu}{\varpi}$$

$$= \nu \left[T + \frac{L}{C} + (k - 1)f \right]. \tag{11.4}$$

In the case of a very heavy load, $\chi \geq 1$, which means that there are always packets awaiting for transmission, and the contention behavior of a terminal is fully determined by its decision following the **p**-persistent MAC contention policy. However, this situation is undesirable since the system will be unstable in this case, so it will not be discussed below.

In a stable $G/G/1$ queueing system, we should have $\chi < 1$. In this case, the probability for a terminal to contend for the channel (q) is given by

$$q = \chi \mathbf{p}. \tag{11.5}$$

In this case, the per-terminal throughput is equal to ν. Given $\mathbf{n}$, ν, and χ, we can have the throughput given by $\mathbf{n}$ terminals G as follows:

$$G = \nu \sum_{i=1}^{\mathbf{n}} i \binom{\mathbf{n}}{i} \chi^i (1 - \chi)^{\mathbf{n}-i}. \tag{11.6}$$

In a shared-media network, a packet usually cannot be transmitted immediately upon its arrival in the MAC layer due to the MAC overhead mentioned above. Therefore, for a terminal with a transmission bit rate C, its effective transmission rate ($\bar{C}$) actually is given by

$$\bar{C} = \frac{kL}{T + \frac{L}{C} + (k - 1)f}, \tag{11.7}$$

where $\frac{L}{C}$ is the per-packet transmission time, and f for a frame consisting of r request slots and $\mathbf{K}$ data slots (when $\mathbf{K} = 1$, f corresponds to the shortest frame) is calculated by

$$f = \frac{rl + \mathbf{K}L}{C}.$$ (11.8)

Note that in a practical system, the transmission rate for request submission is usually set lower than C for high reliability. Here since the request segment (i.e., rl) is usually much smaller than the data segment (i.e., $\mathbf{K}L$), in the following discussion, we ignore this difference.

With $k = 1$, a terminal can only use one data access for only a packet transmission, and has no reservation for its future transmission. When $k > 1$, a reservation of k data slots has been made for a burst transmission. If $k \to \infty$, $\bar{C} = \frac{L}{f}$, which indicates that the effect of the MAC overhead T on $\bar{C}$ becomes trivial with a large k. As discussed earlier, the phyMIMO MAC intends to increase C with a shorter per-packet transmission time. But it cannot reduce the MAC overhead, since at one time, only one terminal is allowed to transmit at one frequency. In contrast, the logMIMO MAC allows different terminals to transmit simultaneously at the same frequency to reduce the MAC overhead. But its transmission rate is still c, which is lower than C, resulting in a longer per-packet transmission time.

Now we need to find out T and C to determine χ for the phyMIMO and log-MIMO MAC schemes in the case of $\chi < 1$ for $k = 1$ and $k > 1$, respectively, which is discussed below.

11.4.2 Request Without Reservation

In this case, a terminal needs to contend for the channel access for every packet to be transmitted, i.e., $k = 1$. To simplify the analysis, we assume that the number of request slots (r) is equal to the number of simultaneous transmissions allowed by the channel (s). In this case, once a terminal succeeds in request submission, it can surely get channel access.

For an active terminal (say A) that is going to contend for the channel, whether it can win the channel competition depends on the activities of the other $\mathbf{n} - 1$ terminals. As mentioned earlier, the contention probability of a terminal (q) is determined by the product of its active probability (χ) and its MAC persistent probability ($\mathbf{p}$), and is given by Eq. (11.5). Then the probability for terminal A to succeed in MAC contention (η) is the probability that the s simultaneous channel accesses are not over contended. That is, the total number of competing terminals from the remaining $\mathbf{n} - 1$ ones should not exceed the remaining $s - 1$ channel accesses, where "$s - 1$" means that one slot access should be given to terminal A for its successful MAC contention. Therefore, we have

$$\eta = \begin{cases} 1, & \mathbf{n} \leq s, \\ \sum_{i=1}^{s-1} \binom{\mathbf{n}-1}{i} q^i (1-q)^{\mathbf{n}-1-i}, & \mathbf{n} > s. \end{cases}$$ (11.9)

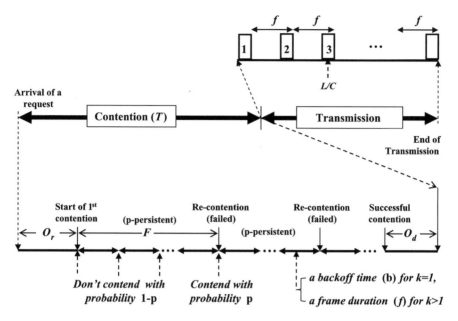

Fig. 11.4 MAC contention process from the arrival to the departure of a packet ($k = 1$) or a burst ($k > 1$)

For $s = 1$, this request slot can only be contended by the current terminal under consideration, and the other terminals need to wait; thus $\eta = (1 - q)^{n-1}$.

Now we calculate the MAC overhead T. As illustrated in Fig. 11.4, once a packet arrives at a terminal, it may not contend for the channel access immediately for request submission if the channel is busy, resulting in an offset to its first contention attempt (O_r). Due to the durable MAC behavior defined earlier, the terminal will retry contention with a mean time interval of F until it succeeds in request submission as depicted in the figure. Similar to O_r, there is also an offset from request submission to packet transmission (O_d) because the request can be only submitted in the request segment, while data must be transmitted in the data segment. Let j denote the number of trials conducted by the terminal for having a successful contention. Then, we have

$$T = O_r + \sum_{j=1}^{\infty}(j - 1)F(1 - \eta)^{j-1}\eta + O_d$$

$$= F\left(\frac{1}{\eta} - 1\right) + O_r + O_d. \tag{11.10}$$

Here it is assumed that a terminal can know the result of a submitted request immediately after its submission as mentioned earlier.

F is affected by the **p**-persistent MAC contention policy, by which, once a terminal decides to contend for the channel access, it needs to further determine whether to do it now or to consider it later. That is, the terminal contends for the channel now with probability $\mathbf{p}$ and reconsiders it later with probability $1 - \mathbf{p}$. In the latter case, the terminal differs its action by a backoff time ($\mathbf{b}$). At the end of this period, it makes a decision again, as illustrated in Fig. 11.4. Let i denote the number of decisions. Similar to T, we have

$$F = \sum_{i=1}^{\infty} (i - 1)\mathbf{b}(1 - \mathbf{p})^{i-1}\mathbf{p}$$

$$= \mathbf{b}\left(\frac{1}{\mathbf{p}} - 1\right). \tag{11.11}$$

Regarding O_r and O_d, they are relatively small compared to F and can be approximated as follows. If the current transmission is completed just at the time when a packet arrives at the terminal, this packet can start contention immediately so $O_r = 0$. Similarly, $O_r = \frac{L}{C}$ if the packet arrives just at the time when the current transmission starts. Then, on average, $O_r = \frac{L}{2C}$ if the packet arrival at the transmitter is uniformly distributed over a packet transmission period. Similarly for O_d, on average, a terminal can submit its request at the middle of the request segment, which means that a terminal needs to wait $\frac{rl}{2C}$ before starting transmission after a successful request submission; hence $O_d = \frac{rl}{2C}$. Therefore, we have

$$O_r + O_d = \frac{L + rl}{2C}. \tag{11.12}$$

Similarly for $\mathbf{b}$, once a terminal decides not to contend, it just waits till the end of the current contention and transmission process, i.e.,

$$\mathbf{b} = \frac{rl + L}{C}. \tag{11.13}$$

Then substituting Eqs. (11.11) and (11.12) into Eq. (11.10), we have

$$T = \frac{L + rl}{C}\left[\left(\frac{1}{\mathbf{p}} - 1\right)\left(\frac{1}{\eta} - 1\right) + \frac{1}{2}\right]. \tag{11.14}$$

11.4.3 Request with Reservation

As mentioned earlier, a reservation with $k > 1$ needs to go through (i) request submission from a terminal and (ii) request granting by the central unit. Let γ denote the probability for a successful request submission and g the probability for a successful granting; then the probability for a successful reservation is given by $\gamma \times g$.

Given the number of simultaneous accesses to a common data slot (s) and the number of data slots available per frame ($\mathbf{K}$), $s\mathbf{K}$ is the total number of data slot accesses available per frame. We assume that a terminal can only be granted one data slot access per frame and cannot request another slot access if the current one is not released. Note that here the term "data slot access" is adopted to distinguish it from the conventional "data slot." A conventional slot with time division multiple access (TDMA) can only be used by one terminal at one time. But with logMIMO, a data slot may be used by more than one terminal simultaneously. Therefore, one data slot access indicates one terminal access to this slot, and the total number of accesses to a data slot is equal to the number of terminals that can simultaneously have access to this data slot.

Suppose now that there are h out of the total $\mathbf{n}$ terminals with $h \leq \min(\mathbf{n}, s\mathbf{K})$, each of which has been allocated one slot access per frame. Similar to η given in Eq. (11.9), the probability for a successful request submission (γ) is the probability that the total $(r-1)$ request slots are not over contended by the remaining $(\mathbf{n} - h - 1)$ terminals that have not been granted with reservation. Apparently, if the number of such terminals is less than r, we have $\gamma = 1$.

Below γ is expressed as a function of h for discussion, i.e., $\gamma(h)$. Since the request channel is still a SISO channel, which does not allow simultaneous request submissions at the same frequency, we have

$$\gamma(h) = \begin{cases} 1, & \mathbf{n} - h \leq r \\ \sum_{i=1}^{r-1} \binom{\mathbf{n}-h-1}{i} q^i (1-q)^{\mathbf{n}-h-1-i}, & \mathbf{n} - h > r, \end{cases} \tag{11.15}$$

which is equal to $(1-q)^{\mathbf{n}-h-1}$ when $r = 1$ for $\mathbf{n} - h > r$, where the subtraction of 1 corresponds to the requesting terminal under consideration.

Once a terminal succeeds in request submission, if $h < s\mathbf{K}$, there is at least a free slot access available in this frame, and its request can be granted, hence $g = 1$; otherwise $g = 0$. Now we only need to find out the probability that there are h slot accesses occupied in a frame in the case of $h < s\mathbf{K}$, which is denoted by $w(h)$ below.

Apparently, $w(h) = 0$ for $h > \min(\mathbf{n}, s\mathbf{K})$. For $h \leq \min(\mathbf{n}, s\mathbf{K})$, due to the durable MAC behavior defined earlier, once a terminal has data to transmit, it will continue to contend for a data slot access until it succeeds. Thus, a request can eventually be granted if there is a free data slot access available in the frame. In this case, $w(h)$ can be approximated by the probability that there are h actively requesting terminals in the network. The probability for a terminal to be active is the probability that the queue is not idle, i.e., χ. Then for $h \leq \min(\mathbf{n}, s\mathbf{K})$, we have

$$w(h) = \binom{\mathbf{n}}{h} \chi^h (1-\chi)^{\mathbf{n}-h}. \tag{11.16}$$

Then we can use Eqs. (11.15) and (11.16) to calculate the probability for a successful slot access reservation, η, as follows:

$$\eta = \sum_{h=0}^{\varepsilon-1} w(h)\gamma(h), \tag{11.17}$$

where $\varepsilon = \min(\mathbf{n}, s\mathbf{K})$, and the subtraction of 1 is due to the following facts. (i) If $\mathbf{n} > s\mathbf{K}$, then $\min(\mathbf{n}, s\mathbf{K}) = s\mathbf{K}$, and in this case, at least one free data slot access needs to be available for a successful reservation. (ii) If $\mathbf{n} \leq s\mathbf{K}$, then $\min(\mathbf{n}, s\mathbf{K}) = \mathbf{n}$; in this case, the maximum number of granted terminals cannot exceed $\mathbf{n} - 1$ since the current requesting one is still contending.

Here the MAC overhead T is the average trial time for a terminal to successfully get channel access for the first packet transmission, and it can be calculated with Eq. (11.10), but with different settings of F, O_r, and O_d, which are discussed below.

For F, the only difference from that in the case of $k = 1$ discussed earlier is that the time interval between two consecutive decision points is a frame duration (f) rather than the backoff time ($\mathbf{b}$) as indicated in Fig. 11.4. Therefore, we have

$$F = f\left(\frac{1}{\mathbf{p}} - 1\right). \tag{11.18}$$

In this case, O_r refers to the mean waiting time before a request is submitted, since a request can be submitted only in the request segment located at the beginning of a frame. Similar to the O_r discussed in Sect. 11.4.2, we can have $O_r = \frac{\mathbf{K}L}{2C}$. Similarly for O_d, on average, a request is submitted at the middle of the request segment; hence there is an offset to the beginning of the data segment equal to $\frac{rl}{2C}$. If the granted data slot access is located at the first slot, the terminal can transmit immediately; otherwise, it needs to wait $(i - 1)$ slots, where $1 \leq i \leq \mathbf{K}$ is the index of the granted slot. Suppose granted slots are uniformly distributed over the $\mathbf{K}$ slots. Then on average, a granted terminal still needs to wait

$$\sum_{i=1}^{\mathbf{K}} \frac{(i - 1)L}{\mathbf{K}C} = \frac{L(\mathbf{K} - 1)}{2C} \tag{11.19}$$

before data transmission. Therefore,

$$O_d = \frac{rl + L(\mathbf{K} - 1)}{2C}, \tag{11.20}$$

and then

$$O_r + O_d = \frac{rl + L(2\mathbf{K} - 1)}{2C}$$

$$= \frac{f}{2} + \frac{L(\mathbf{K} - 1)}{2C}. \tag{11.21}$$

Then substituting Eqs. (11.18) and (11.21) into Eq. (11.10), we have

$$T = f\left(\frac{1}{\mathbf{p}} - 1\right)\left(\frac{1}{\eta} - 1\right) + \frac{f}{2} + \frac{L(\mathbf{K} - 1)}{2C}, \tag{11.22}$$

which is the same as Eq. (11.14) for the request without reservation ($k = 1$) when $\mathbf{K} = 1$.

Note that the above formulas for T are a function of η, while η is determined by q as indicated by Eqs. (11.9) and (11.17) with $q = \chi\mathbf{p}$. On the other hand, χ is also a function of T, as indicated by Eq. (11.4). Therefore, in the remaining discussion in this chapter as well as in Chap. 12, χ is given to calculate T first; then we calculate the traffic load ν allowed by χ in the case of a stable network, as discussed below.

11.4.4 Stability Condition of Networks

Here we discuss in more detail the settings of some parameters to satisfy the stability condition $\chi < 1$ with the generalized formula (11.22) for requests both with and without reservation, i.e., $k = 1$ and $k > 1$.

In order to have $\chi < 1$, from Eq. (11.4), we have

$$T < \frac{1}{\nu} - \frac{L}{C} - (k-1)f, \tag{11.23}$$

and further with Eq. (11.22), we have

$$\left(\frac{1}{\mathbf{p}} - 1\right)\left(\frac{1}{\eta} - 1\right) < \frac{1}{f}\left[\frac{1}{\nu} - \frac{(\mathbf{K}+1)L}{2C}\right] - k + \frac{1}{2}, \tag{11.24}$$

which bounds $\mathbf{p}$ and η to satisfy the stability condition. Since η is also determined by $\mathbf{p}$ for given $\mathbf{n}$, s, r, and $\mathbf{K}$ as indicated by Eqs. (11.9) and (11.17), the bound of $\mathbf{p}$ can be calculated by Eq. (11.24) numerically. When $\eta = 1$, MAC efficiency reaches the maximum, and we have the upper bound of ν from Eq. (11.24) for a given C and frame structure as follows:

$$\nu < \frac{C}{\left(k\mathbf{K} + \frac{1}{2}\right)L + \left(k - \frac{1}{2}\right)rl} \tag{11.25}$$

since $f = \frac{rl + \mathbf{K}L}{C}$. For the request without reservation, $k = \mathbf{K} = 1$, the above bounds are further simplified as

$$\left(\frac{1}{\mathbf{p}} - 1\right)\left(\frac{1}{\eta} - 1\right) < \frac{1}{f}\left[\frac{1}{\nu} - \frac{L}{2C}\right] - \frac{1}{2}, \tag{11.26}$$

and

$$\nu < \frac{2C}{3L + rl}. \tag{11.27}$$

11.5 Conclusion

Although phyMIMO can offer a much higher per-terminal transmission bit rate, in the MAC layer, a terminal may suffer from long waiting times before having access to the channel. The logMIMO just reverses this situation. This chapter provides a mathematical analysis of the performance of MAC schemes based on phyMIMO and logMIMO. It is much easier to implement logMIMO than phyMIMO since, like virMIMO, logMIMO only requires one antenna per transmitting terminal. Furthermore, logMIMO is simpler than virMIMO since it does not need inter-terminal cooperative communication. These features make logMIMO a probable potential method to upgrade existing centralized wireless networks to increase uplink sharing efficiency. A numerical discussion will be given in Chap. 12.

References

1. Alamouti, S.M.: A simple transmit diversity technique for wireless communications. IEEE J. Sel. Areas Commun. **16**(8), 1451–1458 (1998)
2. Paulraj, A.J., Gore, D.A., Nabar, R.U., Bolcskei, H.: An overview of MIMO communications – a key to gigabit wireless. Proc. IEEE **92**(2), 198–218 (2004)
3. Stuber, G.L., Barry, J.R., McLaughlin, S.W., Li, Y., Ingram, M.A., Pratt, T.G.: Broadband MIMO-OFDM wireless communications. Proc. IEEE **92**(2), 271–294 (2004)
4. Ganesan, A., Sayeed, A.M.: A virtual MIMO framework for multipath fading channels. In: Proc. Asilomar Conf. Signals, Systems & Computers (ACSSC), Pacific Grove, CA, USA, vol. 1, pp. 537–541 (2000)
5. Sendonaris, A., Erkip, E., Aazhang, B.: User cooperation diversity. Part I. System description. IEEE Trans. Commun. **51**(11), 1927–1938 (2003)
6. Ryu, H.S., Kang, C.G., Kwon, D.S.: Transmission protocol for cooperative MIMO with full rate: design and analysis. In: Proc. IEEE Veh. Tech. Conf. (VTC) – Spring, Dublin, Ireland, pp. 934–938 (2007)
7. Yin, H.J., Liu, H.: Performance of space-division multiple-access (SDMA) with scheduling. IEEE Trans. Wirel. Commun. **1**(4), 611–618 (2002)
8. Lotter, M.P., Van Rooyen, P.: An overview of space division multiple access techniques in cellular systems. In: Proc. South African Symp. Comm. & Signal Processing (COMSIG), Rondebosch, pp. 161–164 (1998)
9. Lal, D., Toshniwal, R., Radhakrishnan, R., Agrawal, D.P., Caffery, J.: A novel MAC layer protocol for space division multiple access in wireless ad hoc networks. In: Proc. IEEE Conf. Comp. Commun. Net. (ICCCN), Miami, Florida, USA, pp. 614–619 (2002)
10. Lal, D., Jain, V., Zeng, Q.A., Agrawal, D.P.: Performance evaluation of medium access control for multiple-beam antenna nodes in a wireless LAN. IEEE Trans. Parallel Distrib. Syst. **15**(12), 1117–1129 (2004)
11. Prasad, N., Varanasi, M.K., Venturino, L., Wang, X.D.: An analysis of the MIMO-SDMA channel with space-time orthogonal and quasi-orthogonal user transmissions and efficient successive cancellation decoders. IEEE Trans. Inf. Theory **54**(12), 5427–5446 (2008)
12. Jayaweera, S.K.: V-BLAST-based virtual MIMO for distributed wireless sensor networks. IEEE Trans. Commun. **55**(10), 1867–1872 (2007)
13. Tang, S.H., Shagdar, O., Shirazi, M.N., Suzuki, R., Obana, S.: Opportunistic cooperation and selective forwarding, a virtual MIMO scheme for wireless networks. In: Proc. IEEE Symp. Personal, Indoor & Mobile Radio Commun. (PIMRC), Cannes, France, pp. 1–6 (2008)
14. Yang, H.M., Shen, H.Y., Sikdar, B., Kalyanaraman, S.: A threshold based MAC protocol for cooperative MIMO transmissions. In: Proc. IEEE INFOCOM, Rio de Janeiro, Brazil, pp. 2996–3000 (2009)
15. Mundarath, J.C., Ramanathan, P., Veen, B.D.V.: NULLHOC: a MAC protocol for adaptive antenna array based wireless ad hoc networks in multipath environments. In: Proc. IEEE Global Tele. Conf. (GLOBOCOM), vol. 5, pp. 2765–2769 (2004)

16. Sundaresan, K., Sivakumar, R., Ann, M.A., Chang, T.Y.: Medium access control in ad hoc networks with MIMO links: optimization considerations and algorithms. IEEE Trans. Mob. Comput. **3**(4), 350–365 (2004)
17. Park, J.S., Nandan, A., Gerla, M., Lee, H.: SPACE-MAC: enabling spatial reuse using MIMO channel-aware MAC. In: Proc. IEEE Int. Conf. Commun. (ICC), Seoul, Korea, vol. 5, pp. 3642–3646 (2005)
18. Redi, J., Watson, B., Ramanathan, R., Basu, P., Tchakountio, F., Girone, M., Steenstrup, M.: Design and implementation of a MIMO MAC protocol for ad hoc networking. Proc. SPIE **6248**, 624802 (2006) (12 pages)
19. Park, M.Y., Choi, S.H., Nettles, S.M.: Cross-layer MAC Design for Wireless Network Using MIMO. In: Proc. IEEE Global Tele. Conf. (GLOBOCOM), Missouri, USA, vol. 5, pp. 2870–2874 (2005)
20. Rossetto, F., Zorzi, M.: A low-delay MAC solution for MIMO ad hoc networks. IEEE Trans. Wirel. Commun. **8**(1), 130–135 (2009)
21. Hu, M., Zhang, J.S.: MIMO ad hoc networks with spatial diversity: medium access control and saturation throughput. J. Commun. Netw. **6**(4), 317–330 (2004)
22. Hoang, D., Iltis, R.A.: An efficient MAC protocol for MIMO-OFDM ad hoc networks. In: Proc. Asilomar Conf. Signals, Systems & Computers (ACSSC), Pacific Grove, CA, USA, pp. 814–818 (2006)
23. Nabar, R.U., Bolcskei, H., Kneubuhler, F.W.: Fading relay channels: performance limits and space-time signal design. IEEE J. Sel. Areas Commun. **22**(6), 1099–1109 (2004)
24. Buratti, C., Zanella, A.: Capacity analysis of two-hop virtual MIMO systems in a Poisson field of nodes. In: Proc. IEEE Veh. Tech. Conf. (VTC) – Spring, Barcelona, Spain, pp. 1–6 (2009)

Chapter 12
Numerical Evaluation of MAC Schemes Based on Physical and Logical MIMO

Abstract Chapter 11 analyzes the performance of MAC schemes based on physical and logical MIMO for uplink sharing in a centralized wireless network. These analytical results are used in this chapter to provide a numerical comparison of the schemes. This comparison shows that, without a per-frame reservation, the MAC based on the logical MIMO can very much outperform that with the physical MIMO in most of the investigated scenarios. With a per-frame reservation, the physical MIMO-based MAC can outperform the logical one mainly when the number of data slots available per frame is large. This finding may suggest an alternative way to exploit MIMO in centralized wireless networks such as cellular networks, since almost no change in mobile terminal hardware is required.

12.1 Introduction

As mentioned earlier, since it is infeasible to exploit the multiple-input-multiple-output (MIMO) feature to realize both phyMIMO and logMIMO simultaneously in one terminal, Chap. 11 analyzes the performance of medium access control (MAC) schemes based, respectively, on phyMIMO and logMIMO for uplink sharing in a centralized wireless network. Following these analytical results, this chapter conducts a numerical comparison between phyMIMO and logMIMO in terms of MAC performance. We make the following observations from this comparison. (i) Without a periodic slot reservation in every frame, the phyMIMO MAC can slightly outperform the logMIMO MAC if the MAC contention degree is very low; otherwise, the latter can greatly outperform the former. (ii) With a periodic slot reservation per frame, the phyMIMO MAC can outperform the logMIMO MAC even in the case of high MAC contention if the number of data slots available per frame is large; otherwise, the logMIMO MAC can perform almost the same as the phyMIMO MAC, and even better if this number is too small or the traffic load is very heavy.

The remainder of this chapter is organized as follows. Section 12.2 discusses a channel capacity model for phyMIMO and logMIMO. The performances of MAC schemes with and without per-frame reservation are discussed in Sects. 12.3 and 12.4, respectively, and the chapter is summarized in Sect. 12.5.

S.M. Jiang, *Future Wireless and Optical Networks*,   185
Computer Communications and Networks,
DOI 10.1007/978-1-4471-2822-9_12, © Springer-Verlag London Limited 2012

12.2 MIMO Channel Capacity

This section first discusses a MIMO channel capacity model reported in the literature and then compares numerically the capacities given by physical MIMO (phyMIMO) and logical MIMO (logMIMO), respectively.

12.2.1 A Capacity Model

The availability of channel state information (CSI) at either the transmitter or receiver and the channel quality will affect the MIMO channel capacity. The analysis of MIMO channel capacity is complex, and usually only a bound or region is provided mainly due to the difficulty in determining the distribution of eigenvalues for the covariance matrix [1, 2]. Here, a non-random channel capacity model proposed in [3] is adopted for the discussion.

According to [3], if the elements of the transmitter array are far apart from each other, and the total transmitted power ($P_{TX,\text{total}}$) is uniformly allocated to each antenna at the transmitter, the capacity of a Rayleigh channel measured in Bps/Hz converges to a non-random quantity as follows:

$$R = \log_2[\det(\mathbf{I}_m + \text{SNR} \cdot \mathcal{R}_{RX})], \tag{12.1}$$

where

$$\text{SNR} = \frac{P_{TX,\text{total}}}{P_{\text{noise}}} \tag{12.2}$$

and $\mathcal{R}_{RX}$ is the correlation matrix of the receiver array with

$$[\mathcal{R}_{RX}(\tau)]_{vw} = \rho_{vy,wy}(\tau). \tag{12.3}$$

Here $\rho_{vy,wy}(\tau)$ indicates the space-time cross-correlation between the gains of two arbitrary communication links vy and wy where $y \in \{1, 2, \ldots, \mathbf{n}\}$ is the index of the transmit antennas, and $\mathbf{I_m}$ is an $\mathbf{m} \times \mathbf{m}$ real identity matrix while P_{noise} is the noise power at each receiver.

Similar to [3], here we only discuss a special case for non-isotropic scattering around the receiver, in which both the transmitter and receiver are equipped with linear uniform arrays, i.e., $\delta_{x,x+1} = \delta$ and $d_{v,v+1} = d$ with $\alpha_{xy} = \beta_{vw} = 90°$ (refer to Fig. 12.1 for the parameter definition). In this case, for a Rayleigh channel at time $\tau = 0$, from Eqs. (12) and (18) provided in [3], we can obtain

$$\rho_{vy,wy}(\tau) \approx \frac{I_0\left(\sqrt{\kappa^2 - \frac{4\pi^2(d+\delta\Delta)^2}{\lambda^2}} + j\frac{4\kappa\pi(d+\delta\Delta)\sin(\mu)}{\lambda}\right)}{I_0(\kappa)}, \tag{12.4}$$

where I_0 is the zero-order modified Bessel function of the first kind, $j^2 = -1$, $\mu \in [-\pi, \pi]$ is the mean direction of the angle of arrival (AOA) seen by the receiver,

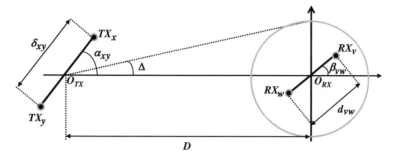

Fig. 12.1 Geometric configuration for transmitter (TX) and receiver (RX) antennas with parameters listed below: δ (d) = distance between transmit (receive) antennas, D = distance between the sender and receiver, α, β, Δ = angles as indicated in the figure [3]

and $\kappa \geq 0$ controls the width of AOA [4]. Furthermore, only the receiver knows the channel transfer matrix without using transmit beamforming, and $\mathcal{R}_{RX}$ is common to $[\mathcal{R}_{RX}(\tau)]_{vw}$ for all transmit antennas, so their contributions to the correlation between the receiver antennas are the same [3].

From Eq. (12.4), we find that $\rho_{vy,wy}(0)$ is independent of the antenna indices, and therefore ρ is used instead of $\rho_{vy,wy}(0)$ henceforth. In this case, $[\mathcal{R}_{RX}]_{ij} = 1$ for $i = j$ and $[\mathcal{R}_{RX}]_{ij} = |\rho|$ otherwise. Note that since D needs to be very large to keep the far field assumption meaningful [3], $\delta\Delta$ is set very small, and in this case, Eq. (12.4) can be simplified into Eq. (27) provided in [3].

Equation (12.1) along with Eq. (12.4) can also be used to study the effect of spatial gain on channel capacity. Spatial gain depends on spatial diversity. With phyMIMO, multiple antennas are installed in a terminal which usually is highly compact. In this case, the distance between antennas (δ_{phy}) is very small especially compared with that of logMIMO (δ_{log}), which actually is the distance between terminals. This feature enables logMIMO to have a larger spatial diversity than phyMIMO, resulting in more spatial gain. For comparison, below R is rewritten as a function of $\mathbf{m}$ and δ. Given a bandwidth of B for a MIMO channel, its capacity $\mathcal{C}$ is given by

$$\mathcal{C}(\delta, \mathbf{m}) = B \times R(\delta, \mathbf{m}). \tag{12.5}$$

Thus, the transmission bit rate per terminal with phyMIMO is simply given by

$$C_{\text{phy}} = \mathcal{C}(\delta_{\text{phy}}, \mathbf{m}), \tag{12.6}$$

which is not affected by the number of transmitting terminals since the number of antennas used by both the transmitter and the receiver is fixed at $\mathbf{m}$.

For logMIMO, every transmitting terminal has one antenna, and multiple terminals of this kind form a MIMO channel with the central unit. The number of antennas of this MIMO channel depends not only on the number of receive antennas at the central unit (i.e., $\mathbf{m}$) but also on the number of transmitting terminals (i.e., $\mathbf{n}$). Therefore, the number of antennas of this MIMO channel is min[$\mathbf{m}$, $\mathbf{n}$] with an overall capacity equal to $\mathcal{C}(\delta_{\text{phy}}, \min[\mathbf{m}, \mathbf{n}])$, which is shared by min[$\mathbf{m}$, $\mathbf{n}$] transmitting terminals. Now the question is to determine the per-terminal transmission bit rate ($C_{\log}$) in this case.

In the literature, a channel decoupling approach is often used in the analysis of multi-element antennas (MEAs). For example, reference [1] states that "with linear operation at both the transmitter and the receiver, the MEA can be transferred into an equivalent system consisting of $\min(\mathbf{n}_T, n_R)$ decoupled SISO subchannels", where $\mathbf{n}_T$ and $\mathbf{n}_R$ denote the numbers of transmit and receive antennas, respectively. Regarding channel separating, with logMIMO, it should be easier than with phyMIMO to separate the uplink channel because there is a much larger distance between transmit antennas with logMIMO as mentioned earlier, while the receive antennas at the central unit can also be set large enough for high reception performance. Therefore, if each involved terminal contributes equally to the power of the signal received by the central unit, $C_{\log}$ can be approximated by

$$C_{\log} \approx \frac{\mathcal{C}(\delta_{\text{phy}}, \min[\mathbf{m}, \mathbf{n}])}{\min[\mathbf{m}, \mathbf{n}]}. \tag{12.7}$$

12.2.2 Numerical Discussion of Capacity

This section compares logMIMO and phyMIMO in terms of their channel capacities by using the same settings of $\mathbf{m}$ and the MIMO channel capacity model discussed in Sect. 12.2.1. The following settings are adopted for both phyMIMO and log-MIMO: (i) $d = 2\lambda$ for the distance in wavelength between antennas implemented at the central receiver; (ii) $B = 200$ kHz for the spectrum bandwidth, which is equivalent to one GSM channel; (iii) SNR $= 17$ dB [3], (iv) $\Delta = 1°$, (v) $L = 1000$ bytes, and (vi) $l = 10$ bytes. Both κ and μ are correlated and related to the antenna array and signal propagation path. Here, we simply take the following three sets of (κ, μ) listed in Table I provided in [4] for the numerical discussion: $(39, 259.2°)$, $(700, 108°)$, and $(59, 79.2°)$.

Figures 12.2 and 12.3 depict the MIMO channel capacity (R) in bps/Hz against the distance between transmit antennas (δ) and that between receive antennas (d) for the first two sets of (κ, μ). We find that R increases with both distance parameters, since spatial diversity increases with them. For phyMIMO, δ_{phy} usually ranges from millimeters to micrometers, which is roughly equivalent to a fraction of or up to several wavelengths and further depends on the carrier. For example, with the 1800 MHz carrier, its wavelength is about 16.7 cm, which is almost double the size of a typical mobile phone. In this case, δ_{phy} can be only a small fraction of a wavelength. With logMIMO, $\delta_{\log}$ usually ranges from meters even up to hundreds of meters, resulting in much larger spatial diversity than with phyMIMO. These two figures show that a large spatial diversity with longer δ can be transferred into channel capacity gain. This means that logMIMO can outperform phyMIMO in terms of R. Comparing Fig. 12.2 and Fig. 12.3, we find that κ and μ also affect the channel capacity. For example, the difference in R for setting $[\delta = 100\lambda, d = 0.1\lambda]$ in these figures is around 2 bps/Hz. A detailed discussion of this issue is beyond the scope

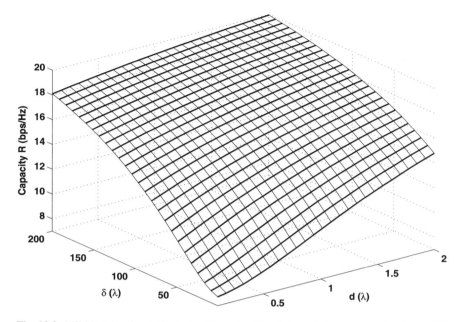

Fig. 12.2 MIMO channel capacity in bps/Hz against the distance between transmit antennas (δ) and that between receive antennas (d) in wavelength: $\kappa = 39$, $\mu = 259.20°$, $\mathbf{m} = 4$

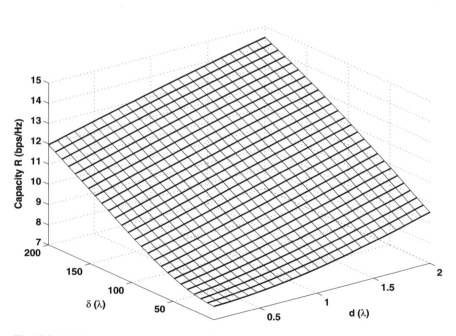

Fig. 12.3 MIMO channel capacity R in bps/Hz against the distance between transmit antennas (δ) and that between receive antennas (d) in wavelength: $\kappa = 700$, $\mu = 108°$, $\mathbf{m} = 4$

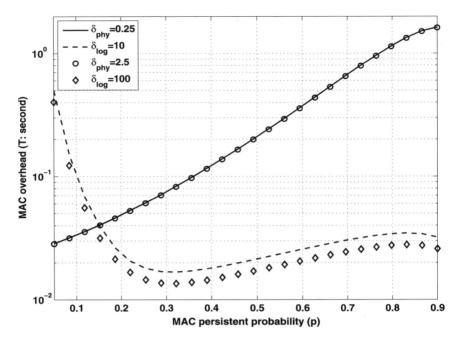

Fig. 12.4 MAC overhead (T) versus MAC persistent probability (**p**) for two settings of distance between transmit antennas (δ): $\chi = 0.4$, **m** $= 4$, and **n** $= 20$ (using "phy" for phyMIMO MAC and "log" for logMIMO MAC as legend in the figure henceforth)

of this chapter and can be found in the literature. We will fix $\kappa = 59$ and $\mu = 79.2°$ for the remaining discussion.

12.3   Request Without Reservation

In this case, $k = 1$. Below we compare the logMIMO and phyMIMO MAC schemes by using the same settings of **m** for both, while we set $s = 1$ for phyMIMO and $s =$ **m** for logMIMO due to their characteristics as discussed earlier.

12.3.1 MAC Overhead

Figures 12.4 and 12.5 plot the MAC overhead (T) and mean packet arrival rate (ν) against MAC persistent probability (**p**) by fixing the terminal active probability (χ) for two settings of δ, one of which is 10 times larger than the other. For both settings, δ for logMIMO ($\delta_{\log}$) is set to be 40 times that for phyMIMO (δ_{phy}), since logMIMO can allow much larger distances between antennas than phyMIMO. This difference causes different spatial diversities, resulting in a difference in the overall

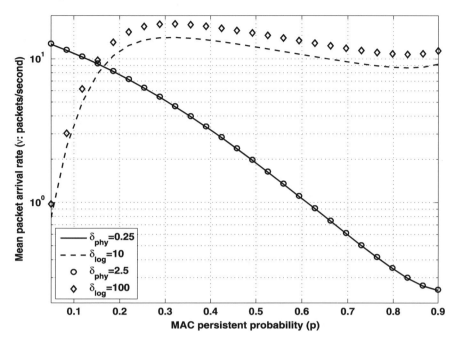

Fig. 12.5 Mean packet arrival rate (ν) versus MAC persistent probability (**p**) for two settings of distance between transmit antennas (δ), with the same setting as in Fig. 12.4

MIMO channel capacities given by logMIMO and phyMIMO. For the phyMIMO MAC, since δ_{phy} is too small to yield many differences in the capacity given by the two settings of δ_{phy}, the corresponding results of T almost overlap, and the same occurs for ν. But for the logMIMO MAC, there are still some differences especially with a large **p** due to the much larger inter-antenna distances (δ_{log}) with logMIMO.

As illustrated in Fig. 12.4, the relationship between T and **p** is not monotonic with the logMIMO MAC. That is, T first decreases and then increases with **p**, because **p** can affect the performance in the following manner. A larger **p** makes a terminal have more contention opportunities; but, on the other hand, it also increases the MAC contention degree to reduce MAC contention success. This joint effect on T can be further explained by Eq. (11.14), which shows that T decreases as **p** and η increase. For ν depicted in Fig. 12.5, it is actually given by $\frac{\chi}{S}$ according to its definition, where S is the average MAC service time calculated by Eq. (11.3). Since $k = 1$ here, S is simplified as

$$S = T + \frac{L}{C}, \tag{12.8}$$

where $\frac{L}{C}$ is a constant against **p**. This explains why ν changes against **p** in the manner as illustrated in Fig. 12.5. However, for the phyMIMO MAC, increasing **p** mainly reduces its successful contention probability, since it cannot support simultaneous transmissions in the MAC layer as mentioned earlier.

Figures 12.4 and 12.5 clearly show that the logMIMO MAC can greatly outperform the phyMIMO MAC especially with large **p**, mainly due to their difference in MAC efficiency. This effect can be reflected by the ratio of the MAC overhead (T) over per-packet transmission time ($\frac{L}{C}$), which can be obtained with Eq. (11.14) directly as follows:

$$\frac{T}{L/C} = \frac{L+rl}{L}\left[\left(\frac{1}{p}-1\right)\left(\frac{1}{\eta}-1\right)+\frac{1}{2}\right]. \qquad (12.9)$$

The larger this ratio, the less efficient the MAC is. Since C is canceled out in Eq. (12.9), increasing C cannot bring a gain in MAC efficiency, but increasing successful MAC contention probability (η) can. This demonstrates the weakness of the phyMIMO MAC versus the logMIMO MAC.

12.3.2 Average MAC Service Time

Now we discuss the average MAC service time (S) with a setting of $\delta_{phy} = 0.25\lambda$ and $\delta_{log} = 10\lambda$. It is mainly determined by T, as indicated by (11.3). To simplify the comparison, here the ratio of the S of the phyMIMO MAC (S_{phy}) to that of the logMIMO MAC (S_{log}), i.e., $\frac{S_{phy}}{S_{log}}$, is plotted. $\frac{S_{phy}}{S_{log}} > 1$ means that the logMIMO MAC outperforms the phyMIMO MAC.

As shown in Fig. 12.6, the phyMIMO MAC is better than the logMIMO MAC only when the MAC occupancy (χ) and the number of terminals (**n**) are small, while the logMIMO MAC becomes much better as **n** and χ increase. The superiority of the phyMIMO MAC over the logMIMO MAC is much smaller compared to that of the logMIMO MAC over the phyMIMO MAC.

Figure 12.7 plots this ratio against the number of receive antennas **m** and χ. It shows that, with a large χ, as **m** increases, the superiority of the logMIMO MAC first increases and then decreases with **m**. This happens because the MAC efficiency of the logMIMO MAC increases with **m**. However, given a traffic load, the gain of the increased MAC efficiency will converge if the transmission capacity offered by increasing **m** is more than what the traffic load needs. With the phyMIMO MAC, increasing **m** mainly increases channel transmission bit rate (C) rather than MAC efficiency, as discussed above. This explains the following phenomenon: even with a large **m** setting, the superiority of the logMIMO MAC is still large.

12.3.3 Network Throughput

Figures 12.8 and 12.9 plot the network throughput (G) against **p** and χ. As discussed earlier, it is not surprising that the logMIMO MAC is better than the phyMIMO MAC in most cases. However, both the logMIMO and phyMIMO MAC schemes

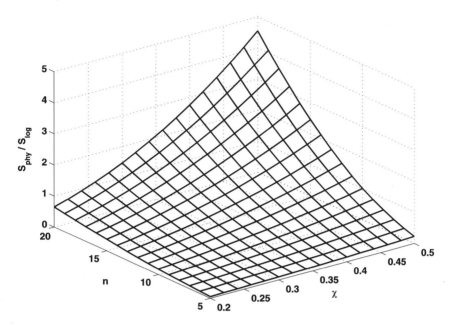

Fig. 12.6 Ratio of the average packet MAC service time with the phyMIMO MAC to that with the logMIMO MAC ($\frac{S_{phy}}{S_{log}}$) versus the number of terminals (**n**) and MAC occupancy (χ): **p** = 0.3, **m** = 4

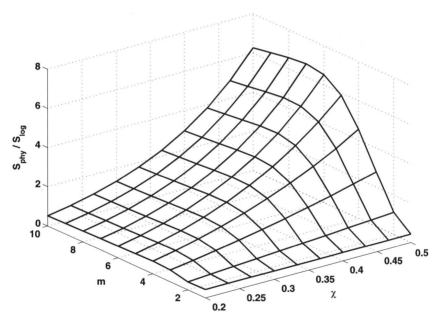

Fig. 12.7 Ratio of the average packet MAC service time with the phyMIMO MAC to that with the logMIMO MAC ($\frac{S_{phy}}{S_{log}}$) versus the number of receive antennas (**m**) and MAC occupancy (χ): **p** = 0.3, **n** = 20

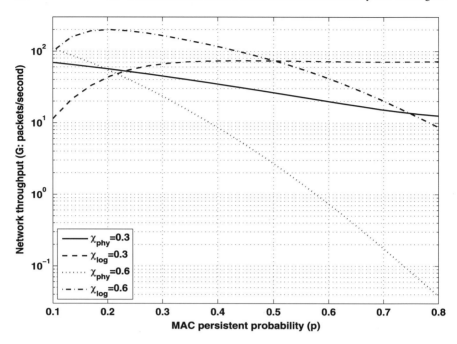

Fig. 12.8 Network throughput (G) versus MAC persistent probability (**p**) without a reservation ($k = 1$): **m** $= 4$, **n** $= 20$

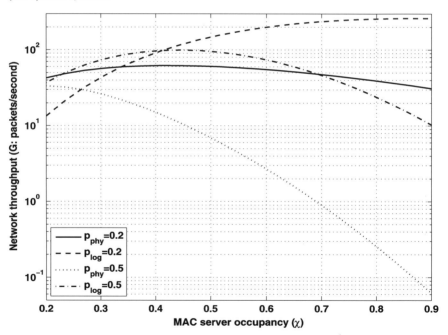

Fig. 12.9 Network throughput (G) against MAC occupancy (χ) without a reservation ($k = 1$), with the same setting as used in Fig. 12.8

suffer from high MAC contention, which is determined by the terminal contention probability. This probability is given by $q = \chi \mathbf{p}$, which shows that increasing either $\mathbf{p}$ or χ will lead to an increase in MAC contention. But the logMIMO MAC is more resilient than the phyMIMO MAC against the increased MAC contention due to its support of simultaneous transmissions in the MAC layer.

12.4 Request with Reservation

In this case, the number of data slot accesses per request exceeds 1, i.e., $k > 1$.

12.4.1 MAC Overhead

As discussed earlier, it is expected that reservation can dilute the impact of the MAC overhead on the performance, which can make the phyMIMO MAC perform better. As illustrated in Fig. 12.10, for $\chi = 0.3$, with which the terminal's activity is very low, the T given by the phyMIMO MAC is lower than that given by the logMIMO MAC. The reason is that the low load makes the MAC contention degree smaller, so the effect of the frame duration (f) on T indicated in Eq. (11.22) is bigger than the MAC efficiency. Given a frame structure, f is fully determined by channel capacity C as indicated by Eq. (11.8). As mentioned earlier, the phyMIMO MAC offers higher C than the logMIMO MAC, resulting in a shorter f. Furthermore, a reservation request is still submitted via a single-input-single-output (SISO) channel, which cannot take advantage of the simultaneous MAC transmission capability of the logMIMO MAC. However, for a heavy traffic load with $\chi = 0.7$ as illustrated in this figure, this capability can enable a data slot to be used by different terminals simultaneously, making the logMIMO MAC more efficient than the phyMIMO MAC, resulting in much shorter T.

Figure 12.11 plots mean burst arrival rates (i.e., $\nu = \frac{\chi}{S}$) against the number of slots reserved per request (k). This figure does show the superiority of the phyMIMO MAC over the logMIMO MAC even in the case of $\chi = 0.7$, where the T given by the phyMIMO MAC is much longer than that given by the logMIMO MAC. It also shows that the gap in their performance becomes wider and both perform worse as k increases. This happens because the MAC service time (S) increases with k as indicated by Eq. (11.3), while the S given by the logMIMO MAC grows faster because the f given by the phyMIMO MAC is shorter due to its higher transmission rate C. However, Fig. 12.11 also suggests using small k to accommodate more traffic load (i.e., higher ν). In this case, the difference in their performance becomes small.

Note that it is not practical to set $\mathbf{m}$ and r large, since it is difficult to implement many antennas in a small-sized terminal for the phyMIMO MAC. On the other hand, too many request slots per frame causes a large frame overhead.

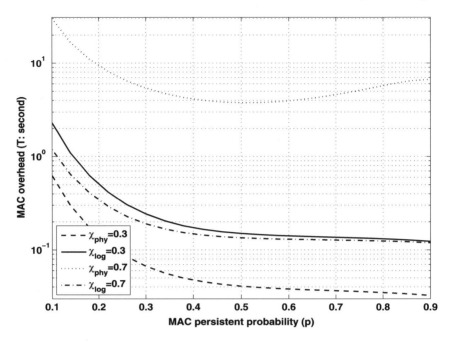

Fig. 12.10 MAC overhead (T) against MAC persistent probability (**p**) for two χ settings: **n** $= 20$, $r = m = 4$, and **K** $= 10$

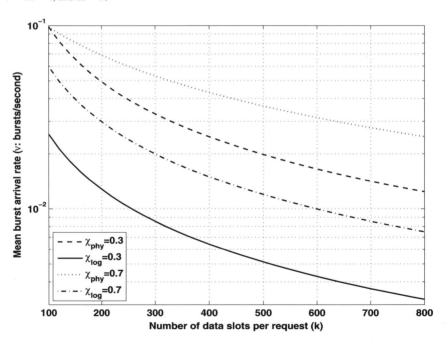

Fig. 12.11 Mean burst arrival rate (v) against the number of data slots reserved per request (k) for two χ settings, with the same setting as used in Fig. 12.10 with $p = 0.4$

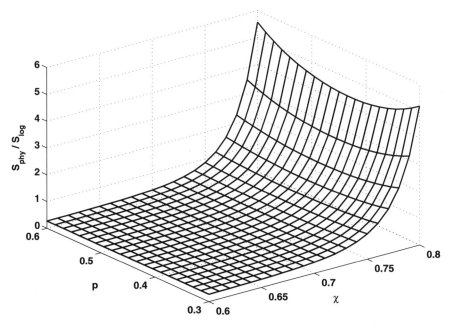

Fig. 12.12 Ratio of average burst MAC service time (S) with the phyMIMO MAC to that with the logMIMO MAC ($\frac{S_{\text{phy}}}{S_{\text{log}}}$) versus MAC occupancy ($\chi$) and MAC persistent probability (**p**): $\mathbf{m} = r = 4, \mathbf{n} = 20, \mathbf{K} = 10, k = 300$

12.4.2 Average MAC Service Time

Figure 12.12 depicts $\frac{S_{\text{phy}}}{S_{\text{log}}}$ against χ and **p**. We find that the superiority of the log-MIMO MAC over the phyMIMO MAC increases quickly as χ and **p** increase, which demonstrates again the advantage of the simultaneous transmission capability of logMIMO MAC under heavy traffic loads. In this case, with the same **K** setting, although the phyMIMO MAC can offer higher C to each individual terminal, it cannot grant more terminals than the logMIMO MAC for data channel access. For heavy traffic loads, as **p** increases, this ratio first decreases and then increases, because, in this case, the average MAC service time for a burst (S) is mainly determined by the MAC overhead (T).

Figure 12.13 plots the ratio of the average MAC service time for a burst (S) given by the phyMIMO MAC to that by the logMIMO MAC, i.e., $\frac{S_{\text{phy}}}{S_{\text{log}}}$, against the number of antennas (**m**) and the number of request slots per frame (r). It is not surprising that the superiority of the logMIMO MAC over the phyMIMO MAC becomes smaller as **m** and r increase. As **m** increases, the C given by phyMIMO increases proportionally to **m** almost linearly, resulting in shorter f. However, this does not happen to the logMIMO MAC, since it can only provide **m** simultaneous transmissions for accommodating more traffic, each at a lower rate of c. Naturally as r increases, the probability for successful request submission increases for both

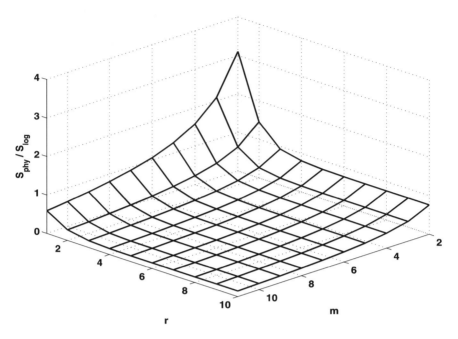

Fig. 12.13 Ratio of the average burst MAC service time (S) with the phyMIMO MAC to that with the logMIMO MAC ($\frac{S_{phy}}{S_{log}}$) versus the number of receive antennas (**m**) and the number of per-frame request slots (r): $\mathbf{p} = 0.4$, $\mathbf{n} = 20$, $\mathbf{K} = 10$, $k = 300$

schemes. However, with a fixed traffic load, this gain becomes smaller as r continues to increase, so the effect of the simultaneous transmission of the logMIMO MAC on S becomes weaker.

As shown in Fig. 12.14 for $\frac{S_{phy}}{S_{log}}$ against the per-frame number of data slots (**K**) and the number of active terminals (**n**), the logMIMO MAC can outperform the phyMIMO MAC only when **n** increases to a certain point since **n** determines MAC contention degree, which is stronger than C in influencing S with a large **n**. On the other hand, **K** is very important in order for the phyMIMO MAC to outperform the logMIMO MAC. With a large **K**, there are more data slots available per frame, which dilutes the impact of the advantage of the simultaneous transmission capability of the logMIMO MAC. With the same **K** setting, the frame duration (f) of the phyMIMO MAC is shorter due to its higher bit rate (C), so the phyMIMO MAC becomes better as **K** increases. However, a frame with a large **K** will cause bandwidth waste if the traffic load is too low to fulfill each data slot in every frame.

12.4.3 Network Throughput

Figures 12.15 and 12.16 plot the network throughput (G) against χ and **K**. As illustrated in Fig. 12.15, the phyMIMO MAC is better in most cases, and G increases

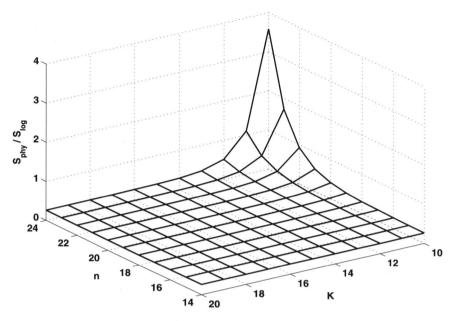

Fig. 12.14 Ratio of the average burst MAC service time (S) with the phyMIMO MAC to that with the logMIMO MAC versus data slots (K) and the number of nodes (n): $\chi = 0.7, p = 0.3, m = r = 4, k = 300$

with χ for both MAC schemes since the traffic load (v) also increases with χ, which causes G to increase too. However, with the phyMIMO MAC, G starts to reduce quickly from about $\chi = 0.65$ because, as the traffic load continues to increase, the MAC contention becomes higher, resulting in lower successful contention probability (η). However, with the same $\mathbf{K}$, the logMIMO MAC is more resilient than the phyMIMO MAC against increased MAC contention degree, as mentioned earlier. This is why G continues to grow with χ with the logMIMO MAC. It is more interesting to find that the logMIMO MAC can perform almost the same as and even better than the phyMIMO MAC with a small $\mathbf{K}$ setting in the case of heavy loads, as illustrated Fig. 12.16. This happens because, even with a small number of data slots per frame, the logMIMO MAC can still accommodate much more traffic due to its simultaneous MAC transmission capability. Furthermore, the frame duration (f) becomes shorter with a small $\mathbf{K}$, resulting in a shorter MAC service time (S). However, the phyMIMO MAC needs a large $\mathbf{K}$ in order to accommodate more traffic at the expense of a larger frame duration (f), which increases S.

12.5 Conclusion

We have made the following observations from this chapter. For the MAC without a reservation, the phyMIMO MAC can outperform the logMIMO MAC only if the

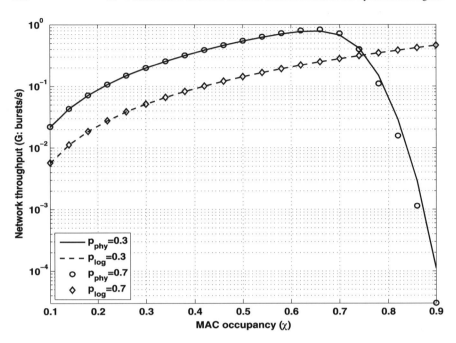

Fig. 12.15 Network throughput (G) against MAC occupancy (χ) for $k = 300$: $K = 10$, $\mathbf{m} = 4$, and $\mathbf{n} = 20$

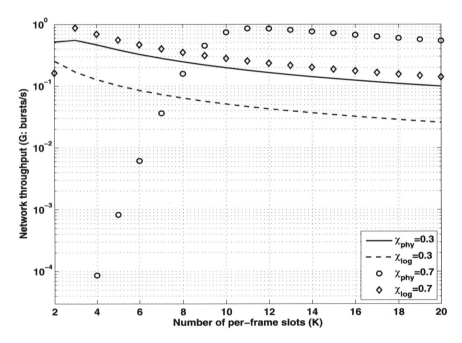

Fig. 12.16 Network throughput (G) against the number of per-frame data slots ($\mathbf{K}$) for $k = 300$: $\mathbf{m} = 4$, $\mathbf{n} = 20$, and $p = 0.4$

MAC contention is very low; otherwise, the logMIMO MAC is much better. With a periodic slot reservation, the phyMIMO MAC can perform better than the log-MIMO MAC under one of the following conditions: (i) a large number of transmit and receive antennas are implemented in the transmitter and receiver; (ii) a large number of request slots are available per frame; (iii) a large number of data slots are available per frame. All these conditions can dilute the impact of the MAC overhead on network throughput. However, it is impractical to have a large number of receive antennas because of the difficulty in implementing many antennas in a small-sized terminal. It is also undesirable to have too many request slots per frame, as it causes large frame overheads. Furthermore, a frame with a large number of data slots per frame may also cause waste if the traffic load is too low to fulfill each data slot in every frame.

References

1. Shiu, D.S., Foschini, G.J., Gans, M.J., Kahn, J.M.: Fading correlation and its effect on the capacity of multielement antenna systems. IEEE Trans. Commun. **48**(3), 502–513 (2000)
2. Gesbert, D., Shafi, M., Shiu, D., Foschini, P.J., Golden, G.D., Valenzuela, R.A.: From theory to practice: an overview of MIMO SpaceTime coded wireless systems. IEEE J. Sel. Areas Commun. **21**(3), 281–301 (2003)
3. Abdi, A., Kaveh, M.: A space-time correlation model for multielement antenna systems in mobile fading channels. IEEE J. Sel. Areas Commun. **20**(3), 550–560 (2002)
4. Abdi, A., Barger, J.A., Kaveh, M.: A parametric model for the distribution of the angle of arrival and the associated correlation function and power spectrum at the mobile station. IEEE Trans. Veh. Technol. **51**(3), 425–434 (2002)

Chapter 13
Green Networking Strategies Versus Networking Modes

Abstract Green networking has becomes a hot research topic due to the ever-growing concern about global warming, and many green networking strategies are proposed in the literature. Despite the many differences in these proposals, they have some similar fundamental elements in addressing green networking issues. Therefore, this chapter tries to formulate these issues through a quantification of the fundamental elements. Furthermore, the implementation issues of each strategy are investigated to check possible changes to be carried out in the existing network protocols, algorithms, and infrastructure. The discussion is taken to a deeper level by investigating how green networking efficiency is affected by networking modes.

13.1 Introduction

The Internet has achieved great success over the past three decades. However during its development, the privileged issues deeply addressed have primarily included network performance and reliability rather than energy efficiency, especially in wired networks. As reported in [1], in 2002, the Internet consumed about 8% of the electrical power in the United States, and this number is doubled as of 2012. This is due to the ever-increasing demand for high network capacity driven by the growing number of access networks and users equipped with various types of personal mobile devices. These devices typically include smart phones, iPads, laptop computers, and desktop computers. Meanwhile, the emergence of bandwidth-greedy applications such as video conference, video-on-demand, networked games, and high definition TV is another driving factor. These demands can only be satisfied by increasing the network capacity, which leads to an increase in the power consumption of the Internet [2]. Some detailed investigations on energy consumption can be found respectively in [3–5] for access networks and wireless networks, in [6] for optical networks, and in [7, 8] for the Internet as a whole.

In wireless networks, energy efficiency has been studied extensively in order to prolong the lifetime of battery-operated devices such as mobile phones. This efficiency also affects the lifetime of certain ad hoc networks such as wireless sensor networks, in which it is battery-operated nodes that compose the network. Although much effort has been made on the terminal side to improve energy efficiency, more studies are still needed on how to make wireless networks more energy efficient. For example, in wireless local area networks (LANs), wireless routers with the always-on mode waste lots of energy when they are in an idle state, where there is no application traffic passing through the router. Similarly, in cellular networks, "always-on" base stations are dominant in the energy consumption of the whole network [4].

It is a consensus that optical networks will play a critical role in the future Internet due to their immense network capacity that metallic media like copper wire cannot offer [9]. However, for the time being, neither cost-effective photonic computers nor optical buffers, especially optical random access memory, are available for optical networking. Since all these elements are essential for network functions like routing and congestion control, realizing green optical networks is a difficult issue, since energy consumption will become the major factor in limiting super-high speed optical core networks in the future Internet [8, 10].

Since the green Internet approach was discussed in 2003 [11], many research works on green networking have been reported in the literature. In general, green networking refers to efforts that can improve network energy efficiency without degradation of the network performance. Recently, several surveys of green networking from different perspectives were published. For example, a survey of energy consumption of electronic network elements is conducted in [12], and one for optical network elements in [10]. Various green networking schemes are evaluated in [2, 13–15], and a taxonomy for green networking is also discussed in [15]. Furthermore, energy efficiency for optical networks is investigated in [9, 16], while references [17, 18] focus on telecom networks. For wireless networks, some earlier surveys of energy consumption can be found in [19].

Although there are many differences in the various green networking strategies, they share some similar fundamental elements in addressing green networking issues. Therefore, this chapter first formulates the major green networking issues through a quantification of these elements. Then it further evaluates some typical green networking strategies by discussing how these quantities may be affected by a particular strategy. Furthermore, the implementation issue of each strategy is also discussed to check possible changes required in the existing network protocols, algorithms, and infrastructure. The discussion is taken to a deeper level by evaluating how green networking efficiency will be affected by networking modes. Note that here we do not discuss green networking issues related to renewable energy and green computing.

The remainder of this chapter is organized as follows. Section 13.2 discusses the definition and formulation of energy efficiency and the green networking approach. Some green networking strategies at different levels are discussed in Sects. 13.3–13.5, and the chapter is summarized in Sect. 13.6.

13.2 Energy Efficiency for Networking

This section first defines and formulates some quantities that reflect networking energy efficiency and then classifies green networking strategies into three levels according to the effect of a green strategy on energy efficiency and the existing network implementation.

13.2.1 Measurements of Energy Efficiency

As discussed in [16], there are several quantities measuring energy efficiencies (in joules/bit) for green networking to reflect how green a network is. These are redefined below with some modification.

- Designed energy efficiency (Υ_d): This reflects the relation between the system capacity and the total energy to be used to support this capacity at the design level. It is defined mathematically as follows:

$$\Upsilon_d = \frac{\text{Power consumption rate in joules/second } (\mathbf{E})}{\text{Designed network capacity in bits/second } (\mathbf{U})}. \tag{13.1}$$

The energy efficiency of a newly implemented network operating at its full capacity under high traffic load can be considered at this level. The energy efficiency at this level is the maximum that can be achieved by the system.

- Operational energy efficiency (Υ_o): For the network operator, maximizing the network throughput with a given amount of energy consumption is a reasonable option, which can be achieved through the optimization of network protocol and algorithm design as well as network operation. This level of energy efficiency is defined mathematically as follows:

$$\Upsilon_o = \frac{\text{Power consumption rate in joules/second } (\mathbf{E})}{\text{Maximum network throughput in bits/second } (\mathbf{U}_{\max})}. \tag{13.2}$$

Here $\mathbf{U}_{\max}$ can be rewritten as follows:

$$\mathbf{U}_{\max} = \zeta \cdot U, \tag{13.3}$$

where ζ ($\zeta \leq 1$) denotes the maximum utilization of the network capacity.

- Effective energy efficiency (Υ_e): For users, what is important is how many bits can be successfully received by their destination nodes; this is often called goodput in the literature. The goodput can be calculated as

$$\text{Goodput} = \zeta \cdot \mathbf{U} \cdot (1 - \mathbf{f}), \tag{13.4}$$

where $\mathbf{f}$ indicates the packet failure probability across the network, which can be estimated theoretically by the CAC-level packet failure ratio defined in Sect. 6.2. Thus the effective energy efficiency is defined mathematically as follows:

$$\Upsilon_e = \frac{\text{Power consumption rate in joules/second } (\mathbf{E})}{\text{Maximum network goodput in bits/second } (\zeta[1 - \mathbf{f}]\mathbf{U})}. \tag{13.5}$$

As indicated by Eqs. (13.1)–(13.5), both the maximum throughput and goodput are bounded by the designed network capacity, i.e.,

$$\mathbf{U} \geq \zeta \mathbf{U} \geq \zeta(1 - \mathbf{f})\mathbf{U}. \tag{13.6}$$

Then we have the following relationship between the three quantities:

$$\Upsilon_d \leq \Upsilon_o \leq \Upsilon_e. \tag{13.7}$$

Note that the smaller Υ is, the higher energy efficiency it indicates.

Precisely, we can obtain

$$\Upsilon_o = \frac{\Upsilon_d}{\zeta} \quad \text{and}$$

$$\Upsilon_e = \frac{\Upsilon_o}{1 - \mathbf{f}} \tag{13.8}$$

$$= \frac{\Upsilon_d}{\zeta(1 - \mathbf{f})}.$$

Equation (13.9) indicates that changing Υ_d can change both Υ_o and Υ_e, while changing Υ_o can only affect Υ_e. Here ζ and $\mathbf{f}$ are determined by the efficiency of the network protocols and algorithms.

13.2.2 Energy Consumption Rate

The energy consumption rate denoted by $\mathbf{E}$, which indicates the average amount of energy consumption per time unit, can be divided into two parts: one corresponding to network devices and the other to supporting systems (e.g., cooling and lighting etc.); these are denoted by $\mathbf{E}_d$ and $\mathbf{E}_s$, respectively. Since the supporting system is mainly used to dissipate the heat generated by network devices, $\mathbf{E}_s$ can be determined proportionally to $\mathbf{E}_d$. That is, we can define a ratio of energy consumption rates (σ) as follows:

$$\sigma \triangleq \frac{\mathbf{E}_s}{\mathbf{E}_d}. \tag{13.9}$$

Given a location and a time period, σ can be set to a constant; for example, σ is set to 1 in [6]. Then $\mathbf{E}$ can be expressed by

$$\mathbf{E} = (1 + \sigma)\mathbf{E}_d. \tag{13.10}$$

Note that $\mathbf{E}_d$ can also be further divided into two parts according to the working state of the device. One part corresponds to the busy period of the device, during which the device has application traffic in transmission, and is denoted by $\mathcal{E}$. The other corresponds to the idle period of the device, during which there is no application traffic loaded in the device, and is denoted by $\mathcal{E}'$. Then, $\mathbf{E}_d$ can be expressed as follows:

$$\mathbf{E}_d = \mathcal{E} + \mathcal{E}'. \tag{13.11}$$

Note that $\mathcal{E}'$ primarily depends on the following factors.

- Energy efficiency of devices during the idle period: This is determined by the amount of energy consumed by the device during this period.
- Device operation modes: This is affected by whether the device is turned off or put into sleeping mode during the idle period.
- Operation of network protocols: This refers to whether there is some background traffic for control or signaling used by the protocol during the idle period. This kind of traffic will affect whether a device can be shut down or go to sleep during the idle period.

$\mathcal{E}$ mainly depends on the number of operations to be carried out by the network device to transmit application traffic. The following notation is used here to calculate $\mathcal{E}$:

- Φ_j: set of operations of network node j;
- ξ_y: energy consumption rate of operation y;
- $\mathbb{N}$: set of the nodes in the network under consideration.

Then the total energy consumption rate of this network during a busy period is calculated by

$$\mathcal{E} = \sum_{\forall j \in \mathbb{N}} \sum_{\forall y \in \Phi_j} \xi_y. \tag{13.12}$$

Note that Φ_j further depends on the networking modes, which will be discussed in detail in Sect. 13.5.

13.2.3 Formulation of Green Networking Strategies

Here a function combing Eqs. (13.10) and (13.9) is used to denote the above three quantities for networking energy efficiencies. That is,

$$\Upsilon(\zeta, \mathbf{f}, \sigma) = \frac{(1 + \sigma)(\mathcal{E} + \mathcal{E}')}{\zeta(1 - \mathbf{f})\mathbf{U}}, \tag{13.13}$$

with which Υ_d, Υ_e, and Υ_o defined earlier can be expressed as follows:

$$\Upsilon_d = \Upsilon(1, 0, \sigma),$$

$$\Upsilon_o = \Upsilon(\zeta, 0, \sigma),$$

$$\Upsilon_e = \Upsilon(\zeta, \mathbf{f}, \sigma).$$

Note that, except in those schemes exploiting renewable energy, a green networking scheme tries to improve energy efficiency, i.e., it tries to minimize $\Upsilon(\zeta, \mathbf{f}, \sigma)$ without or with trivial network performance degradation. We can formulate this as follows:

Green networking $\triangleq$ {Minimizing $\Upsilon(\zeta, \mathbf{f}, \sigma)$|No performance degradation}. (13.14)

Regarding the minimization of $\Upsilon(\zeta, \mathbf{f}, \sigma)$, following Eq. (13.13), we can achieve this by improving the network capability, which includes maximizing $\mathbf{U}$, ζ and minimizing $\mathbf{f}$. It can also be realized through reducing the energy consumption, which includes minimizing $\mathcal{E}$, $\mathcal{E}'$, and σ. To minimize $\mathcal{E}$, from Eq. (13.12), one way is to reduce ξ_y for each operation. However, this part is related to the efficiency of devices rather than the efficiency of network protocols and algorithms. Another method to save energy is to reduce the number of operations for a network function, i.e., shrinking set Φ_j.

How to prevent a green networking scheme from degrading network performance should be considered carefully in the first place. Actually, it is difficult to guarantee zero performance degradation; aiming at negligible degradation is more feasible, as will be discussed later.

13.2.4 Categories of Green Networking Strategies

For a green networking strategy, beside its energy efficiency and impact on network performance, another important issue is related to its implementation, i.e., how many changes need to be made in the implemented network protocols, algorithms, and network infrastructure? In this context, green networking strategies are categorized into three levels as discussed below.

13.2.4.1 Network Operation Level

At the network operation level, only some settings or changes in network operation modes are needed to implement a green networking scheme, without changes in the implemented network protocols, algorithms, and infrastructure. The main objective of the green scheme at this level is to reduce energy consumption rather than improve network capability (i.e., network capacity plus network performance). As will be discussed in Sect. 13.3, the major energy efficiency parameters affected by this strategy at this level include the energy consumption rate during idle periods ($\mathcal{E}'$) and the ratio of energy consumption rates (σ), which are related to the energy consumption of supporting systems. In this case, the total energy consumed by the network is reduced, and the same is true for the energy efficiency parameters of operational energy efficiency (Υ_o) and effective energy efficiency (Υ_e), which improves the energy efficiency.

13.2.4.2 Network Function Level

The strategy at the network function level tries to improve the network capability and reduce energy consumption by enhancing network protocols and algorithms, such as routing and MAC protocols as well as scheduling algorithms, without changes in network infrastructure including routers, switches, gateways, and communication media for the implementation of a green scheme at this level. As discussed in Sect. 13.4, this strategy may affect the following parameters: the utilization of the network capacity (ζ), the packet failure ratio (**f**), and the energy consumption rate during idle periods ($\mathcal{E}'$).

13.2.4.3 Network System Level

With the strategy at the network system level, changes in the network infrastructure and even networking modes are needed to realize a green networking strategy. Although these changes are costly, they may be transparent to higher layers, especially the application layer. As discussed in Sect. 13.5, the strategy at this level may affect almost every energy efficiency parameter related to both the network capacity and energy consumption except that related to supporting systems, i.e., the ratio of energy consumption rate (σ).

13.3 Strategies at Operation Level

At this level, energy saving is realized primarily through the dynamic management and displacement of network equipment, typically including routers, switches, access points (APs), and base stations. Mechanisms at this level may be time-based, location-based, or based on configuration optimization as discussed below.

13.3.1 Time-Based Schemes

In the Internet today, a network equipment must always be at its full working rate no matter how much application traffic it has to transmit. However, the traffic load in the network fluctuates with time and depends on user activities. For example, in a home network, some network equipment (e.g., networked computers and the gateway) and even the whole network are not necessarily powered on if they are not in use, especially when the user is asleep at night. Furthermore, now there are many wireless WiFi routers and hubs installed in many sites such as home and commercial centers. But at the present time, they cannot automatically scale power consumption according to traffic load. In this case, a simple way to save energy is for the user to manually turn off these devices if they are not in use. "Just do it!"

Similarly, in backbone networks, the network capacity is actually often over-provisioned to simplify the implementation of QoS provisioning, and selectively shutting down links during low traffic periods can greatly reduce power consumption, as discussed in [20]. This is due to the fact that many links are bundles of multiple physical cables and line cards that can be shut down independently. Unlike home environments, in which power switching operations can be carried out manually, for a remote switching operation, a signaling protocol is needed to perform the remote control operations. Reference [21] discusses how a dynamic operation of base stations can yield a big energy saving in cellular networks by switching off redundant base stations for low traffic loads.

In general, this strategy usually affects the parameter of energy consumption rate during idle periods ($\mathcal{E}'$), and can operate periodically, e.g., daily, weekly, or even monthly. The operation period depends on the user activities and traffic load distribution, which mathematically can be simply modeled in comparison with the always-on mode as discussed below.

Let $\mathcal{T}_{on}$ denote the on segment of a period $\mathcal{T}$, during which there is application traffic for processing at the node. With the always-on mode, the operation energy efficiency is calculated by

$$\Upsilon_o = \mathbf{E} \times \frac{\mathcal{T}}{\mathbb{L}}, \tag{13.15}$$

where $\mathbb{L}$ indicates the total number of bits transmitted during the entire period $\mathcal{T}$.

With the turning-off mode, in which the device is powered off during the idle period, its operation energy efficiency is given by

$$\Upsilon'_o = \mathbf{E} \times \frac{\mathcal{T}_{on}}{\mathbb{L}_{on}}, \tag{13.16}$$

where $\mathbb{L}_{on}$ indicates the total number of bits sent during the on segment. Since application traffic arrives only during the on segment of period $\mathcal{T}$, then $\mathbb{L} = \mathbb{L}_{on}$.

Then following Eqs. (13.15) and (13.16), the operation energy efficiency with the turning-off mode is given by

$$\Upsilon'_o = \Upsilon_o \times \frac{\mathcal{T}_{on}}{\mathcal{T}}. \tag{13.17}$$

Similarly, we can obtain the effective energy efficiency with the turning-off mode (Υ'_e) as follows:

$$\Upsilon'_e = \Upsilon_e \times \frac{\mathcal{T}_{on}}{\mathcal{T}}. \tag{13.18}$$

For example, the turning-off mode can save about one-third of the power consumed by the always-on mode in the case of an 8-hour sleeping time per day.

13.3.2 Location-Based Schemes

As mentioned earlier, a portion of the network energy is consumed by supporting systems such as air-cooling systems, as indicated by Eq. (13.10). Thus reducing this energy consumption, i.e., reducing σ in Eq. (13.10), can also greatly improve the network energy efficiency. To this end, we should place network facilities such as switching centers in colder or windy locations as much as possible to use natural forces to dissipate the heat generated by network devices during their operation. Examples of these locations include open and windy sites and the shadowed sides of mountains. This kind of scheme can reduce the total energy consumption and improve network energy efficiency by reducing the operational and effective energy efficiency quantities, i.e., Υ_o and Υ_e, respectively.

Actually, this strategy is very attractive for green computing, especially for green server farms because they have more options for location selection, which can range from cities to countries through network technologies. An example can be found in [22]. However, a detailed discussion of this issue is out the scope of this monograph, since it is related to green computing [23].

13.3.3 Configuration Optimization

The performance and energy consumption of a network operation are also affected by the network configuration. A comprehensive measurement of energy consumption in a large network is discussed in [24], where an Urja system is used for an enterprise network, which is composed of 90 switches supplied by various vendors. This system monitors the power usage as a function of traffic loads flowing through the network, and gathers configuration and traffic information. Based on the collected information, the system can suggest various configurations and rewiring changes that can be made to improve network energy efficiency. Those configuration changes can be easily carried out by network administrators. The data collected over a period of four months indicate a saving of over 30% of the network energy consumption without performance impact.

13.4 Strategies at Network Function Level

The strategy at the operation level only aims at energy saving; it does not improve network performance. However, the strategy at the network function level not only can reduce energy consumption, but can also improve network performance. The cost is that some changes in the implemented network protocols and algorithms are inevitable. There are many such kinds of proposals available in the literature, which are further classified following Eq. (13.13) for the discussion. That is, the way in which a green networking scheme at this level can improve energy efficiency depends on how the parameters in this formula will be changed. These are listed as follows:

- Improving network performance by reducing the packet loss ratio ($\mathbf{f}$) and improving the network capacity utilization (ζ),
- Reducing energy consumption by reducing the ratio of energy consumption rate (σ), the energy consumption rates during busy and idle periods, respectively, i.e., $\mathcal{E}$ and $\mathcal{E}'$,

- Both improving network performance and reducing energy consumption.

Note that, although changing the designed network capacity (U) can also affect the network energy efficiency following this formula, this part belongs to the strategy at the network system level, since it requires changes in the implemented network infrastructure. This part will be discussed in detail in Sect. 13.5.

13.4.1 Improving Network Performance

Schemes of this kind aim to improve network throughput or goodput but without efforts to reduce energy consumption in the network. Actually, many conventional schemes trying to improve network throughput (i.e., ζU) and reduce packet failure ratio (i.e., f) belong in this category, although they have not explicitly addressed energy efficiency issues. For example, there are many schemes proposed to improve TCP performance in multi-hop wireless networks through cross-layer design and optimization. Since the network performance is improved by increasing the network capacity utilization (ζ) and reducing the packet loss ratio (f), which almost do not change energy consumption, both the operational and effective energy efficiencies can be improved; i.e., Υ_o and Υ_e are reduced according to Eq. (13.13). There are many surveys of such kinds of schemes in the literature such as [25] but not in the context of green networking, so their details are not discussed here.

13.4.2 Reducing Energy Consumption

This kind of scheme aims at reducing energy consumption but without efforts to improve network performance. Instead, it may slightly degrade network performance in order to improve network energy efficiency by improving the original performance-oriented network protocols and algorithms. Usually the performance degradation is controlled at an acceptable level or can even be negligible. This kind of scheme was studied for wireless networks long before green communication and networking became a hot research topic. For example, how to prolong the lifetime of mobile terminals and networks has been studied in wireless ad hoc networks, especially in wireless sensor networks, since the network units in these kinds of networks are often battery-operated. A survey of green wireless communication can be found in [26], so this part is not discussed here in detail.

Recently, some new approaches have been proposed for green networking, such as automated sleeping, load-aware adjustment, aggregation policy, and energy-aware routing, as well as their hybrids; these are discussed in more detail below.

13.4.2.1 Lifetime Prolonging

Since many mobile terminals are battery-operated, prolonging their lifetimes is an important issue, especially when they also function as routers in a network such as mobile ad hoc networks (MANETs) and wireless sensor networks. In this case the lifetime of terminals may impact the performance and even the lifetime of the whole network. Thus a lot of research is being conducted to improve the transmission efficiency over the air interface, such as the optimization of frame size selection, frame compression, and channel-state-dependent scheduling. Some relevant surveys can be found in [27].

For wireless sensor networks, when numerous battery-operated nodes are deployed spaciously and randomly, their batteries are usually unreplaceable in the case of battery exhaustion. Thus, extensive research has been conducted to design energy-efficient schemes for signal processing, raw data collection and sampling, and coding and data transportation. For networking, medium access control (MAC) and routing protocols are two important research issues, so many proposals have been studied to improve energy efficiency. For example, a sleeping mode is proposed to let nodes sleep during an idle period to reduce power consumption. Several energy-aware routing protocols have been studied to find routes with less energy consumption in [19, 28]. Some of these approaches have been extended to other networks for green networking, as discussed below.

13.4.2.2 Automated Sleeping Mode

To avoid network nodes from being always in a full-rate working state when there is no application traffic in transmission, some proposals have been studied to allow a node to automatically sleep in the idle state and return to the working state upon traffic arrival. This scheme is similar to the time-based one at the network operation level discussed in Sect. 13.3.1. Their major differences include the time scale and randomness for switching operation between sleeping and working states. The switching time scale at the network operation level is very large and the point at which to switch is also predictable, so this operation can even be carried out manually. Here, the time scale is much smaller and usually at the packet or burst level, and it is hard to predict when a switching operation should be carried out.

Despite the above differences between these two-level strategies, the gain offered by this strategy over the always-on mode can be estimated in a similar way as that at the network operation level discussed in Sect. 13.3.1; i.e., following Eqs. (13.17) and (13.18), we have

$$\Upsilon'_o = \Upsilon_o \times \frac{\alpha}{\alpha + \beta}, \tag{13.19}$$

and

$$\Upsilon'_e = \Upsilon_e \times \frac{\alpha}{\alpha + \beta}, \tag{13.20}$$

where α indicates the average on period and β the average off period. The major energy efficiency parameter affected by this scheme is the energy consumption rate during idle periods ($\mathcal{E}'$).

Below some examples of using the automated sleeping mode for green networking are briefly described.

TCP/IP   This strategy has been adopted by many proposals such as the green TCP/IP, which was proposed as early as 1998 [29] and is among the earliest proposals that adopted the automated sleeping mode to save energy. This scheme suggests turning an active TCP connection into the sleeping state during the idle period and resumes the connection upon the arrival of application traffic.

Local Area Networks (LANs)   Recently, the IEEE 802.3az [30] also adopted a similar idea. It defines an Energy Efficient Ethernet (EEE) based on the concept of a low power idle (LPI) mode to reduce the energy consumption of a link during the idle period. EEE can make a quick stop and resume of frame transmissions according to traffic loads. It defines a long period for no signal transmission and a short period for signal transmission. Reference [31] conducted a simulation-based evaluation of an IEEE 802.3az network, which shows that for 10 Gbps links, packet coalescing can increase energy saving with a small impact on network performance. A variant of this strategy is to switch active channels within a multi-channel Ethernet link according to the actual traffic rates [32].

Optical Networks   For wavelength division multiplexing (WDM)-based optical networks, a sleep cycle protocol using a multi-path selection scheme is proposed in [33]. This scheme tries to select paths such that the overall energy consumption of optical core networks is minimized, while maintaining the service threshold condition. To this end, a clustering approach is adopted jointly with an optical control management scheme, which can turn a cluster into an on cycle or an off cycle. These two cycles are similar to the idle and busy states mentioned earlier. That is, during the off cycle, the nodes within this cluster run in the sleeping mode to cut down the traffic load through them.

Endpoints   For endpoints like desktop computers, workstations, and servers, a sleeping mode in an extreme case is discussed in [34]. This scheme is called selective connectivity, in which an endpoint can choose whether to be connected to or disconnected from the network. When an endpoint is disconnected from the network, it simply goes to sleep in order to save energy. This proposal is targeted at delay/disruption-tolerant networks (DTNs). Unlike conventional networks like IP, where end-to-end connectivity disruption is assumed as a rare event by network protocols and algorithms, this kind of event will happen frequently in DTNs.

Switching Between States   The difficult issue for this strategy is to determine when a network node should go to sleep and when to resume its work. Usually some traffic-probing mechanisms or schedulers are needed to switch between sleeping and working states in time. There are two options available [35]: the timer-driven sleeping and waking-on-arrival. With the former, a network node enters and exits the sleeping state at well-defined time points, while with the latter, a network node wakes up automatically upon sensing incoming traffic, which is achieved by a circuitry powered-on during the sleeping period [11].

13.4.2.3 Load-Aware Adjustment

The automated sleeping mode discussed above may cause unnecessary interruption of network connectivity and services if a node fails in resuming its work in time. Thus a less aggressive scheme is proposed. Instead of letting nodes go to sleep, this scheme tries to automatically adjust the service capacity according to instant traffic loads. This is due to the fact that power consumption actually depends on the working frequency and voltage, and usually slow operating can save energy. Low frequency can be realized with low voltage, and working under low voltage can greatly reduce energy consumption [35].

Furthermore, this strategy can be applied jointly with the automated sleeping mode to further reduce energy consumption during the busy period. The adaptability of this strategy can be applied to adjust transmission rates and network topologies as well as power control, as we discuss below.

Transmission Rate Adjustment   Besides the sleeping mode discussed above, a rate adaptation scheme is also discussed in [35]. This scheme uses the history of packet arrivals to predict the future packet arrival rate so that transmission rates can be adjusted to scale the working voltage or frequency accordingly. This study shows that using rate adaptation and sleeping jointly can greatly reduce energy consumption in typical networks with little degradation of network performance.

A high-layer channel-number scaling scheme is proposed for IPTV networks in [36]. It aims to reduce the number of broadcast channels to save both network bandwidth and energy. The conventional scheme tries to simplify QoS provisioning by broadcasting all TV channels to everywhere at all times whether or not a channel is being viewed by the user. This leads to a big waste of channels. Thus, the proposed scheme tries to let each network node pre-join only a selection of channels, which consists of the active channels and a small number of inactive ones, rather than every channel.

Topology Adjustment   Reference [37] studies the effect of cell sizes on the power consumption in cellular networks. It shows that the optimal cell size from an energy-saving perspective depends on several factors, and dynamically adjusting cell sizes can help reduce power consumption. Then a cell-size adjusting scheme is proposed to adjust cell sizes according to the actual traffic situation, leading to an energy saving of up to 40% of the original consumption.

Similarly, reference [38] also discusses a cell zooming concept, which suggests allowing cell sizes to be adaptively adjusted according to traffic loads. The simulation results show that this concept not only can balance traffic loads among different cells but can also reduce the overall power consumption of the network.

Power Management   Reference [39] discusses an enhanced power management scheme based on previous work of the same authors. This enhanced scheme tries to dynamically trade off between network performance and power consumption by using a governor scheme, which is prototyped on the Linux operation system. This governor scheme consists of the following elements: a traffic estimator, an optimization module, and an Advanced Configuration and Power Interface (ACPI). The traffic estimator is responsible for the monitoring and sampling of arrival and loss rates under the current traffic load. Then this information is passed to the optimization module, which is responsible for finding an optimal device configuration for power consumption. Finally the selected configuration is passed to the hardware through ACPI to set the configuration accordingly.

13.4.2.4 Aggregation Policy

Due to the unpredictable nature of traffic loads in the network, neither the automated sleeping mode nor the load-aware adjustment approach mentioned above can always offer a big energy saving. On the other hand, they may cause additional packet losses and delay to application traffic. Therefore, reference [40] proposes an alternative method, which suggests aggregating the traffic from multiple input links before it is injected into the switching fabric in a node. The reason is that the multiplexed traffic of several individual flows is more smooth than an individual flow. It was found that, with this method, the power consumption scales linearly with traffic loads without packet losses. However, some changes in the implemented network units are needed to support the traffic aggregation.

Note that the current Internet implicitly assumes a full-time connectivity between endpoints. Thus an endpoint needs to stay powered to maintain its presence even if there is no application traffic in transmission. Some background traffic, such as the Internet Control Message Protocol (ICMP) packets for network management, must be processed in order to maintain the connectivity [14]. To reduce the power consumption in this case, another sort of aggregation policy called proxying is proposed. By proxying, a node can delegate the processing task of the background traffic to a proxying node, which can also provide the proxying service for other nodes. Thus using one proxying node can allow many other nodes to go to sleep in order to save power consumption. A detailed survey of several proxying schemes can be found in [14].

13.4.2.5 Energy-Aware Routing

A simple energy-aware routing approach was proposed early in 2003 in reference [11], which suggests switching off energy-inefficient network components and allowing some network components to be inactive. But this scheme handles only two energy states, i.e., either the on state or the off state. Here the on state is equivalent to the node state during the busy period and the off state to that during the idle period mentioned earlier. Thus this scheme cannot provide enough granularity of energy states.

Recently, reference [41] has proposed a novel energy reduction approach, which adopts a granular energy profile. This profile for a particular network component is defined as the dependence of its power consumption as a function of its traffic load or throughput. Based on such granular energy states, an energy-profile-aware routing is proposed by including energy profiles in dimensioning, routing, and traffic engineering decisions. The case study provided by this reference shows that a power saving of more than 35% can be achieved.

A green routing protocol is proposed for a hybrid hierarchical network. In this kind of network, a network node consists of two switches in two signal domains; one is an optical-to-optical (OOO) switch and the other an optical-electrical-optical (OEO) switch [42]. The OOO switch is used to route wavebands that aggregate multiple carriers, each of which corresponds to a particular wavelength. The OEO switch is used to add/drop a carrier and convert wavelengths. The port cost refers to the power consumption at transmitting ports, which are used to switch wavebands in the optical domain. Some power is consumed for OEO conversion in processing individual wavelengths. This protocol jointly considers the power saving and port cost to save energy by using two heuristic algorithms based on the end-to-end waveband merging strategy and the sub-path waveband merging strategy.

13.4.2.6 Hybrid Schemes

Reference [35] proposes and models a method to reduce the overall power consumption in the network by jointly using the automated sleeping mode and the load-adaptive rate scheme mentioned earlier. This method assumes that the network equipment is equipped with power management primitives at the hardware level, and that they can be invoked by network protocols for power management. Power consumption is reduced by putting sub-components of the whole system to sleep in the idle state, which is equivalent to the state during the idle period mentioned earlier.

A hybrid approach jointly using the above-mentioned automated sleeping mode, adaptive link rate, and merging policies can be found in the green network technology (GNT) [43] developed by a European project. The GNT consists of two parts: dynamic power scaling and smart standby. The dynamic power scaling method allows one to dynamically reduce the working rate through the use of the adaptive rate and low power idle (LPI) methods mentioned earlier. The smart standby method allows devices or parts of them to turn themselves almost completely off by shifting their functionalities to proxying nodes. The analytical results show that the GNT can offer an energy saving of about 68% of that to be consumed by the whole network.

13.5 Strategies at Network System Level

As mentioned earlier, in the future Internet, the challenge of power consumption will become a critical issue in core networks due to a rapid increase in the traffic load driven by the ever-increasing number of users and applications [8, 10]. More network capacity will consume more power accordingly.

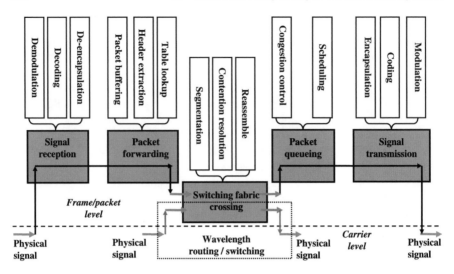

Fig. 13.1 Major operations performed per node in the store-and-forward networking mode

The strategy at the network system level may greatly affect energy efficiency, since it can change both network capacity and power consumption. To this end, changes in the implemented network infrastructure and the current networking modes are needed to implement the green networking strategy at this level. However, so far just a few references are explicitly addressing energy efficiency at this level. Therefore, this section mainly discusses how networking modes may affect network energy efficiencies.

13.5.1 Energy Consumption in Store-and-Forward Mode

Many studies show that the store-and-forward networking mode used in the current Internet is a major hindrance of achieving high energy efficiency, especially in optical networks [16]. This section discusses the breakdown of energy consumption during the busy period in the network element ($\mathcal{E}$) in this networking mode.

As illustrated in Fig. 13.1, with this mode, every network node such as switches or routers needs to reassemble the incoming physical signal into frames. These frames are decapsulated into packets, which are further processed for routing in higher layers such as the network layer. If this node is not the destination of the packet, after the packet crosses the switching fabric, the reverse process is carried out to encapsulate the packet into frames, which then are converted into the physical signal again to be sent to the next hop through physical media. A process can be further divided into several operations, each of which contributes to the total energy consumption of a node, as discussed below.

13.5.1.1 Energy Consumption of Network Node

Usually a network node consists of an input module, an output module, and a switching fabric in between [10]. Accordingly, the energy consumption rate of a node (say node j), $\mathcal{E}_j$ can also be broken down into three parts: $\mathcal{E}^I$ for the input module, $\mathcal{E}^X$ for the switching fabric, and $\mathcal{E}^O$ for the output module. That is, $\mathcal{E}_j$ can be calculated by

$$\mathcal{E}_j = \mathcal{E}_j^I + \mathcal{E}_j^X + \mathcal{E}_j^O. \tag{13.21}$$

Note that $\mathcal{E}^X$ is mainly determined by fabric switching technologies like the Banyan network [44]. The function of the switching fabric is to make a packet arriving at an input port cross the fabric so as to reach an output port corresponding to the destination of the packet. Therefore, a contention similar to the MAC contention may occur somewhere inside the fabric if multiple packets arrive at different input ports and are going to the same output port simultaneously. However, usually the method of design of a switching fabric is transparent to the design of network protocols and algorithms. So here we only focus on $\mathcal{E}^I$ and $\mathcal{E}^O$, because $\mathcal{E}^X$ should be discussed separately in the context of fabric switching technologies.

13.5.1.2 Network Operation

Here an operation set is used to describe the major operations to be processed in the input module (Φ^I) and the output module (Φ^O) for physical signal processing. For a hybrid of optical and electrical networks, certain signal conversions between the optical and electrical domains are needed. These conversions include optical-electrical (OE) conversion and electrical-optical (EO) conversion; they are marked with superscript * below to indicate that they are used only in this kind of hybrid network.

As indicated in Fig. 13.1, which shows the major operations to be conducted for an incoming physical signal, we can have Φ^I and Φ^O as follows:

$$\Phi^I = \{\text{signal reception, OE conversion*, demodulation, decoding, decapsulation,}$$
$$\text{packet buffering, packet header extraction, table lookup}\}, \tag{13.22}$$

and

$$\Phi^O = \{\text{packet queueing, scheduling, packet header rewriting, encapsulation,}$$
$$\text{coding, modulation, EO conversion*, signal transmission}\}. \tag{13.23}$$

Particularly in Φ^I, the table lookup operation is used to find the output port that an arriving packet should be forwarded to after crossing the switching fabric in order to arrive at its destination.

13.5.1.3 Network Energy Consumption

Let $\Phi_j = \Phi_j^I \cup \Phi_j^O$. Then the total amount of energy consumed by a network per time unit is given by

$$\mathcal{E} = \sum_{\forall j \in \mathbb{N}} \left(\mathcal{E}_j^I + \mathcal{E}_j^X + \mathcal{E}_j^O \right)$$

$$= \sum_{\forall j \in \mathbb{N}} \left(\sum_{\forall y \in \Phi_j} \xi_y + \mathcal{E}_j^X \right). \tag{13.24}$$

Thus the major effort to reduce energy consumption is by shrinking set Φ_j for every network element as much as possible, especially avoiding energy-greedy operations such as OEO conversions [10]. Therefore, the following sections discuss how different networking modes can achieve this objective.

13.5.2 Switching Versus Routing

At the time being, the connectionless IP is the dominant networking technology for the Internet. IP uses routing for packet forwarding according to a globally unique IP address. This feature simplifies the IP implementation, making it so popular today. Alternatively, with the connection-oriented ATM and MPLS upon which a network connection has been set up, packet switching is used for packet forwarding according to switching labels, which are much shorter than the IP address. For ATM in particular, the packet is fixed at a size of 53 bytes and is called a cell, and the switching label includes a 12-bit long virtual channel identifier (VCI) and a 14-bit long virtual path identity (VPI) for two levels of network connections. However, for IP, the IPv4 address is 32 bits long, while the IPv6 address is 128 bits long.

Both packet routing and switching rely on table lookup operations. These tables are called switching table and routing table, respectively, for switching and routing operations. The major difference between these two tables is their size. The switching table size (S_s) is usually much smaller than the routing table size (S_r). If packet switching is used instead of packet routing for packet forwarding, energy efficiency can be improved due to the following features. First, less energy is consumed for switching table lookup than for routing table lookup, which affects the energy consumption rate during the busy period ($\mathcal{E}$). Second, the table lookup time of the switching table is much shorter than that of the routing table due to the difference in their sizes, which affects the maximum utilization of network capacity (ζ) in Eq. (13.13). If both energy consumption and search time for table lookup are linearly proportional to table size, the above improvement ratio roughly ranges from $\frac{S_s}{S_r}$ to $(\frac{S_s}{S_r})^2$ following Eq. (13.13), but at a cost of a connection setup overhead since packet switching can be provided only in the connection-oriented network.

13.5.3 Wavelength Routing and Switching

Since the use of optical networks is the only enabling networking technology available today that can cost-effectively provide the immense network capacity to satisfy the bandwidth requirement of the future Internet, making optical networks more energy efficient is critical to green networking for the future Internet—a large capacity usually consumes more power, as mentioned earlier. Instead of using the store-and-forward mode in wavelength division multiplexing (WDM) networks, wavelength routing and switching technologies are developed. With wavelength routing, there is no change in the wavelength associated with a route from source to destination, as illustrated in Fig. 2.9, while the wavelength can be changed per hop with wavelength switching as depicted in Fig. 2.10.

Wavelength routing exploits the physical characteristics of a light wave to make the optical signal cross the switching fabric without OEO conversion. In this case, numerous operations of the store-and-forward mode can be avoided, which leads to a remarkable energy saving, since the major energy consumption here is the energy consumed by the switching fabric in the optical domain ($\mathcal{E}_j^X$). That is, the energy consumption rate of node j ($\mathcal{E}_j$) given by Eq. (13.21) in the store-and-forward mode is reduced here as follows:

$$\mathcal{E}_j = \xi_j^r + \mathcal{E}_j^X + \xi_j^t, \tag{13.25}$$

where ξ_j^r and ξ_j^t indicate the per-operation energy consumption rate for the signal reception and transmission in node j, respectively.

Slightly different from wavelength routing in terms of energy consumption, wavelength switching requires wavelength conversion operations [10], which consumes additional energy. Let ξ_j^c denote the energy consumption rate for wavelength conversion in node j. Then the energy consumption rate of node j in this case is given by

$$\mathcal{E}_j = \xi_j^r + \mathcal{E}_j^X + \xi_j^c + \xi_j^t. \tag{13.26}$$

13.5.4 Optical Burst Switching

Both wavelength routing and switching are types of circuit switching technologies since the network capacity is fixed per wavelength, and one path is associated to a particular wavelength for routing or a series of wavelengths for switching. Thus they cannot benefit from traffic multiplexing. Therefore, methods of jointly using electronic and photonic technologies to find a practical solution to large network capacity provisioning have been studied for some time.

A typical example is the optical burst switching (OBS) network [45]. With OBS, the domain edge first collects packets to the same destination to form a burst. Then a control packet carrying the routing information on this burst is sent via a control light path in order to set up a light path for the burst. Once a node inside the domain

receives this control packet, it converts the optical signal of this packet into electrical signals for information processing. Then according to the routing information
carried by the packet, the node sets a light path for the burst electrically through a
MEMS, for example. Then the burst can travel along the light path all the way to the
domain edge without OEO conversion. As a consequence, much energy is saved by
keeping the majority of traffic (i.e., burst here) in the optical domain in crossing the
switching fabric. Therefore, OBS can reduce the average energy consumption rate
per packet (ξ_j'), which can be estimated as follows:

$$\xi_j' = \frac{1}{L + \iota}[\mathcal{E}_j \iota + (\xi_j^r + \mathcal{E}_j^X + \xi_j^t)L], \qquad (13.27)$$

where L and ι indicate the burst length and control packet length, respectively.

13.5.5 All-Optical Packet Switching

With OBS, the processing of the control packet for the light path setting may become a bottleneck of the network, since the electrical setting speed of the light
path is much slower than the optical transmission speed [16]. Therefore, all-optical
packet switching (AOPS) is becoming a promising research direction. With AOPS,
it is supposed that no OEO conversion is needed; packet routing and/or switching
operations should be carried out in the optical domain. To this end, optical buffering
is probably needed along with a packet header rewriting operation, similar to the
electrical packet switching operation. Let ξ_j^b indicate the energy consumption rate
for optical buffering and ξ_j^w that for the optical packet header rewriting operation in
node j. The energy consumption rate in node j is given by

$$\mathcal{E}_j = \xi_j^r + \mathcal{E}_j^X + \xi_j^b + \xi_j^w + \xi_j^t. \qquad (13.28)$$

However, at this time, no mature photonic computing and buffering technologies are available to realize AOPS, especially the optical random access memory
(RAM), which is a fundamental component for routers and switches to avoid packet
losses. The state-of-the-art buffering technique is the optical fiber delay line (FDL).
However, an FDL buffer is not only large in size but also energy-greedy [10]. In
this situation, a possible research direction toward realizing AOPS is to simplify
the network structure such that neither table lookup nor packet header rewriting operations are needed by AOPS nodes for packet forwarding with less information
processing.This proposal, called two-level source routing (TLSR), was discussed in
Chaps. 3–4.

13.5.6 Green Reconfigurable Routers

Reference [46] proposes a conceptual architecture for a green reconfigurable router,
which has the following features different from conventional ones. First, each func-

Table 13.1 Energy efficiency parameters affected by green networking strategies

Strategy levels	Performance		Capacity	Energy consumption				Energy efficiency			CI	Example of proposals
	ζ	f	U	σ	$\mathcal{E}'$	ξ_y	Φ_j	Υ_d	Υ_o	Υ_e		
Operation				✓	✓			✓	✓		0	[20]~[24]
Function	✓	✓		✓	✓			✓	✓		1	[29]~[43]
System	✓	✓	✓	✓	✓	✓	✓	✓	✓		2	[46]

CI = Changes in the implemented network protocols and algorithms: 0/1/2 indicates no/less/more changes, respectively

tion block of the router is designed to be energy efficient by reducing the peak power consumption. Second, some rate-adaptive mechanisms are installed inside the router. The function blocks of these mechanisms are designed to be flexibly configured so that they can operate in a specific state according to the traffic load in the network, such as the on state, off state, or other low-energy-consumption states. Based on the above green reconfigurable router, a power-aware routing protocol is further applied to determine routes that consume the minimum energy in packet forwarding. This can be achieved through the aggregation policy and automated sleeping mode mentioned earlier.

13.6 Conclusion

Table 13.1 summarizes the energy efficiency parameters that are affected by green networking strategies following Eqs. (13.12) and (13.13).

A short-term green solution is the operational-level strategy. This strategy can offer remarkable energy saving without modification to the implemented network system. This kind of operation can even be carried out manually by turning off network devices not in use, for example. A long-term green solution is the network system-level strategy. This strategy may require changes not only in network infrastructure, such as routers and communication media, but also in networking modes, which should be designed according to the characteristics of the communication media. The mid-term green solution is the network function-level strategy, which requires changes mainly in implemented network protocols and algorithms.

Although there are many works studying the strategy at the network function level, it will be difficult for these schemes to be implemented in practice unless the following conditions are satisfied. First, the gain in energy saving offered by this kind of scheme should be large enough to attract the network operators. Second, the impact of implementing this kind of scheme on the network performance should be so trivial that it can be negligible. Although there are many schemes at this level either improving network performance and capacity or reducing energy consumption, few of them can do both simultaneously.

On the other hand, how to design next generation networks for the future Internet is still a hot research topic under discussion. This provides a good opportunity for us to take into account green networking issues in network design. However, so far there are few references addressing this issue at the network system level, especially for optical networks.

References

1. Plepys, A.: The grey side of ICT. J. Environ. Impact Assess. Rev. **22**(5), 509–523 (2002)
2. Zeadally, S., Khan, S.U., Chilamkurti, N.: Energy-efficient networking: past, present, and future. J. Supercomput. (2011, to appear)
3. Baliga, J., Ayre, R., Sorin, W.V., Hinton, K., Tucker, R.S.: Energy consumption in access networks. In: Proc. IEEE Optical Fiber Commun. Conf. (OFC), San Diego, USA, pp. 1–3 (2008)
4. Etoh, M., Ohya, T., Nakayama, Y.: Energy consumption issues on mobile network systems. In: Proc. IEEE Int. Symp. on App. & the Internet (SAINT), Turku, Finland, pp. 365–368 (2008)
5. Baliga, J., Ayre, R., Hinton, K., Tucker, R.S.: Energy consumption in wired and wireless access networks. IEEE Commun. Mag. **49**(6), 70–77 (2011)
6. Baliga, J., Ayre, R., Hinton, K., Sorin, W.V., Tucker, R.S.: Energy consumption in optical IP networks. J. Lightwave Technol. **27**(13), 2391–2403 (2009)
7. Baliga, J., Ayre, R., Hinton, K., Tucker, R.S.: Photonic switching and the energy bottleneck. In: Proc. Photonics in Switching, San Francisco, USA, pp. 125–126 (2007)
8. Tucker, R.S.: A green Internet. In: Proc. Annual Meeting of the IEEE Lasers and Electro-Optics Society, Acapulco, Mexico, pp. 4–5 (2008)
9. Zhang, Y., Chowdhury, C., Tornatore, M., Mukherjee, B.: Energy efficiency in Telecom optical networks. IEEE Commun. Surv. Tutor. **12**(4), 441–455 (2010)
10. Aleksić, S.: Energy efficiency of electronic and optical network elements. IEEE J. Sel. Top. Quantum Electron. **17**(2), 296–308 (2011)
11. Gupta, M., Singh, S.: Greening of the Internet. In: Proc. ACM SIGCOMM, Karlsruhe, Germany, pp. 19–26 (2003)
12. Ceuppens, L., Sardella, A., Kharitonov, D.: Power saving strategies and technologies in network equipment opportunities and challenges, risk and rewards. In: Proc. IEEE Int. Symp. on App. & the Internet (SAINT), Turku, Finland, pp. 381–384 (2008)
13. Chilamkurti, N., Zeadally, S., Mentiplay, F.: Green networking for major components of information communication technology systems. EURASIP J. Wirel. Commun. Netw. **2009**, 5208–5219 (2009)
14. Bianzino, A.P., Chaudet, C., Rossi, D., Rougier, J.L.: A survey of green networking research. IEEE Commun. Surv. Tutor. **PP**(99), 1–18 (2010)
15. Bolla, R., Bruschi, R., Davoli, F., Cucchietti, F.: Energy efficiency in the future Internet: a survey of existing approaches and trends in energy-aware fixed network infrastructures. IEEE Commun. Surv. Tutor. **13**(2), 223–244 (2011)
16. Yoo, S.J.B.: Energy efficiency in the future Internet: the role of optical packet switching and optical-label switching. IEEE J. Sel. Top. Quantum Electron. **17**(2), 406–418 (2011)
17. Koutitas, G., Demestichas, P.: A review of energy efficiency in telecommunication networks. TELFOR J. **2**(1), 2–7 (2010)
18. Vereecken, W., Heddeghem, W.V., Deruyck, M., Puype, B., Lannoo, B., Joseph, W., Colle, D., Martens, L., Demeester, P.: Power consumption in telecommunication networks: overview and reduction strategies. IEEE Commun. Mag. **49**(6), 62–69 (2011)
19. Pantazis, N.A., Vergados, D.D.: A survey on power control issues in wireless sensor networks. IEEE Commun. Surv. Tutor. **9**(4), 86–107 (2007)
20. Fisher, W., Suchara, M., Rexford, J.: Greening backbone networks: reducing energy consumption by shutting off cables in bundled links. In: Proc. ACM WS Green Networking, New Delhi, India, pp. 29–34 (2010)

21. Oh, E.S., Krishnamachari, B., Liu, X., Niu, Z.S.: Toward dynamic energy-efficient operation of cellular network infrastructure. IEEE Commun. Mag. **49**(6), 56–61 (2011)
22. Pervilä, W., Kangasharju, M.: Running servers around zero degrees. In: Proc. ACM WS green networking, New Delhi, India, pp. 9–14 (2010)
23. Kurp, P.: Green computing. Commun. ACM **51**(10), 11–13 (2008)
24. Mahadevan, P., Banerjee, S., Sharma, P.: Energy proportionality of an enterprise network. In: Proc. ACM WS Green Networking, New Delhi, India, pp. 53–59 (2010)
25. Leung, K.C., Li, V.O.K.: Transmission control protocol (TCP) in wireless networks: issues, approaches, and challenges. IEEE Commun. Surv. Tutor. **8**(4), 64–79 (2006)
26. Sanctis, M.D., Cianca, E., Joshi, V.: Energy efficient wireless networks towards green communications. Wirel. Pers. Commun. **59**, 537–552 (2011)
27. Jones, C.E., Sivalingam, K.M., Agrawal, P., Chen, J.C.: A survey of energy efficient network protocols for wireless networks. Wirel. Netw. **7**(4), 343–358 (2001)
28. Akkaya, K., Younis, M.: A survey on routing protocols for wireless sensor networks. Ad Hoc Netw. **3**(3), 325–349 (2005)
29. Irish, L., Christensen, K.: A "green TCP/IP" to reduce electricity consumed by computers. In: Proc. IEEE Southeastcon, Orlando, USA, pp. 302–305 (1998)
30. IEEE Standard 802.3az: Amendment 5: Media Access Control Parameters, Physical Layers, and Management Parameters for Energy-Efficient Ethernet, Oct. 2010
31. Christensen, K., Reviriego, P., Nordman, B., Bennett, M., Mostowfi, M., Maestro, J.A.: IEEE 802.3az: the road to energy efficient Ethernet. IEEE Commun. Mag. **48**(11), 50–56 (2010)
32. Imaizumi, H., Nagata, T., Kunito, G., Yamazaki, K., Morikawa, H.: Power saving technique based on simple moving average for multi-channel Ethernet. In: Proc. OptoElectronics & Commu. Conf. (OECC), Hong Kong, China, pp. 1–2 (2009)
33. Bathula, B.G., Elmirghani, J.M.H.: Green networks: energy efficient design for optical networks. In: Proc. IFIP Int. Conf. Wireless & Optical Commun. Net. (WOCN), Cairo, Egypt, pp. 1–5 (2009)
34. Allmany, M., Christensenz, K., Nordman, B., Paxson, V.: Enabling an energy-efficient future Internet through selectively connected end systems. In: Proc. ACM WS Hot Topics in Networks (HotNets)
35. Nedevschi, S., Popa, L., Iannaccone, G., Ratnasamy, S., Wetherall, D.: Reducing network energy consumption via sleeping and rate-adaptation. In: Proc. USENIX Symp. Networked Sys. Design & Implementation, Berkeley, USA, pp. 323–336 (2008)
36. Ramos, F.M.V., Gibbens, R.J., Song, F., Rodriguez, P., Crowcroft, J., White, I.H.: Reducing energy consumption in IPTV networks by selective pre-joining of channels. In: Proc. ACM WS Green Networking, New Delhi, India, pp. 47–52 (2010)
37. Bhaumik, S., Narlikar, G., Chattopadhyay, S., Kanugovi, S.: Breathe to stay cool: adjusting cell sizes to reduce energy consumption. In: Proc. ACM WS Green Networking, New Delhi, India, pp. 41–46 (2010)
38. Niu, Z.S., Wu, Y.Q., Gong, J., Yang, Z.X.: Cell zooming for cost-efficient green cellular networks. IEEE Commun. Mag. **48**(11), 74–79 (2010)
39. Bolla, R., Bruschi, R., Davoli, F., Ranieri, A.: Energy-aware performance optimization for next-generation green network equipment. In: Proc. ACM SIGCOMM Workshop on Programmable Routers for Extensible Services of Tomorrow (PRESTO), Barcelona, Spain (2009)
40. Singh, S., Yiu, C.: Putting the cart before the horse: merging traffic for energy conservation. IEEE Commun. Mag. **49**(6), 78–82 (2011)
41. Restrepo, J.C.C., Gruber, C.G., Machuca, C.M.: Energy profile aware routing. In: Proc. Int. WS Green Commu., Dresden, Germany, pp. 1–5 (2009)
42. Hou, W.G., Guo, L., Wang, X.W., Wei, X.T.: Joint port-cost and power-consumption savings in hybrid hierarchical optical networks. Opt. Switch. Netw. **8**(3), 214–224 (2011)
43. Bolla, R., Bruschi, R., Christensen, K., Cucchietti, F.: The potential impact of green technologies in next-generation wireline networks – is there room for energy saving optimization? IEEE Commun. Mag. **49**(8), 80–86 (2011)

44. Sibal, S., Zhang, J.: On a class of Banyan networks and tandem Banyan switching fabrics. IEEE Trans. Commun. **43**(7), 2231–2240 (1995)
45. Battestilli, T., Perros, H.: An introduction to optical burst switching for the next generation Internet. IEEE Optical Commun., S10–S15 (2003)
46. Hu, C.C., Wu, C.M., Xiong, W., Wang, B.Q., Wu, J.X., Jiang, M.: On the design of green reconfigurable router toward energy efficient Internet. IEEE Commun. Mag. **49**(6), 83–87 (2011)

Chapter 14
To Be Continued

Abstract Chapters 1~13 have discussed many networking issues, old and new, and have proposed some new approaches and methods for wireless and optical networks in the future. However, much follow-up research effort is still needed in order to make them complete and practical. Furthermore, some networking issues have not been addressed so far. One important question without a clear answer yet is where we should go further to develop new network technologies for the future Internet. Therefore, this last chapter of the monograph first gives a summary of the major networking issues discussed in the preceding chapters, which is followed by a brief evolution of network technology development. A strategic vision on possible developments of network technology for the future Internet is then briefly discussed.

14.1 Summary of the Monograph

As mentioned in Chap. 2, a good network technology has to satisfy the requirements of both today's applications and those to appear in the future Internet. It should also take into account the characteristics of the communication media in the physical layer so that the media capacity can be best utilized to support applications in higher layers. For applications, the major concerns include quality of service (QoS) and the security that a network can provide, as well as the cost of using the provided service. For communication media, network protocols and algorithms must be designed such that the utilization of media capacity can be maximized.

To achieve this goal, this monograph discussed several new networking approaches: the two-level source routing (TLSR) structure to realize all-optical packet switching (AOPS), the differentiated queueing service (DQS) for granular end-to-end QoS provisioning, the quantitative end-to-end arguments to evaluate various reliable end-to-end transmission schemes, Semi-TCP to handle the TCP's problem present in multi-hop wireless networks and all-optical networks, and the logical MIMO (logMIMO) to improve the performance of medium access control (MAC) protocols in centralized wireless networks without increasing the implementation complexity of mobile terminals.

Note that the above approaches are primarily related to Open Systems Interconnection (OSI) layers 1 to 4 with cross-layer design as much as possible, summarized as follows.

- Crossing layers 1 and 2: A MIMO-based MAC approach for the uplink sharing in centralized wireless networks is discussed in Chaps. 11–12. This approach exploits the feature of the MIMO originally used in the physical layer to enable simultaneous MAC transmissions in the data link layer.
- Crossing layers 1 and 3: A structure to facilitate the realization of AOPS networks is discussed in Chaps. 3–4. It enables the routing function originally performed only in the network layer (i.e., layer 3) to be carried out in the optical domain.
- Crossing layers 2 and 3: A granular end-to-end QoS provisioning approach is discussed in Chaps. 5–6. It can exploit the information on routes available in the network layer for the QoS scheduling in the data link layer.
- Crossing layers 2, 3, and 4: An end-to-end transmission reliability control approach called Semi-TCP is discussed in Chap. 10. It tries to overcome the weakness of the original TCP by decoupling the congestion control function from TCP and shifting it down to lower layers. That is, this function is shifted down to either the network layer for all-optical networks or the data link layer for shared-media networks. Some theoretical analysis was also conducted earlier in Chaps. 7–9.

Finally, a brief survey of green networking strategies is conducted in Chap. 13, and cross-layer design and optimization have also been used to address some issues of energy efficiency as discussed therein.

However, these works reported in this monograph are far from completion, and more research work is still needed, as summarized at the ends of Chaps. 3, 5, 6, 8, and 13, respectively. Meanwhile, some important network issues have not been addressed here, including network security, network management, and mobility support.

14.2 Development of Network Technologies

"To be continued" is often used between episodes of a movie or TV series to indicate the continuation of a story. Actually, the development of communication network technologies is just like a long story, which is briefly summarized as follows: (i) from the telephone network only for voice communication to integrated service networks for multimedia, (ii) from stationary communication to mobile communication and finally to pervasive communication for anything, anyhow, anywhere, and anytime, and (iii) from primarily focusing on the capability and performance of networks to having to additionally consider energy efficiency, and so forth. Accordingly, many new network technologies have been invented and later replaced by newer ones, such as (i) circuit switching to packet switching, (ii) hierarchical routing to non-hierarchical routing, (iii) metallic communication media to optical fibers, and (iv) homogeneous and simple network technology to heterogeneous network technologies and finally to a converged but versatile one, and so on.

At this time IP is the only dominant network technology for the Internet. Thus, there is a trend to converge different networks to IP, i.e., the all-IP network, such as the IP Multimedia Subsystem (IMS) [1] for wireless cellular networks. But IP itself is not ready to complete this mission, because originally it was not designed to function in this role. Although a lot of incremental efforts have been made to enable IP to fit this position, it was found that only modifying the original IP cannot satisfy the requirements of the future Internet. Thus a clean slate design seems inevitable. A comprehensive survey of research activities of the next generation network and the future Internet can be found in [2], and many of the activities reported therein are still undergoing.

Indeed, there are numerous issues to be addressed for next generation networks for the future Internet. But the upmost important strategic question is where we should go further. As mentioned earlier, so far there is no clear picture of the future Internet, and it is almost impossible to perceive now the requirements of new applications probably to appear in the future. On the other hand, the final decision on whether a new network technology will be deployed in practice is made by relevant stakeholders like network operators and service providers [3]. Of course, their major concern is the economic profit that a new network technology can offer them. An important factor influencing the profit is the lifetime of the new network technology. For example, the 3G cellular network is in a dilemma, since the beyond-3G technologies, such as 4G and Long Term Evolution (LTE), have also begun to penetrate the market before the maturity of the 3G market. This makes investors hesitate to continually invest in 3G technologies, since implementing a new network technology is often very costly. Therefore, it is necessary to avoid a similar situation from happening to the network technologies for the future Internet.

14.3 A Strategic Vision of Possible Network Development

This section discusses a strategic vision of a possible development of network technologies for the future Internet based on the cross-layer design and optimization approach.

Since a cross-layer design often occurs between adjacent layers, OSI layers 1 to 4 that are related to communication and network can be roughly grouped into three super-layers for research, as illustrated in Fig. 14.1, with a mapping between the OSI and TCP/IP layered models. The remaining OSI layers 5 to 7 are grouped into a cyberspace super-layer. Each layer of this super-layer model is described below.

- Cyberspace super-layer: Sits on the top and directly interfaces with Internet applications, and also accommodates the application layer of the TCP/IP model.
- Transport super-layer: Its major function is to provide end-to-end transport services to applications according to their QoS requirements. Unlike the similar layer of the OSI and TCP/IP layered models, besides satisfying application requirements, this super-layer should also adapt to the characteristics of network routes, which may cross multiple types of networks, to maximize the end-to-end transport performance. For example, the conventional TCP works well in wired networks in the case of acceptable packet loss rates. But for multi-hop wireless networks and all-optical networks, some new types of TCP such as Semi-TCP should be better.

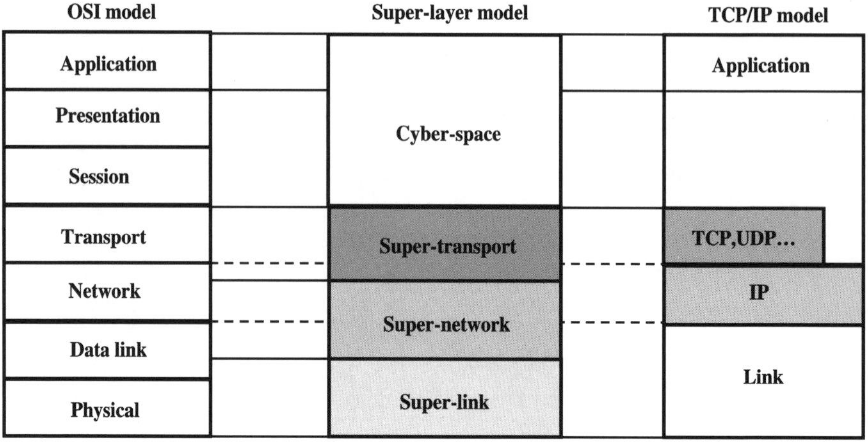

OSI model		Super-layer model		TCP/IP model
Application		**Cyber-space**		**Application**
Presentation				
Session				
Transport		**Super-transport**		**TCP,UDP...**
Network		**Super-network**		**IP**
Data link				**Link**
Physical		**Super-link**		

Fig. 14.1 A super-layer model versus the OSI and TCP/IP layered models with cross-layer design and optimization

- Network super-layer: Aims at providing network services for traffic forwarding across the entire network. It can exploit the information available in lower layers or redistribute certain functions to optimize the network performance. For example, the MAC contention degree and wireless channel quality can be exploited by routing protocols to make an optimal routing decision. The congestion control function can be imbedded into MAC protocols in the data link layer for shared-media networks. On the other hand, the data link layer may also exploit the information available in the network layer to improve channel utilization. For example, the network layer has the information on network topologies, traffic distribution, and end-to-end delays, which can be used by the data link layer to make scheduling and MAC decisions.

- Link super-layer: Sits at the bottom and is similar to the link layer defined by the TCP/IP layered model as illustrated in Fig. 14.1, but with more emphasis on communication media-specific design. It aims at handling different physical media used in the network by providing medium-specific access control to them in order to maximize the utilization of the network capacity. For example, for shared-media networks like wireless networks, MAC protocols are needed. MAC design should try to exploit some features of physical media to maximize the utilization such as the MIMO-based MAC discussed in Chaps. 11–12. There are many technologies developed or under development to maximize media utilization, which can be jointly used by higher layers to maximize network capacity. Typical technologies include, e.g., space division multiple access (SDMA), MIMO, orthogonal frequency division multiplexing (OFDM), cognitive radio and cooperative communication, and topology control. For optical networks, the optical node can exploit wavelength-based technologies such as wavelength routing and switching for contention resolution inside the switching fabric.

The transport super-layer can be designed to be so flexible that new transport protocols can be designed as necessary to support any future applications that appear without impacting the existing applications and network systems. The link super-layer is primarily determined by the communication media used in the physical layer. One can perceive that, for the future Internet, the dominant media will be optical fibers and wireless radio. Therefore, we can focus on these two types of media to develop the link super-layer to maximize the network capacity.

Now the remaining question is where the network super-layer should go. Traditionally, a network is designed according to the requirements of the applications that the network will support. These requirements are assumed known to the network design, and the traffic characteristic and QoS requirements of these applications can be studied extensively. For example, the telephone network was originally dedicated to voice communication. The Integrated Services Digital Network (ISDN) is designed to support multimedia applications, which include data, voice, and video. The IP network was originally designed for data applications.

However, besides those well-known applications, the next generation network should also be able to support unknown applications that will appear in the future. But at this time, it is impossible for us to learn the characteristics of these unknown applications for the network design. Obviously, the above application-specific design approach cannot be used here to guide the research on the next generation network. In this case, a possible answer to the question of where to go is to study how to maximize the capability of a network using optical fibers and wireless radio as communication media instead of how to support some particular applications.

References

1. Camarillo, G., García-Martín, M.A.: The 3G IP Multimedia Subsystem (IMS) – Merging the Internet and the Cellular Worlds, 2nd edn. Wiley, Chichester (2006)
2. Paul, S., Pan, J.L., Jain, R.: Architectures for the future networks and the next generation Internet: A survey. Comput. Commun. **34**(1), 2–42 (2011)
3. Clark, D.D., Wroclawski, J., Sollins, K.R., Braden, R.: Tussle in cyberspace: defining tomorrow's Internet. IEEE/ACM Trans. Netw. **13**(3), 462–475 (2005)

Index

S.M. Jiang, *Future Wireless and Optical Networks*,
Computer Communications and Networks,
DOI 10.1007/978-1-4471-2822-9, © Springer-Verlag London Limited 2012